Prais

MW00325459

The Winning Family

"An inspiring book that can improve the quality of family life."
—*Library Journal*

"Never has a book been so meaningful and timely! It has all the essentials: theory, practicality, application, and passion for kids." —*Dr. Michele Borba*, author of *Thrivers, Unselfie, The Big Book of Parenting Solutions, Esteem Builders*, and *Self-Esteem: A Classroom Affair*

"*The Winning Family* came to my attention when first published. I am so happy for this two-generational edition; it is a miraculous gift that validates the first edition and includes what has been learned and applied in the past thirty-five years. It was far ahead of its time then, and is now timeless. The excitement, healing, and shifts in perception—from fear-based parenting to love-based parenting—has changed many lives." —*Nevin Valentine MA*, early childhood college instructor and parent educator

"This book goes beyond parenting to focusing on the personal development of parents along with the development of their children." —*Jeanne Gibbs*, author and founder of Tribes Learning Communities

"Uniquely inspiring, accessible, and non-guilt-provoking!" —*Mothering Magazine*

"*The Winning Family* was the only book I took to the hospital when I gave birth to our daughter thirty-three years ago. The wise words have been my unfailing support for both our children all these years through all stages of their lives. They are now confident, insightful, self-reliant, extremely caring beautiful adults who are kind kind kind. I recommend this book to friends at all stages of their parenthood." —*Laurel Hameon*, Brisbane, Australia

"This book is a must for parents who want to raise children with understanding, nurturing, and healing, instead of blame, shame and punishment."
—*Patricia G. Palmer Ed.D.*, clinical psychologist, author of *Liking Myself, The Mouse, the Monster, and Me*, and *Teen Esteem*

"*The Winning Family* is a book you will return to again and again for the reassuring words, lighthearted confidence in the love of parents for their children, and down-to-earth ideas about making the parenting journey a path of self-discovery." —*Julianne Idleman*, Hand in Hand Parenting

"This book is life changing. If you truly care about the happiness of your children and the world they live in, this book is for you. It can be used as a daily resource and a fun text to help you bond, heal, and improve your life."
—*J. Madrigal*

i

"Very well written, empowering, uplifting, enlightening, interesting, and easy reading. It's wonderful!" —*Rochelle Ford*, director of the Avanta Satir Network

"Practical and insightful. A super book!" —*Dr. Christopher Green*, Australian pediatrician, author of *Toddler Taming*

"Packed with helpful insights and suggestions. I highly recommend it!" —*Jean Illsley Clarke*, author of *Self-Esteem: A Family Affair*

"The most critical issue of the decade is the well-being of our children. This is the right book at the right time!" —*Sheila Murray Bethel*, author of *Making a Difference: 12 Qualities that Make You a Leader*

"This positive and hopeful book covers in a very insightful way all of the major stumbling blocks which lead to major dysfunctions in nuclear families." —*Dr. Constance A. Jones*, Associate Professor of Sociology, Mills College

"This is the number one book I recommend to families." —Teacher, California

"This book has become our second Bible." —*Linda Schuler*, mother, Illinois

"I wish I had had this book twenty-one years ago, when I first became a parent. This is 'must reading' for all caregivers of children. I read it cover to cover in one day." —*Sandra Gellert*, National Association for Family Day Care

"I am a recovering alcoholic, and it's helped me very much. My self-esteem has really gone up and so has my boys'. Our lives are an adventure today. We are able to love each other like never before." —*Jane M.*, mother, Florida

"Every page is an invitation and a challenge to put every word into action. The insights helped bridge the gap between me and my son." —*Bob Hill*, father, New York

"I am an Adult Child of an Alcoholic and have been in group therapy for some time. This book covers so many of the topics that are involved in therapy." —*Nancy Gants*, Ohio

"I use this book all the time in counseling suicidal teenagers." —*Don Burchfield*, Counselor, Phoenix, Arizona

"The best book I have read in years! It captured my interest from beginning to end. I'm a single mother raising a boy diagnosed with neurological problems. I was 'losing it.' Reading a bit of this book every day put a lot of things into perspective for me and helped me in this difficult time." —*Mother*, New Jersey

"I am a mother of four children who is currently going through a divorce. *The Winning Family* is what I needed to help with the rebuilding of my family." —*Mother*, Kentucky

"A wealth of forthright information." —*Parenting Magazine*

THE
Winning Family

Where No One Has to Lose

Dr. Louise Hart
and
Kristen Caven

UPLIFT PRESS

www.upliftpress.com

This book is dedicated to our children and grandchildren for seven generations.

Uplift Press
www.upliftpress.com

Text Design by Cowgirl Creative
Cover design by Cowgirl Creative featuring. Michele Shubert

Library of Congress Cataloging-in-Publication Data

Hart, Louise.
    The winning family: increasing self-esteem in your children and yourself / Louise Hart. — Rev
        p. cm.
    Includes bibliographical references and index.
    ISBN-13: 978-0-89087-689-3 / ISBN-10: 0-89087-689-4
        1. Self-esteem. 2. Self-esteem in children. 3. Child rearing
I. Title.
BF697.5.S46H37 1993
649'.7 — dc20

                                                                93-6844
                                                                CIP

Contents

Preface

"The true character of a society is revealed in how it treats its children." —Nelson Mandela

There have been major changes in our society—a sea change—since I raised my children fifty years ago. Instead of supporting parents to provide a nurturing foundation for their children, society has placed increased responsibilities and burdens on them. Their time, attention, and focus have been distracted and diverted from the most important cultural work: supporting the healthy development of children.

Although today's parents enjoy benefits of modern life, we have challenges, as well. Our families all have deep roots in the lives and experiences of our ancestors. Some were positive. Some negative. The positive ones may be benefitting our life today; the negative ones may be repeating and causing trouble for our children—we may even have to deal with events that happened before we were born.

According to the Happiness Research Institute, Nordic countries are the best places for raising children. They are safe, family-friendly, and care about human rights, and they have well-developed public-education and health-care systems. In 2021, the United States was ranked 22 in the world, and many other countries have room for improvement.[1]

A stark warning was recently issued by the US Surgeon General about the state of mental health among our youth. Between 2009 and 2019, suicide rates went up by 57 percent among youth between ten and twenty-four years old, and the pandemic made issues worse.[2] Childhood trauma is an underreported public health crisis in this country, impacting millions of Americans with devastating consequences that can have a lasting emotional and physical impact.[3]

Adverse Childhood Experiences (ACEs) are a root cause of mental health and relationship problems, addictions, and violence. ACEs affect the mental and physical health of individuals, families, and society, yet few people are aware of it. Many are grappling with the lifelong effects, without knowing they are dealing with abuse, neglect, and household dysfunction that happened before they were born.

Patterns can repeat from generation to generation without our intending it, without our awareness. However, once we become conscious of old wounds, we can begin to release them. Trauma is a fact of life. So is resilience. So is healing.

In the face of our compounded epidemics of anxiety, depression, rage, addiction, and violence, I am eager to share with you what I learned during my lifetime from a desire to change harmful family patterns. My stories and strategies for our challenges and successes have proven, during my lifetime in psychology, to be best practices. And my adult children are proof that prevention and positive parenting work!

Instead of parenting on automatic, this book helps you parent on purpose. Mothers and fathers have the power — and the opportunity — to create a nurturing foundation. So do grandparents, foster parents, and anyone who cares for children. This book will help you.

It is a well-documented fact that Positive Childhood Experiences (PCEs) — respect, kindness, empathy, love, protection — can bring out the best in your children and yourself.[4] They can transform negative patterns and stop childhood trauma.

If you have negative family patterns to break, choosing to create Positive Childhood Experiences will change the future of your family, including your kids and your grandkids. This is the work of heroes. Your children will thank you, literally! And you will thank yourself when you feel their love later in life.

How you shape your children affects the quality of life for your youngsters and your growing family for the rest of your life. I've always warned parents, *if you don't shape your children, they will be shaped by forces that don't care what shape they are in.*

Families come in different forms and sizes. Over the course of a lifetime, a person might live in several of them, as I did. I was born to German immigrant parents in an extended family with relatives who ate and lived with us.

After college, I married and taught elementary school for four years. After my first pregnancy, I committed to the full-time profession of a stay-at-home mom—a common role in times past. Another baby (Kristen, who you will get to know well in this book) arrived just eleven months later. Our nuclear family moved to Colorado, a thousand miles away from relatives.

Childhood is a time of amazing discovery and growth. For parents, it is a time for meeting their needs for safety, for attention, for love and belonging. I watched the amazing development of the bodies and brains of my babies. Those years were difficult, but also lots of fun.

As I learned how to nurture and connect with my kids, I got to know myself at a deeper level. While growing into my role of mom, I peeled back layers of awareness and filled in some of my own developmental holes. I recalled the vow I made as a lonely five-year-old girl: *I would raise my kids better than I'd been raised.* I committed to giving my little ones what I had needed and hadn't received—especially unconditional love and nurturing.

My mother had been the first of thirteen children born in an impoverished Bavarian town before World War I. The first of thirteen children, she was overworked filling everyone else's needs, while her own emotional and physical needs were not being met. Much later in life, she asked, *"How could I love when I hadn't been loved?"* She added, *"I always missed the love of my mother."* Her question broke my heart.

I vowed to become the mother I wish I'd had and also the mother I wished *she'd* had. Love became paramount for me. When I nurtured my babies, they loved me back. That primal bonding was the beginning of our lifelong loving relationships.

Fast-forward through many years. My long marriage ended. As a single mom, I helped launch my youngsters into college and then entered graduate school myself. In studying mental health and healthy families, I learned that self-worth/self-esteem is key.

As "Dr. Mom," I wrote *The Winning Family*, packed with uplifting knowledge that develops healthy, happy, and peaceful children. And then I created my first presentation for a small group of parents, and I expanded it for larger audiences — schools, communities, and conferences held far and wide.

My daughter helped develop my career, which turned into our family business. I am honored and thrilled that she has now taken the lead on bringing forth this new edition for the next generation.

Positive parenting can bring out the best in yourself, in your children, and even in your grandchildren. Changing patterns is easier to do when children are young. You cannot turn back the clock, but no matter when you start, more happiness is possible. Start now. This book will teach, encourage, and support you in the process of transforming your family. On this journey, you will find much support, for as much of a sea change as there has been in our society since I was a child and Kristen was young, much of it has been for the good, lifting us all up with the tide of greater awareness.

> *"If you bungle raising your children, I don't think whatever else you do matters very much."* —Jackie Kennedy

— Dr. Louise Hart, 2022, aka Grama Lulu

1.

The Idea of Winning

"No one wins until everyone wins." — Bruce Springsteen[1]

You might think a winning family has a trophy case, poolside parties, fabulous vacations, political connections, and Ivy League educations. But none of these things matter. To my mom, Louise Hart, the original author of this book, a winning family is not defined by externals — although success may be a side effect. In a family where love can truly be experienced without limits, parents use common warm practices that make everyone feel like they belong. My mom taught audiences of hundreds, sometimes thousands, of parents and caregivers about turning their own pain into power. Her work gave a generation of parents fresh inspiration and real tools to teach their kids to feel worthy and strong.

Behind every great man, they say, is a great woman. I'm pretty sure that's true for great women too. I have had the great fortune in my life to help my mother fulfill her mission to make a real difference in the world.

When I was in college, my mom was too. I remember the night she told me she was the "most improved student" in her public speaking class, going from terrified to terrific. Her dissertation morphed into the first edition of this book. She asked me to illustrate it and create overhead graphics and illustrations for her presentations. She traveled around the world, speaking to parents and caregivers in PTA meetings, hospitals, military bases, and conferences. Back home, I was her assistant, her graphic design department, her vision department, and, eventually, her coauthor.

Now, at last, I can tell the world what inspired her to write this famous book. It was a secret I needed to keep to protect myself,

1

but I'm a grown-up now, and it's safe for me to share.

My parents divorced when I was in sixth grade. It surprised us all — they never fought. My dad was a big personality, and Mom played the role of a good wife. Married at twenty-two and a mother at twenty-five, she struggled to take care of herself, because, back then, "self-care" was seen as selfishness. She had no idea who she was outside her roles of wife and mother. Fortunately for us and for you, the reader, mothering inspired and motivated her.

My dad got full custody of the children because my mom, having nothing of her own, couldn't fight him, much less provide for us. We saw her on Thursdays, one weekend a month, and one month in the summer. She was our oasis. My dad, who had ADHD (attention-deficit/hyperactivity disorder), struggled to take care of himself and my two brothers while working full time as a physician. He married a woman who had three kids of her own. For a year, we were like the Brady Bunch, but then the screaming started.

Our time away with Mom was easy and uncomplicated. We dreaded going home, where we would be greeted by complaints about all we had done wrong. In public, we were a big happy family, filling up a pew at church. But at home, we walked on eggshells, trying to avoid land mines, and hid in our rooms, wondering what we had done wrong.

For the next six years, until all three of us were able to escape to college, we suffered emotional pain and violence on a weekly, if not daily, basis. There were no sticks or stones, but we got hurt. We went to school with our self-esteem in shreds and relied on our friends and teachers to build us back up. When we were with Mom, we felt listened to and loved.

My stepmother, who needed total control to keep from feeling undermined, would not speak to my mother or let her call our house. We were even forbidden to say our mom's name. We felt forced to keep secrets and lie or all hell would break loose. The difference between our two families was like night and day.

2

When Mom wrote her doctoral dissertation (which became this book), she was able to see the sharp contrast between a dysfunctional family and a functional one. In our blended family, there were losers, usually her three children, who longed to cooperate with, and not compete with, siblings and build friendships, not walls. In my mom's family, we could all feel like winners.

To be fair, there were some very good times in the blended family. Our basic needs were met, and we had stability; and when everything was in its place, we had moments of peace and connection. And in my mom's family, we had challenges as well as positive experiences. But one day my brother spelled out the difference: "It's like we can win when we're in Mom's family. At home we lose nine-tenths of the time." The idea was that everyone was responsible, together, for creating a winning family. Mom created space for us to celebrate our successes, even the littlest things, such as, "I made it to school on time today." When my mom held up an advance copy of her book at our weekly dinner, we applauded. The idea of a winning family has continued to inspire all of us throughout our lives.

We have had our challenges, as every family does, but we have stayed connected. We appreciate each other's successes and are there for each other when we're struggling. This book has been a part of our lives, and so has Mom's success.

Two years before I became a mother, I helped Mom develop the The Winning Family into an updated, expanded edition. Upon the birth of my son, Donald, with the wisdom of this book fresh in my mind, I was more interested in understanding my baby than controlling him. The skills I'd learned while writing the book applied to my work helping other kids and parents in our schools, social groups, and in fact all of my relationships.

Mom retired from her speaking career when Donald was a toddler, and then a few years later, she flunked retirement for the first time and went back on the road because of her passion for the next generation of kids. When we tried to publish a new edition of this book, the publisher asked for a whole new book instead, focused on the bullying. We thought *The Bullying Antidote* would be the last book we'd write together before she *really* retired.

But a new generation of parents still needs *The Winning Family*, perhaps more than ever. The world has become divided in the same way my family was divided. The word *winning* has taken on a combative spin in politics (annihilation is not winning), and narcissism and privilege eclipse the conversation about who gets to feel good about themselves. Parents, children, and teens have their self-esteem attacked every day in new and unexpected ways, and the basics get lost in the shuffle.

In Mom's retirement she wanted to focus on ancestry research and travel memoirs, so I decided to accept her challenge to reboot *The Winning Family* in my own voice. I added my own wisdom, stories, and academic expertises, since my son is now the age I was when Mom and I wrote the previous edition. His generation, which struggles more than ever with "all the feels," is beginning its parenting journey, and though much has changed in the world since his grandma was a kid, her keys will still unlock family well-being for him and my own grandkids.

Much has changed since I became a mom. Mental illness is no longer a dirty secret, and mental health is considered as important as physical health. Neuroscience has validated all of this book's wisdom, and studies on psychological strengths have, in fact, created a new field of psychology focused on flourishing — the state of growth above and beyond recovering. In fact, the term *positive parenting*, which we coined in one of Mom's brochures, is now widely used for reinforcing positive behavior. Positive parenting isn't about getting good *behavior* now through means that might cause pain and disconnection. Instead of the outside-in word *behavior*, we prefer the inside-out word *agency*. We focus on building inner authority, creativity, and positive self-esteem.

Today, writers, bloggers, coaches, and teachers offer many parenting styles: helicopter parenting, gentle parenting, goodenough parenting. What we want to encourage in this book is real enthusiasm for the power of love — empathy, understanding, and connection — when expressed in the family.

Positive parenting is based on the foundational concept that nurturing positive emotion makes us more capable and happy. The goal of this book is to "improve family life by better understanding the dynamics of love, parenthood, and commitment."[2] However, our philosophy goes even further than that; the tools we teach can help end cycles of trauma and violence that have gripped humanity for millennia.

My blended win-lose family was not a rarity. Among the many changes to this edition is the addition of a chapter on the divided family, with insights into what makes blended families work. I don't know much about my stepmom's upbringing, but my father's was certainly traumatic and tumultuous, in spite of his cheerful spirit. Of my three parents, my mom was the only one who transformed herself, by taking the time to know herself more deeply through therapy and self-examination. She worked hard to free herself from the trauma that shaped her, and now she shows others how to do it. One of her readers said, "This book is better than years of therapy."

Currently, the world is having an awakening about the intergenerational effects of ancestral, generational, and childhood toxic stress, trauma, and violence. The Kaiser study that powered *The Bullying Antidote* revealed that Adverse Childhood Experiences (ACEs)[3] negatively affect our mental, emotional, and physical health all our lives, even into old age, and into the lives of our grandchildren.

The Winning Family has always been about creating Positive Childhood Experiences (PCEs or PACEs) that build resilience. Many of us have experienced childhood trauma, and our "natural" responses to the world are "off," but we now know more about overcoming, healing, and well-being. In trauma, we lose. In resilience, we win.

We encourage all who have been wounded by the combative

definition of *winning* to adopt the word's more expansive concept, which is not about competition. Winning finds strength, accomplishment, and goodness wherever it occurs. Imagine a family in which everyone has a voice, gets their needs met, and feels like mistakes lead to learning and success. Imagine a family that teaches children how living in a democracy requires self-esteem instead of selfishness, control, and greed. The idea of a family like this can guide every member into goodness, and even greatness.

2.

You Are Creating a Masterpiece

"Our children give us the opportunity to become the parents we always wished we'd had." — Louise Hart[1]

This book originally started with a chapter called "You Are Building a Cathedral." The story went like this: Many years ago, two men were working at the same job on the outskirts of a European city. A stranger approached them and asked, "What are you doing?" The first man replied with an edge of resentment, "I'm hauling rocks." The second man enthusiastically replied, "I'm building a cathedral!" Just as skilled craftsmen designed cathedrals to inspire7, stand tall and strong, and resist the elements over the years, we who raise and teach and care for children work to build in them the strength, integrity, and inspiration to live happy, creative, productive lives. This vitally important work is too often unsupported and undervalued.

Cathedrals are structures of Christian power, and their magnificent presence in the world is certainly Eurocentric. But in this edition, we want to be clear that principles are human and universal. Parenting is a spiritual journey. If you substitute the words temple or synagogue for cathedral in the story, it might work just as well, as might theme park or library. These places represent bigger ideas than the individual. It's completely appropriate to approach parenting like that. Because raising healthy children is the most important work of the culture.

If you have children, parenting is your most important job. What you do when your children are small will contribute to the pain or the joy of the rest of your life and the lives of others. Little other work has such far-reaching effects. You are shaping the future and who your children will become, and it matters how they feel about themselves.

We are all products of our families, culture, and time—and of these three, family has the strongest influence over shaping our beliefs and emotional realities. Mom's parents gave her more than they had ever received from their parents. As children, they both had had difficult times in Germany. The first of twelve children, my grandmother had grown up with adult responsibilities; her mother had died delivering the fourth baby, and her father's new wife had born and raised nine more children.

The primary focus in that family was survival; the primary value was work. She and my grandfather transmitted those values to my mom and her siblings. With the best of intentions, they did all they could for their children, but they couldn't give what they didn't have. My grandmother once asked Mom, "How can I love when I never was loved?" She talked about how much she had always missed the love of her own mother. History repeats . . . unless we do something about it.

Many people operate under the assumption that since parenting is a natural adult function, we instinctively know how to do it. But doing it well requires study and practice, as does any other skilled profession. Who would even consider turning an untrained surgeon loose in an operating room? Yet we "operate" on our children every day.

Things just weren't right for Mom as a child. She was confused, lost, and lonely. She felt unloved. She had no self-esteem, no sense of self. When she got pregnant with my brother in the early 1960s, she made the most important decision of her life, and of mine. She made a commitment to raise her children the way she would like to have been raised. This was not easy to do since she had no models. Along with other parents of her generation, she became a pioneer into new ways of mothering. After examining and reexamining everything she knew about parenting, she gave my brothers and I what she thought was best.

Ideally, while we grow up, we have to become emotionally skilled adults who take responsibility for our own happiness. Ideally, in parenting, we pass on this new way of being to our own kids. Mom continues to delight in getting back everything she gave us: acceptance, respect, love, and support. Children deserve the best, and, *over time, what goes around comes around.*

As children, we had no choice about how we were parented. As parents, we have the choice to *unconsciously* repeat the patterns used with us or *consciously* pass on only those values we would like to see repeated.

For better or worse, you learned how to parent from those who raised you. You learned from the examples they set. If you felt loved and valued as a child, you were fortunate to have had good modeling. If you've become a competent, healthy adult, thank your parents, or whoever modeled that for you. Raising kids should be easier for you. But if you were rejected, neglected, or abused in any way, or if you grew up in an alcoholic or otherwise dysfunctional family system, you can — and you *must* — choose differently in order to rise above old destructive patterns and create a healthy life for yourself and your family.

Take an honest look at your own childhood. Remember what it was like growing up in your family. What did your parents do to make you feel loved? How did they discipline you? How did they communicate and resolve problems with you and with each other? What experiences helped you feel good about yourself, and what led you to conclude that you were "bad" or that there was something wrong with you?

> "*Children are compelled to give meaning to what is happening to them. When there is no clear explanation, they make one up; the intersection of trauma and the developmentally appropriate egocentrism of childhood often leads a little kid to think, I made it happen.*" — CA Surgeon General Dr. Nadine Burke Harris, author of *The Deepest Well*

Parents, being human, make mistakes. We can choose to learn

from mistakes our parents made rather than repeat them. We can choose to heal ourselves rather than wound our children.

To become conscious parents, we need to question, sift, and sort through old "tapes" (what psychologists before the digital age called unconscious habits, patterns, and conditioning). *Pass on the best – and throw away the rest.* Taking this motto seriously is our best assurance that negative patterns we may have grown up with will not be repeated in our children's generation.

We live in an exciting time. More and more parents are becoming aware of how they are parenting. Today we think a lot about the impact of our choices on our children's future, and we have countless resources available to help us do so. *With awareness comes choice.* We can assess the results of various parenting strategies and sort them into "growthful" or "harmful." Then we can pick ones we want to hand down to our children.

Both negative and positive experiences contribute to our parenting skills. It's like the game Twenty Questions: a "no" is every bit as valuable as a "yes," because the information helps us narrow our options. If we insist on denying the pain or suffering we have experienced, we run the risk of repeating behaviors with our children—even if we swore we never would. We have all felt wounded at times. Instead of wounding our own children, let's use our love for them as an inspiration to heal ourselves.

Give to your children what you want back from them. If you respect and accept them, they will learn to respect and accept; if you abuse and reject them, they will learn to abuse and reject. It's like a hug—you have to give one away if you want to get one back. Be there for your kids when they're young, and they'll likely be there for you when you're old.

Even though healthy teens typically challenge and rebel against their parents to discover their own values, children are natural imitators. They unconsciously reflect how you think, how you love, what you value, how you solve problems, what you do with feelings, and how you deal with other people. Whether you know it or not, you are teaching self-esteem — or a lack of it — to your children all the time. If they see you working to be your best self, even when you're having trouble doing so, they will want to become their best too.

Self-esteem in families begins with choosing who and how you want to be. Since we can't give what we don't have, we need to learn how to raise our own self-esteem along with our children's. A positive sense of self is the greatest gift a parent can give to a child.

Parents can lay a solid, loving foundation that builds inner strength and resilience before the outside world has a major impact. The old saying "An ounce of prevention is worth a pound of cure" certainly applies to self-esteem and to parenting.

Parents have the ability to help *prevent low self-esteem* — and keep their loved ones away from
- educational failure
- vulnerability to negative peer pressure
- drug and alcohol abuse
- teen pregnancy
- dropping out of school
- eating disorders
- addictive behaviors
- battering relationships
- crime and violence, and
- suicide.

Parents also have the power to *promote high self-esteem* so that their children
- resist dependencies and addictions
- are enthusiastic about life (and school!)
- make friends easily
- trust themselves
- are self-directed
- are cooperative and follow reasonable rules
- take pride in their achievements
- are basically happy individuals, and

- are assets to society and to the world.

Our children are not the only ones who benefit from the practice of positive psychology. Parenting gives grown-ups endless opportunities to create joy and love. It also encourages us to develop strengths, to understand and appreciate ourselves at deeper levels, and to learn and constantly practice new skills. It is universally true that our children can become our best teachers, if we are willing to learn.

If you are at the beginning of your parenting journey, or somewhere in the middle, imagine yourself at the end. When you go to the next life, will your children surround you? Will your legacy live on in terms of the things you taught, the habits you instilled, and the joy you nurtured? Will your grandchildren think fondly of you, talk to each other about you, seek each other out, and talk about the values and strengths on which you focused? Will your love outlast your life?

Now think back as far as you can about an ancestor, someone from whom you are descended. What might their world have been like? What might they have wished and dreamed for? Odds are, their longings were similar to yours: to care and be cared for, to understand and be understood, to learn, to teach, and to do some good in the world. They may never have imagined you as you are, where you are, and how you developed and blossomed. But if you have any affection for yourself, and any for them, you are their monument, their temple, their cathedral, their masterpiece.

3.

The Greatest Gift: Self-Esteem

"What a man thinks of himself, that is which determines, or rather indicates, his fate." —Henry David Thoreau

If you search the term *self-esteem*, you will find it described in dozens of ways—but the dictionary gets it wrong when it suggests that *ego*, *pride*, *pridefulness*, and *self-regard* are all synonyms.[1] They're not! No wonder people are confused.

When we hold something in esteem, we value it, think highly of it, and appreciate it. When we have self-esteem, we value our own feelings and needs and know that our strengths and dreams are worthwhile. Those are all part of who we are, part of our "self." Philosophers throughout time have debated what the self is, contrasting it to or equating it with the "soul," but here's what I think: the soul is what regards the self. The self is the soul plus all the mundane details. It includes one's body and brain, one's place in space and time, and all the eternal and noneternal parts of one's being—it is the sum of who we are. The self is endlessly fascinating, and we each have one. When we dismiss or diminish our selves, we disconnect from our stories and our histories, our hearts and our bodies. When we fundamentally cherish our selves, we are more human.

Self-esteem has many parts: the most basic is self-acceptance— knowing deeply that you are okay and care about yourself. Self-concept, self-confidence, self-reliance, self-care, and self-respect follow. The term can be confusing, so looking at what self-esteem is *not* can be helpful. Self-esteem is not egotism, which is about being better than, superior to, or one-up over others. When you are okay with yourself, you don't have to make others wrong or put them down. It is not narcissism — a personality disorder requiring professional treatment characterized by an inflated sense of self-importance, an excessive need for admiration, and a lack of empathy. Self-esteem does not, and cannot, come from others or from anything external. It can't come from money, from status, from social media "Likes," or from people telling you that you are awesome 24/7. Self-esteem is something only you can give to yourself.

Only you can give yourself self-respect.
Only you can give yourself self-acceptance.
Only you can give yourself self-compassion.
Only you can give yourself self-care.
Only you can give yourself self-esteem.

Self-esteem is not what you do or know. It is not based on your appearance, your accomplishments, how you compare with others, or anything temporary. I may feel okay today because I have the coolest car on the block, yet tomorrow I will see a better one and feel unhappy with mine. I may feel impressed with myself today because I've read every book on the best-seller list, yet next year I won't have time to do the same. Today I feel okay because I did a thousand things for my family, yet if I stop doing all those things (possibly because of exhaustion), I will feel like a failure. Straight A's can't give you self-esteem.

Mastery gives us confidence, but those who fail can still have self-esteem. Components of self-esteem include self-acceptance, self-compassion, and self-care. It is an inside job. If you believe in God, this is how God loves us: unconditionally. Even if you don't believe in God, you can still feel unconditional love — from yourself, for yourself.

Unconditional Positive Regard

A term that beautifully describes the foundation of love is "unconditional positive regard." In this book we encourage you to give that to your children, because it helps them build their own self-esteem. We also encourage you to give it to yourself. It begins with self-acceptance — radical self-acceptance — where you unconditionally accept that you are okay, no matter how much of a mess your hair is today, no matter if you lose your job, no matter if you just wrecked the car. Start where you are. Be on your side. Put your hands on your heart and breathe while you imagine feeling love for yourself — and feeling loved by yourself.

Self-esteem grows when we feel love with no strings attached; love with respect, acceptance, appreciation, empathy, sensitivity, and warmth; love that says, "Regardless of what you do, I love and accept you for who you are."

A day-care provider told me about two-and-a-half-year-old Joey, who would say when he got in trouble, "That's okay, because my mom and dad still love me!" His parents had laid a solid loving foundation that had made him resilient.

Conditional love, on the other hand, is turned on and off. It manipulates behavior by saying, "I love you when _____, because _____, or if you do something." Kids who receive only conditional love never really feel loved; when they receive love they can't trust it. These kids try to earn love by becoming people pleasers.

Children have their own life force: their own opinions, dreams, and destinies. The challenge of parenting is to allow and encourage children to be themselves while guiding, supporting, and celebrating their growth process. Successful parents love their children unconditionally and also protect them, set limits, and assume as much responsibility as is necessary for the children's age and developmental stage. This constancy of love and protection is crucial — even in the event of parental separation or divorce.

Where Does Self-Esteem Come From?

Children first look to the adults in their environment, and later to their peers, for a reflection of who and how they are. Keen

15

observers, they soak up every bit of information we provide—our words, facial expressions, posture, tone of voice, and touch. They notice how we react and respond to them: are their physical and emotional needs met, are they taken seriously and listened to, and are they respected and enjoyed? They observe and then draw conclusions. "I am important." "I don't matter." "I am loved." "I'm a nuisance." "I'm too much." "I am beautiful."

To small children, parents and authority figures are all-knowing and all-powerful, and very big. They think, "Those important people treat me as I deserve to be treated. What they say about me is what I am." The conclusions children draw become their "truths"—their basic beliefs about who they are and what they deserve in life. Often, a child's conclusions are faulty. Children may conclude that they are ugly, they are stupid, or they are responsible for their parents' fighting or separation. These truths may embed in their basic, unconscious beliefs about themselves, and last a lifetime. Yet many people's truths are not true. That's why it's important to reexamine (reevaluate) basic beliefs and assumptions throughout our lives (see chapter 20, "Beliefs and Believing").

Pay attention to messages you give children and how you treat them. When children are neglected or abused, they conclude that they deserve it, that they had it coming. They may conclude that they are bad. If they believe they are bad, it could be easy for them to allow others to mistreat them.

On the other hand, when children are respected, they conclude that they deserve respect, and they develop self-respect. When they are valued, when they are cherished, they conclude that they deserve esteem, and they develop self-esteem. Parents are, in effect, mirrors. What we reflect back to our children becomes the basis for self-image and influences every aspect of their lives.

Step outside these beliefs, and it's easy to see the greater truth that no child deserves abuse or harmful punishment. No one deserves to be hit. No one deserves to be abandoned. Every single child—every single person—deserves and needs respect, acceptance, and unconditional love. A parent's job is to fill these needs.

We need to watch our language. Children identify with the labels you give them and may develop a poor self-image and low self-esteem if they are given the wrong ones. When we view our children as being somehow "broken," or as having a "deficit," their self-image becomes one more thing to struggle with. When we find ways to describe kids (and ourselves) in terms of strengths and challenges, we appreciate them as unique, which they are. Everyone has different strengths and weaknesses; some are more apparent than others. Give extra support and encouragement when needed in order to develop and foster positive self-images and self-esteem.[2]

Take a moment to reflect on your own self-esteem as a child and as an adult. Over the years you have had your ups and downs. What affected your self-esteem?

Low self-esteem comes from
- rejection
- conditional love or no love at all
- lack of attention, being ignored, neglect
- not being taken seriously, not being listened to
- disrespect
- emotional abuse — put-downs, name-calling, ridicule, sarcasm, blaming, humiliation, criticism, threats
- needs not being met
- prejudice, bigotry, systemic racism
- comparison; perfectionism; always looking for, and finding, what's wrong
- focusing on externals (appearance, behavior, performance)
- expectations that are too high or too low
- guilt, shame, resentment, and
- physical and sexual abuse or exploitation.

Remember that when children experience treatment of this

nature, they conclude, "I'm not important." "I can't do things right." "I'm not good enough." "I'm not okay." If they accept this as their truth, it damages their self-esteem and puts them at risk.

On the other hand, high self-esteem comes from

- acceptance, respect, love
- attention, care, compassion
- being taken seriously and listened to
- a sense of belonging, bonding, having a support system
- honesty (with tact and sensitivity), integrity
- having needs taken seriously and met
- having one's uniqueness honored
- authentic expression of feelings
- encouragement, support, appreciation
- being believed
- safety, security
- being trustworthy, trusting others
- high standards and attainable expectations
- competence, success, achievement
- doing good and being good
- a sense of personal power, having choices
- pride in one's cultural heritage
- personal and social responsibility
- being healthy and fit
- affectionate and appropriate touch
- forgiveness, allowing and learning from mistakes
- having meaning in life, a sense of purpose
- living up to one's own moral standards
- a sense of connection with a higher power (spirituality)
- gratitude, and
- a sense of humor; laughter and play.

When children observe and experience positive influences in their lives, they conclude, "I'm okay." "I can be me." "Mom and Dad think I'm important; I must matter." "I'm worthwhile." "I'm loved." Self-esteem soars.

In a way, building self-esteem is incredibly simple. When you stop doing the things that lower self-esteem and do more of the things that raise self-esteem, you will notice marked improvements in your family relations. Low self-esteem cannot be "fixed." Over time, however, with attention and care, it can heal.

One parent realized that when he was using low-self-esteem behaviors — criticizing, blaming, and yelling — his kids felt bad, and so did he. On the other hand, when he used his high-self-esteem skills, everyone's self-esteem increased. When we're good to our kids, we all win. When we're being awful, we all suffer. For better or worse, self-esteem is contagious. Families that consciously foster high self-esteem are a lot more fun!

The essence of self-esteem is compassion for yourself and for your children. With compassion you understand and accept yourself. When you make a mistake, you forgive yourself. And you do the same for your kids.

Here's a challenging exercise you can do today. Think of one thing that you heard as a child and accepted as your "truth" — something that was NOT true, but that negatively impacted your life. Before you go to sleep tonight, give yourself some compassion around this untruth. What words will you use? Is there any chance your child might have learned the same "truth" from you? Can you speak those words aloud, in front of your child?

4.

Building Self-Esteem

"If there is no enemy within, the enemy without can do you no harm." – African proverb

Foster Cline, the author of *Parenting with Love and Logic*, joked, "We make butterflies by feeding caterpillars, not by trying to paste wings on them."[1] My mother repeats this metaphor with amusement, the meaning of it crystal clear: we cannot give a child self-esteem. We raise healthy children from the inside out—by cherishing and accepting them as they are, nurturing their growth and development, and having patience. Lots of patience! If we give our children the things they really need, they will develop good self-esteem at their own natural pace and develop wings that will take them places in life.

Good intentions start you on the right path; however, you need new information and skills to really nurture those wings. As little as five minutes a day trying out new strategies with your family can produce powerful, incremental, positive changes.

So what do you do first? Self-esteem begins with self-love, with accepting, respecting, and taking care of *yourself.* That love spills over to your children, who learn to love themselves and to love you. *Love cures people—those who give it and those who receive it.*

Self-esteem begins with bonding. A critical and wonderful event occurs naturally when a newborn and parents have skin-to-skin and other sensory contact. With nursing, cooing, touching, rocking, and cuddling, a newborn bonds quickly and naturally to its mother, and other nurturing adults and children. Because of the remarkably rapid early growth of the brain, the first two months after birth have a disproportionately important impact on development and long-term health.[2] The first ten days are particularly crucial. If a baby feels safe and cared for during this time, its brain forms the foundation for trust, love, self-esteem, and healthy development. What happens during the next months and years is magical: parents attune to their children, learning to read and understand their needs intuitively. It's a myth that you can spoil a baby with attention. On the contrary, bonding and attunement with our children can even heal our own bonding wounds. And attention to our own inner child can begin a process of deep personal healing.[3]

One mother, Anne, shared her discovery. "As I held my beautiful baby, I experienced a totally unconditional love between us and a wonderful sense of euphoria. I was aware and appreciative of my uniqueness. My twenty-two-month-old son has taught me so many lessons. He's taught me what love is, he's taught me self-acceptance, and he's taught me to relax and let him go through his stages."

Not all bonding starts at birth, and bonding happens in many ways over time; mothers should not feel guilty if something goes wrong at the beginning. Throughout life, there are obstacles to bonding, but there are also endless opportunities to fall in love with our children and bond. The closest, and longest, relationships we have in this world are with our children. Family, friends, and society should consistently and predictably support new parents, and parents should not hesitate to get help if they are struggling with this process.

Newborn infants are totally dependent on adults for their well-being, but growing children need the freedom to *be* and *act* their age. It's important to turn over responsibility to children as they become ready and not to "paste wings on them." Learn about child development. Knowing how young brains develop makes it easier for you to work *with* their nature, not *against* it. In other words, "It's easier to ride a horse in the direction it's going!"

The letting-go process of child-raising is a gradual orderly transfer of responsibility and freedom from parent to child, from birth to maturity. Through this process of gaining self-mastery, children build independence, self-confidence, and self-esteem. If children get their needs met, by the time they are young adults, they will be responsible individuals equipped with the skills to function happily and effectively.

Fostering self-esteem in a child from the outset is easier and healthier than trying to repair damaged self-esteem later. Yet, we cannot turn back the clock. We must start where we are now. If your children are older, it's not too late. *The same things that build self-esteem in the first place also repair damaged self-esteem later on —* for your children and yourself. It is always the right time to build self-esteem. New approaches, new skills, and a sense of compassion can begin the healing process at any time.

A thirty-five-year-old woman told me that she barely spoke to her mother from the time she was about eight or nine until she was twenty-six and divorcing her first husband. Only then did they begin to share feelings, develop trust in each other, and work through some of the misunderstandings and unintentional hurts that had come between them. Today they have a warm, supportive, and loving relationship.

Needs vs. Problems

To flourish, plants need good soil, water, and sunshine. To thrive, children also need optimal growing conditions. First and foremost, they need unconditional love. They also need to feel safe at home and at school; they need to know they will not be harmed. It is the job of the family to meet the needs of children. If children's needs are not met, there will be problems. It's really that simple.

If you ignore the needs of your houseplants — soil, water, sunshine — your plants might die. If your car needs maintenance and you don't fix it, you'll obviously have car trouble. If your house needs roof repair and you don't take care of it, you'll be in trouble during the next downpour. Either we tend to needs, or we have problems.

Children and adults have basic physical needs: they must have shelter and food. They also have emotional needs: they must have love and respect, acceptance and understanding, support and encouragement, affection and belonging, and security (founded on structure, freedom, and predictability). Meeting these needs will ensure physical and emotional well-being. Ignore them, and you and your children will have problems. Tending to the basics when children are young can prevent pain, grief, and expensive therapy when they are older. An ounce of prevention is worth at least a pound of cure.

Families that do not meet the basic needs of their members are dysfunctional families. The people society labels "sick," according to Abraham Maslow, have never had their basic human needs met — or the needs of those individuals were at one time satisfied, but then became unmet due to trauma.

What is the best medicine then? "For a child who hasn't been loved enough," wrote Maslow, "obviously the treatment of first choice is to love him — just slop it all over him. Clinical and general human experience is that it works." This also holds true for adults. The same things that build high self-esteem in the first place can heal the damage later on.

If your emotional development was stunted as a kid, there's hope. Healing is possible when you take care of your needs, fill in developmental *holes*, and become *whole*. As you build a solid foundation of love and protection for your children, you also do so for yourself.

Self-Esteem Game

Get a partner to play this with you. Sit facing each other. One person, A, looks the other, B, in the eyes and says, "Tell me how you're terrific!" That's the only thing that A says.

B responds by saying, "I'm terrific because . . ." and completes the sentence. B repeats this sentence with different endings for three or four minutes. At the end of this time you switch roles.

Afterwards, talk about it. How did it feel to hear those terrific things about your partner? How did it feel to say those terrific things about yourself? Exciting? Awkward? Uncomfortable? Exhilarating?

Almost everybody enjoys hearing the wonderful things happening in their partner's life. In fact, after doing this exercise, many people reported a boost in their own self-esteem just by hearing other people's good news. On the other hand, when their partners named their strengths, many felt embarrassed because they hadn't thought of themselves in terms of "terrific-ness." And some felt quite uncomfortable, because they don't value what they do in the line of duty as worth special praise — they felt as if they were bragging. Yet beloved Cherokee humorist Will Rogers said, "If it's the truth, it can't be bragging."

In high school, one of Mom's friends told her she had a nice smile — it was the first time she'd ever gotten a compliment. Mom told another friend that she thought she (Mom) had a nice smile, and that friend said that saying so sounded conceited and she shouldn't toot her own horn. Mom concluded that it was not okay to say good things about herself in this world. Later on, she would make sure to humble herself when she thought well of herself: "I have a nice smile — but I have lots of cavities."

The word *pride* is used both positively — "I'm proud of you" — and negatively — "Don't be proud." Mom raised us to think that being proud meant to feel good about someone and/or their performance. To make one-up/one-down comparisons — "I'm great and you're not" — is false pride or egotism. Feeling good at someone else's expense is not healthy. *Terrific* does not mean "better than."

Helen, a grandmother who attended one of Mom's workshops, shared her insight after the exercise: "I got in touch with my roots — with who I really am. I went back to the joy of the little girl I used to be, before I was contaminated with the negative messages of growing up."

"Flip your focus" from negative to positive. Start catching yourself — and your kids — at being terrific. You are terrific — and so are they. *Whatever you look for, you find.* Notice their effort and progress; don't just focus on results. Catch them being good, and reward them with your attention. Ask them about what they're doing, and show your appreciation. Everyone needs more appreciation; give others what they need. Be sincere.

What you focus on expands. Focus on misbehavior and you'll see it every day. Focus on spills and messiness, on forgetfulness and mistakes, and you'll all be stressed. Focus on good efforts, on good ideas, on follow-through, on actions that make a difference, and you'll see self-esteem. Focus on love and you'll feel more of it. Focus on strengths.

Everyone in your family has strengths. Look for them! What are the positive qualities of each person? Start conversations about strengths with questions such as

- What strengths did you use to overcome that problem? (*patience, curiosity, courage, kindness,* and so forth)
- Do you realize you have *grit*? (or *zest,* or *a sense of beauty,* etc.)
- What positive qualities about yourself/your sister/your dad do you take for granted?

When we obsess or worry about our failings, insecurities, and mistakes, we can easily forget our strengths. We all need help recognizing them. Sometimes we don't even know what our strengths are until someone points them out. It is especially important to special needs kids that their abilities, not their disabilities, are emphasized.

Trust

"*I think we may safely trust a good deal more than we do.*" — Henry David Thoreau[4]

A crucial ingredient when building self-esteem is trust. In her popular self-esteem workshops, Mom asked the audience how important trust was, on a scale of one to ten. She started counting.

When she got to ten, all hands in the room would shoot up.

A child wonders, "Is this world a friendly, safe place for me?" "Can I depend on being fed when I'm hungry and being comforted when I am hurt or frightened?" "Are my needs being fulfilled?" "Can I count on my parents?" "Can I be myself?" The child concludes either "I can trust" or "I cannot trust." We cannot relax our nervous systems if we cannot trust those around us.

In workshops, participants have defined trust as an act of faith, belief in another, confidence, predictability, the absence of fear, a willingness to be vulnerable, feeling safe, and the basis for intimacy. For trust to develop, children must feel safe. The primary task of parents is to create a safe environment for their children. In creating safety, parents lay the foundation for trust and health. Young people who are most vulnerable to peer pressure are those who distrust messages they receive from the significant adults in their lives.[5]

"The single most important ingredient in a nurturing relationship — in any relationship — is honesty," states author Claudia Black[6] You cannot have trust without truth. No one can trust, or be expected to trust, unless people openly and honestly talk about their feelings and what's important. Dishonesty creates confusion and destroys trust. If you do not tell the truth, neither will your kids. They learn from you. Children want honesty. Let's resurrect the old saying "Honesty is the best policy." But be kind.

When a baby is born, new parents often fall headlong into familiar "mom" and "dad" roles, just to get through overwhelming new responsibilities. Yet, in the shift into authoritative positions, we can lose touch with our human failings, feelings, and needs. Mom and dad roles can reinforce power structures that erode family trust and maintain a façade. When the appearance of being a perfect family has a higher priority than having loving, solid relationships within one, unrealistic or impossible expectations breed disappointment and distrust (see chapters 14 and 23, "Parenting Leadership Styles" and "Obsession with Perfection").

Distrust can result from many things: disrespect, fear, neglect, insensitivity, ridicule, humiliation, rejection, neglect, and abuse. Trust must be reasonably and consciously cultivated. However, we can't trust anyone 100 percent of the time; trust is not an all-or-nothing proposition, as many assume. Using good judgment, we must figure out how far and in what situations we can trust people. At what age can you trust your child to carry a cup of water? When are they old enough to cross the street by themselves? When are they ready to be left home alone, to finish their homework without supervision, or to babysit? What about your partner? You might be able to trust them to bring home a paycheck, but not to pick the kids up on time. What about you? Can you be trusted with secrets, but not remembering birthdays?

Trust is always a two-way street. Kids need to be able to trust their parents, and parents need to be able to trust their kids. Parents need to be able to trust each other. Who do we trust? We trust people who are worthy of trust. We must be trustworthy for our families.

We can build trust with our children in a variety of ways:
- Treat them with respect and care.
- Accept them for who they are. Honor differences.
- Meet their needs. Feed them when they're hungry; see that they get enough sleep. Help them feel safe.
- Spend comfortable, quality time together. Be there for them.
- Comfort them when they're afraid. Hold them when they're hurting.
- Avoid unpleasant surprises and punishments. Learn nondamaging discipline (see chapter 17, "Discipline without Damage). Create predictable routines.
- Don't make promises you can't, or won't, keep. If you are not 100 percent committed to something and sure that you can deliver on a promise, don't make that pledge, especially to your kids.

Maintain your own integrity by being accountable to your loved ones.

- Say what you mean—using tact—and mean what you say. Don't give insincere or undeserved praise.
- Respect your family members' boundaries and privacy. Don't force anyone to say things they don't mean.
- Let your children know they can count on you. Tell them when and where you are going and when you'll return.
- Prepare them in advance for big events in their lives. Let them know what to expect.[7]

Sometimes trust begins with a leap of faith on the part of the parents—a gift of respect for and belief in their children. It's important to set high, but attainable, standards for your children and live up to them yourself. Wanting to live up to your expectations, kids become trustworthy. For this reason, we have an obligation to trust them so that they can become trustworthy. We need to focus on their strong points, build on them, and encourage children to be their best.

Eighteen-year-old Katie told her parents that their greatest gift to her was their trust. Her peers would stay out late or do something unacceptable, knowing they would be yelled at, be grounded, or lose driving privileges. Katie's parents' trust was a strong deterrent because she didn't want to lose it. She could be honest with them because she had trust in them, as well. She knew that if an emergency came up, they would be reasonable and understanding, even if they were upset. By being trust*worthy*, she learned to trust herself. Parents also need to learn to trust themselves more and model trustworthiness.

A trusting family environment is one in which honesty, connectedness, and love can flourish. It begins with bonding and building safety and becomes the strongest foundation for building self-esteem.

28

5.

Self-Esteem Protection Skills

"No one can make you feel inferior without your consent." —
Eleanor Roosevelt[1]

The extra-large bumper sticker on the parked truck shouts, in capital letters, "If you can read this, you're an idiot." I'm startled by the random put-down. This seemingly harmless phrase is just one small example of the casual cruelty that people inflict so carelessly on strangers, acquaintances, and members of their own families. Negativity is so common that it seems normal in our culture. Like pollution, it creeps into our homes and under our skin. We have to be aware of toxic levels in our environment and our systems. The drip-drip of negativity damages our self-esteem.

As children we learn quickly that the world can be full of downers. School days are filled with opportunities for humiliation. Typical self-esteem eaters kids encounter daily include being put down by peers, called names, embarrassed by teachers, and abused by bullies; wearing the wrong clothes to school; getting poor grades; dropping the ball in PE; leaving important things at home; feeling awkward around the opposite sex; not knowing where they belong; and not understanding what's being asked of them.

Hopefully, by the time we've reached adulthood, we've begun to learn how to keep these things from sending our self-esteem into a tailspin. But the digs keep coming, at work, in the media, and on random bumper stickers.

Everyone—children and adults alike—needs strategies for *increasing* self-esteem and strategies for *protecting* self-esteem from bullies and toxic people and situations. One of the most important things you can do in your daily life is to keep self-esteem high—and one of the most important things you can do for your kids is to teach them how to protect and nurture themselves. Self-esteem carries its own momentum—the more you have, the less effort it takes to put back together the broken pieces after a blow.

Think of a time when your self-esteem was really high and someone flung an insult your way. In your confidence you let it go right past, thinking they didn't know what they were talking about. The better you feel about yourself, the less vulnerable you are to negativity. Now, remember a time when your self-esteem was sagging and someone gave you a compliment. You may have denied it or found yourself looking between the lines for "what they really meant."

If someone offered you a plate of garbage, would you say, "No thanks," and go on your way? Or would you take it anyway, just to be polite?

Without self-esteem protection skills, many reach for food, alcohol, drugs, or other substances and behaviors to soothe discomfort and pain. With new skills you can set boundaries and teach others how to treat you well. Here are strategies you and your children can use to deal with daily slings and arrows.

- **Inquire.** Asking, "Is something wrong?" or "What do you mean by that?" throws responsibility back on the insult giver and invites them to talk about it. Perhaps there was some miscommunication?
- **Confront.** You don't need to grin and bear it or be a martyr. If a put-down hurts you, you might say, "Ouch," or, "I don't like that." Children can also use a snake sound, hissing at the person and pointing two fingers like the tongue of a threatened dangerous snake. For kids, this may be easier than defending themselves verbally.

- **Outlaw put-downs.** Teachers use this technique. They teach children to be alert to attacks on their self-esteem and that of fellow students. Families with zero tolerance for nastiness at home don't produce bullies.
- **Withdraw.** We don't want to be around people who are unkind, cruel, or annoying. This can be a lifesaver in some cases. But be careful—if you overuse this one, you can lose personal power and your relationships.
- **Don't take it personally.** Mostly kids and other people do things *for* themselves, not *against* you. Maybe they're having a bad day. Maybe they're unaware or simply careless. The put-down probably has nothing to do with you. Instead of reacting, you might find out if there's some pain behind the barb.
- **Humor.** As the shortest kid in his class, José was sometimes called Shrimp. He'd look his teaser right in the eye, smile, and say, "Hmm, I love shrimp."
- **Make a neutral remark.** When they finish, say, "Oh," or, "I see." Leave it at that.
- **Consider the source.** Some people seem to wallow in negativity. Let them express whatever emotions they choose, knowing they have little or nothing to do with the real you. A person who uses racial epithets, for example, advertises their own ugly prejudices and narrow-mindedness.
- **Disagree.** Realize that what people say is their own opinion; you know yourself better than they do. You might disagree, or just say, "You're entitled to your own opinion."

- **Sift through.** Perhaps there is some truth in what they're saying, but they haven't yet learned good, gentle feedback skills.
- **Call a friend.** There's nothing more comforting than a shoulder to cry on. A friend can help you find your strengths when you've lost them.
- **Use positive self-talk.** Repeat over and over to yourself, "No matter what you say or do to me, I am a worthwhile person."[2]

Teach these strategies to your kids. Share them with anyone you know who is in a toxic or abusive situation. It will help them protect their inner core of self-worth.

Here are some strategies that have worked for other people.

- **Wax your back.** A dear friend once told us that every morning in the shower he "waxes his back," and his life is great. No, he doesn't rid himself of superfluous hair; it's a metaphor to protect him from whatever negativity might "rain" on him in the business world, just as oily feathers protect a duck.
- **Duck.** In Arab lore, people supposedly "dodge curses," as if they were avoiding physical objects being thrown at them. You can do this mentally, too. Imagine the negativity just flying over your head.
- **Wear a shield.** In your mind, wrap yourself in white light or an invisible protective bubble. Negativity cannot penetrate it, much less wound you. Mahatma Gandhi said, "Nobody can hurt me without my permission."
- **Give yourself a hug.** Give one to your kid. Hugs are great as a send-off in the morning, a welcome home later on, or an affectionate goodnight. Life is better with hugs. Four a day is the minimum!

- **Clothing and jewelry.** Wonder Woman had bracelets. Working Girl had shoulder pads. People wear power clothes when they want to make a good impression — when, for example, they want to borrow money from a bank. A piece of jewelry or a special garment (maybe Batman underwear?) can impart a sense of personal strength and power.
- **Permission to be different.** Kids (and adults) often get a lot of pressure to be like everyone else. They are teased because they wear the "wrong" clothes. If you teach kids that they are unique and don't have to act and dress like everyone else, they'll be less affected by those pressures. Give them permission to be different — to be who they really are. Give them this exact phrase as a retort: "Permission to be different?"

You don't have to put up with put-downs! You don't have to be a toxic waste dump for other peoples' bad feelings. Try these strategies, or your own, until you find those that help you maintain your self-esteem, and teach them to your children.

These skills can be absolute lifesavers for children who have characteristics that attract attention, such as wearing hearing aids or prosthetics. One student with a malformed ear had a simple answer ready for questions: "It's just special. Only one person out of 440,000 has ears like this." Children who feel good about their unique differences are more tease resistant. Role play to practice self-esteem protection strategies and responses; model the positive language kids can use in these situations. You may discover some interesting things. A child who has a wheelchair may become aware that he or she is an expert at using it and can do things other kids can't. When one mother learned that her young daughter would have to wear glasses, she began to call her "my beautiful four-eyes" in a loving tone of voice. Later on, when kids teased her, she didn't even recognize the intended insult.

Minority students face unfair self-esteem traps in a different way.[3] Dealing with more aggression than usual, they need to build the protective tactic of recognizing stigmatizing stereotypes. However, there is often a nagging doubt whether the attack on their self-esteem was racial or personal. In addition to the above tips, minority kids need cultural heroes, words, and connections that strengthen their identity.

You will not, and should not, always be there to protect your children. Help them learn how to protect themselves. Help them figure out when to put their defenses up and when to let them down. Teach them to seek trustworthy people who are safe to be around. Your kids will catch on and increase the positive energy in the world around them. One young person told her mom, "I help my friends learn to put insults where they belong—in the trash!"

A child with healthy self-esteem is a gift to the world.

6.

"I Know They Love Me, but I Don't Feel It."

"To be fully seen by somebody, then, and be loved anyhow — this is a human offering that can border on miraculous."
—Elizabeth Gilbert[1]

On their twenty-fifth wedding anniversary, a wife told her husband that she had been expressing her love all those years by warming his plates. He replied, "I hate warm plates!" Clearly, they worked through this miscommunication, because they celebrated their thirtieth anniversary — with cold plates.

There are two parts to communication: sending a message and receiving one. Most parents love their children, but because of personal habits, family patterns, and faulty communication styles, many children do not actually feel loved. In Mom's workshops, she asked parents how many of them *knew* while growing up that their parents loved them; usually, many hands were raised up. When she asked how many *felt* loved, fewer hands went up.

Feeling loved is the first and most fundamental need of a child. Sometimes parents who really love their children don't know how to express that love; sometimes something gets in the way of children receiving it. A parent of a teenage bulimic confessed, "My daughter never felt loved, but I love her dearly!" Being loved does not necessarily mean feeling loved.

In our society, many men are taught from childhood not to express their feelings, or to only express them in rigid, structured ways. Many are out of touch with their feelings. Those who

35

experienced trauma and learned to block difficult emotions have a hard time finding access to the kaleidoscope of feelings that love provides. Shere Hite's survey of seven thousand men revealed that almost none of them were close to their fathers.[2] Raising children was typically considered women's work, and fathers, working away from home for long hours, had little contact with their kids. Today, more than twice as many dads stay at home with their kids than did in the 1980s, and they are much more involved in child care.

Still, many dads, like moms who are also breadwinners, feel like they don't spend enough time with their children because they're working so much.[3] Children need closeness with their dads, as well as with their moms, regardless of whether the parents live together or apart. Kids need to feel accepted and cherished by their fathers, and, in turn, dads need to love their children and feel loved and admired by them.

Kids need to connect deeply with both parents on an emotional level, hearing "I love you" and *feeling* loved by them.

What did you get from your father? What did you *need* from him? What do your children need and want from you?

If you did not learn to love as a child, now is the time to do so. Kids are perfect to start on. They're receptive and responsive and can teach you what love is. Infants are full of love. Learn to receive love and to love yourself, and then you can more easily nurture, love, and parent your children.

> *"If we cannot love ourselves, where will we draw our love for anyone else?"* – Mildred Newman and Bernard Berkowitz[4]

What *Does Not* Communicate Love

Much harm has been done in the name of love. Parents with good intentions try to show love in ways that don't work, such as the following:

- **Overpermissiveness.** Parents think, "My kids know that I love them because I let them do anything they want." A high-school friend of mine could stay out as late as she wanted to and concluded that her parents didn't care enough to set a curfew. Children need safe, healthy, and reasonable limits; your willingness to provide boundaries conveys love.

- **Overprotectiveness.** In this sometimes scary world in which we live, our children need protection from danger and harm. Wise parents assess the risk in a situation and increase or decrease protection as needed. However, if we overprotect our kids, they conclude two things: the world is dangerous (so anxiety is normal), and they aren't capable people. Hovering, or helicoptering, doesn't feel loving to kids who need to find their own way. Also, when parents do things for their kids that children should be doing for themselves, they deprive their offspring of the opportunity to learn, gain confidence, and build self-esteem.

- **Underprotectiveness.** Many parents give their children freedom, but kids can feel unloved when their safety is neglected. You need to hold a kid's hand to cross a street until they are at least five years old, and they're not developmentally ready to safely cross alone until they are ten.

- **Martyrdom.** Women in many parts of the world are taught to be self-sacrificing, putting the needs of others above their own. Moms express love for their families by helping and serving, but sometimes they end up being doormats. By putting themselves last and not taking care of themselves, they may eventually feel resentful and depleted. Guess what? The children of martyrs do not feel loved; they feel guilty. It's crucial for parents to take care of themselves and to set

37

boundaries. Children who have learned to expect someone else to always "do it for them" are disempowered and struggle more.

- **Material possessions.** Linda, a thirty-six-year-old mom, told me, "My father would buy me anything I wanted, but he would never hug me or show me any affection. I've spent my whole life feeling that he didn't love me." She felt indulged but not loved. Give your children more presence than presents. Pursuit of material wealth comes at a cost. *The best thing to spend on your children is your time.*

- **Quantity time without quality.** Spending lots of time together does not necessarily communicate love. Many people who were near adults twenty-four hours a day still felt unloved. Kids need so much of our time and attention just for the basics that sometimes parents just don't have the energy to connect in meaningful ways. With simple new skills and habits, however, parents can make time for bonding, nurturing, and loving interactions.

- **Conditions.** Some parents say, "I love you when —," "I love you if —," "I love you because —," or "I love you, but —." Strings attached to love cast long dark shadows. Conditional love does not convey love. It is a manipulation or a maneuver to improve performance. "I love you" is a complete sentence that ends with a period.

What *Does* Communicate Love

Larry, a workshop attendee, said, "I felt loved when my dad carried me on his shoulders and sang to me." One woman felt loved when the family built an ice rink and then went skating together. The love in their families increased, as did self-esteem. Endearing memories came from having fun, or as we say in the biz, from building positive emotion.

What situations made you feel loved as a child? Are you doing things like that for or with your children?

There are many, many ways we can communicate love effectively to children, including the following:

- **Being with, not doing for.** It's easy to get caught up in always doing things for children. It's important, at times, to put aside all the busyness and just be together, especially in times of crisis. With quality of presence, kids conclude, "It's important for you to be with me. I must matter." They feel loved.

- **Taking them seriously.** Things that happen in your children's lives are of tremendous importance to them. Put yourself in their shoes and value what they share with you.

- **Really listening.** This crucial life skill will be discussed fully in chapter 7, "Listening Skills."

- **Nonverbal messages.** Positive facial expressions, eye contact, affectionate touch, and attentiveness make others feel important.

- **Positive words.** We all want to hear good things about ourselves, and everyone needs encouragement. Be sure your words are sincere.

- **Respect and enjoyment.** Children read our attitudes. When we have fun with them, everybody wins.

If you haven't yet explicitly communicated love to your kids, start now and watch what happens. If you don't feel enough love now, look for it and get it!

"If everyone had just one single person in his life to say, 'I will love you no matter what. I will love you if you are stupid, if you slip and fall on your face, if you do the wrong thing, if you make mistakes, if you behave like a human being – I will love you no matter,' then we'd never end up in mental institutions." – Leo Buscaglia[5]

7.

Listening Skills

"What most people really need is a good listening to."
– Mary Lou Casey

Kids who grew up under the children-should-be-seen-and-not-heard rule had a distinct handicap. They were deprived of the opportunity to express their thoughts and opinions and to gain confidence in their own abilities. Many of them came to believe that what they had to say wasn't important, that they weren't important, or even that no one cared about them. Their self-esteem suffered.

My mom was one of these kids. The first time she felt really listened to, she was about seventeen years old. "I spent the night at my friend Annie's home. She and I talked and talked into the early morning. Annie cared about what I had to say and really listened to me! I felt surprise, relief, joy, and closeness." Really listening expresses interest and caring. It is a powerful and intimate experience that enhances self-esteem and friendship.

Remember a time when you had something very important to say, but the person you were talking to was not listening well. The listener either wasn't interested or didn't know how to listen, or perhaps it was just a bad time to bring up that particular subject. What was that like for you? What did you feel? People can feel frustrated, rejected, angry, unimportant, or unloved when they're not heard. They might take it personally and shut down or withdraw. Carl Jung said that people were in institutions because no one would listen to their stories.

Now remember a time when you had something to say and you *were* listened to. Chances are, you felt that you were being taken seriously. You felt important, and your self-esteem went up a few notches. For effective listening, we need to listen to others as we would like them to listen to us.

Communication skills are the most basic important skills that we need in life. Without them we are doomed to continual frustration, misunderstandings, and loneliness. Since the intrusion of digital devices into family time, communication patterns have changed dramatically, and vital connection skills have been lost.

An Australian social planner who conducted extensive research in the suburbs of New South Wales was concerned that "whole generations of women are being lost to us. . . . I've talked to women who've lived for four and a half years across the street from other women and have never even introduced themselves because they seem to have lost the skills of getting to know people."[1] Communication skills enable us to develop friendships and deep love relationships that enrich our lives and enhance our families.

A friend recently returned from a two-month stay in a village in northern Thailand where there was no electricity and telephone service. Every evening the family built a fire outside the home and gathered around it to talk with each other for about two hours. Everyone in that culture naturally learned to tell stories and to listen. Because they had no written language, the transmission of their cultural history depended on people's communication skills.

Listening skills are not difficult to learn. Once you learn to use them and teach them to others, they will transform your relationships and raise self-esteem.

Left-Hand Listening

Nicholas Carlisle, the founder of No Bully, teaches his restorative justice trainers the difference between "right-hand listening" and "left-hand listening." Right-hand listening is what most grown-ups do: they hear a little bit of a story and then jump in to solve a problem. Left-hand listening goes from heart to heart.[2] It's what some call active listening; we just call it *good* listening. Here's how to do it.

- **Show that you are interested.** Let your body say, "I'm interested!" Face the speaker; look into their eyes. When listening to children, sit or crouch down to be at their level.
- **Put aside judgment and criticism.** Put yourself and your own concerns aside. Get into their experience. Feel their emotions. Try to understand.
- **Be aware of nonverbal cues.** Note the speed and inflection of the voice, sighs and gulps, posture, eyes glazing over or tearing up. Reading between the lines gives you important information.
- **Let them finish.** Don't interrupt. While you are the listener, let the speaker do the talking. They have the ball; do not take it away. At times it may be okay to briefly interject something if it enhances the other's story. It's also fair to ask them to repeat a point you're not clear on. This may be difficult for those who are used to communicating competitively — impatiently waiting for a comma and then jumping in.
- **Give them the kind of attention that you enjoy.** It's a gift that says, "I care about you," and, "You are important to me." You'll get your turn afterward.

If you have really listened, you have gathered much information. Next, like a mirror,

- **Reflect the experience.** This direct response lets them know you were paying attention. "So let me get this straight — you were in the car, and . . ."
- **Reflect the feeling(s)** back to the other person *from his or her point of view*. For example, "I bet you were scared," "You must have been really excited," or "You must feel _____ because _____."[3]

If you reflected accurately, the speaker will probably breathe a sigh of relief at having been understood or perhaps will exclaim excitedly, "Yes, that's right!" If you have not reflected accurately, the speaker has an opportunity to clear the misunderstanding. The need for a response is so important that little children can repeat a statement over and over and over again until the parent comments. The response lets them know that they were heard.

The conversation can then take one of several turns. The listener can help the speaker explore the situation (Would you do it that way again?) or offer guidance (How can I help you?). Then the listener can speak, expanding upon the topic. Do NOT give advice unless it is requested. Good listening helps people figure things out for themselves.

Like a tennis match, good communication involves give and take. Taking turns is essential for mutual satisfaction and enjoyment. Interrupting, on the other hand — unless it is respectful — stops the flow. Some people are skilled interrupters who take the speaker's story and run with it, effectively creating a power play that damages communication.

Some speakers tend to derail and wander endlessly into impersonal tangents. When both speaker and listener pay attention to tracking, moving from lighter to deeper issues, conversation is more meaningful.

Practice active listening with someone. Find a time convenient for both of you. Read this section together, and then take turns being the speaker, talking for about two or three minutes each. Afterward, discuss how it felt. If, as the speaker, you were really listened to, you probably experienced some or all of these feelings: excitement, interest, a sense of closeness to the listener, validation, self-worth, understanding, and love. As a listener, you probably felt interest, trust, and enrichment from a new experience, excitement, and closeness to the speaker. You have given a great gift. Self-esteem has increased on both sides. This is win-win communication.

If, on the other hand, you didn't feel listened to, give feedback in a positive way. "When you checked your phone, it made me feel like you weren't interested in what I had to say."

Good listening skills are essential. When someone feels they aren't being heard, who comes out winning? No one.

These skills are no more difficult to learn than how to drive a car. They need to be practiced and road tested. At first they may feel awkward and artificial. That's okay. Keep at it, and they'll get easier. Like driving, listening becomes second nature—and just as effective for getting from place to place.

A good time and place to practice listening skills in a family is at the dinner table. To make sure everyone gets heard, use a talking stick (or spoon) that grants the bearer the right to be listened to. When he or she finishes, the stick is passed along to the next person who has something to share. In one family, every Friday night was free-speech night. Family members could say anything they wanted to without fear of consequences. It was a special time for airing problems and building understanding within their family. Leo Buscaglia says, "If you take time to talk together each day, you'll never become strangers."[4] Daily check-ins before bed, when my husband and I each got to say whatever we felt for 5 minutes, helped my marriage go the distance.

Good listeners take the time to just *be with* those they care about the most. This quiet practice helps people discover that they have stories to tell and thoughts to share. As the saying goes, "There's a reason that we have two eyes, two ears, and only one mouth."

Listening Builds the Self

In an article about the gift of listening, therapist Denise Olesky writes about the momentous difference listening and not listening makes.

When We Are Not Listened To:

Those who do not grow up in a healthy environment may not develop a good sense of self. Perhaps they were raised in a home scarred by emotional or physical abuse, neglect, or overparenting. Their identities may have been minimally acknowledged, if at all.

When feelings and thoughts are ignored in childhood, children may grow up not recognizing that they have their own ideas and sets of behaviors. If children are forced to yield to others' thoughts, wants, and needs continually over time, the development of their identity may suffer. As they grow into adults, they may question, "Who am I?"

When We Are Listened To:

As we grow and develop from children to young adults, we listen to and learn from the world and others around us. When others listen to and learn from us, we learn that our needs are valid and that we are valuable. We learn that we are individuals with our own identities and our own ideas and sets of behaviors. When our environment is healthy, we grow into adults with a healthy sense of self. We learn that our opinions and thoughts are important. We know who we are.[5]

Listening is an amazing gift for anyone. Teach your children how to do it, and they will go farther in life.

"Listen. People start to heal the moment they feel heard."
– Cheryl Richardson

8.

Asking and Refusal Skills

"Half of the troubles of this life can be traced to saying yes too quickly and not saying no soon enough." —Josh Billings

To ride a bicycle, you must know how to make it go and stop and how to make it turn. Communication skills are just as basic. You need sending skills to let others know what you want and don't want, and you need listening skills to understand what others want and don't want.

A Clever Metaphor

A clever approach to teaching kids basic assertiveness skills is with the metaphors 1) monster ways, 2) mouse ways, and 3) "me" ways, or assertive ways.[1]

Monster ways include shouting, recklessly venting anger, hitting, manipulating, and intimidating others. *Mouse ways* include crying, whining, begging, pouting, hinting, getting sick, and hoping someone will read your mind. Monster and mouse communication styles may work, but they usually create bad feelings in the process. Was there ever a time when you whined, yelled, or cried all day and got what you wanted? How did you feel about yourself? How did others feel about you?

In our society, boys are typically taught, or given permission to use, the monster way (aggressive/pushy communication style), and girls are taught, or given permission to use, the mouse way (passive/pushover communication style). Traditionally, we put together one person with each way and tell them to live happily ever after. Of course, that's the stereotype; people of any gender

46

can be passive or aggressive—or assertive.

Assertive communication is direct communication.

Hard to Ask?

If you're not used to asking for what you want and need, it may feel strange. It can be difficult or intimidating at first, but it is worth the risk. It gets easier with practice.

Sometimes it's hard to know what you want, so pay attention to your feelings. Follow your frustration to its roots. Listen to your fears and their messages. Tune in to your desires and wishes. You might need to take some time to figure out what to ask. Do that first to find your way out of confusion.

Direct communication starts with knowing what you want or need (which is sometimes the hardest part), and then asking or telling others what you want or need simply, without bullying or manipulating. "Would you help me?" "I don't like that." "I'd like to get together more often." "Can I have a hug?"

When we ask for what we want, we are much more likely to get it. For example, instead of complaining about how hard you work and how ungrateful everyone is, say, "I worked very hard today and would like some appreciation." A statement like this can work magic. Not only might you receive appreciation, but also others will know that they, too, can be direct and authentic. Unlike mouse and monster communication, direct asking does not cause drama, residual negativity, or codependent behavior, when people respond to unrequested needs.

Being sensitive to the timing of your question or request gives you a greater chance to receive a positive response. Waiting for a good time to speak or asking for a minute of someone's time beforehand is more graceful than asking someone for something when their hands are literally full, when they're hungry, when they just got home, or when they're deep into a project or task.

Some people think that asking questions when you don't know or understand something is a sign of weakness or failure, but it's actually a powerful tool for getting your needs and the needs of others met. Asking increases your sense of self. Asking is a way to find your way out of confusion. Openness leads to honesty, which can be very rewarding — although at first it can make others uncomfortable. If asking for what you want and need is new to you or your family culture, it takes a big effort at first, and it can be frustrating when you don't get good results right away. Don't give up. Keep trying. It's worth it.

Some questions express interest and caring for others. Open-ended questions encourage more talking than questions that can be answered with one word or phrase. Ask, "Would you tell me about your day?" instead of, "How was your day?" To deepen communication, ask, "How do you feel about . . . ?" "What do you want?" or "How can I help?" Asking in a respectful tone of voice can lead to greater understanding.

Teach Kids to Ask

Asking empowers kids to get their needs met and makes life much easier for adults. One of my nieces learned simple sign language before she learned to talk. But when she visited grandma, she couldn't communicate. Mom couldn't tell why she was crying and crying, and she finally said to the child, "Show me." Little Alexa went to the refrigerator and patted the door. She was thirsty! Creativity brought the solution.

I had a "no whining zone" in my house, a trick I also learned from Mom. If a visiting child was whining, I'd say, "I can't hear you in that voice." Then I'd lower my voice and say, "Ask for what you want in a voice like this." No one ever had to act out in my house to get their thirst quenched. And I didn't have to try to read their minds.

Asking Helps Special Needs Get Met

Children — and adults — with physical or cognitive differences need to learn to feel comfortable asking for what they want and need. Children who are able to assert themselves and make their needs known have the best chance of reaching their full potential.

For example, self-advocacy is crucial for a mainstreamed hearing-impaired child who needs to sit toward the front of a class, ask the teacher to face her or him as much as possible, or ask the teacher to wear an auditory microphone apparatus. A child with ADHD may need to ask for extra time to finish a test or permission to wear headphones to minimize distractions. It is not the school's job to offer accommodations, but once they're aware of special needs, most schools are good at providing support. Few teachers are mind readers. Parents can help identify special needs while children get used to asking, which can make them feel very vulnerable or embarrassed. If there's fear around this issue, unmet needs can cause learning problems to snowball.

Saying "No"

"Saying no can be the ultimate self-care." —Claudia Black

In general, it's easier to ask directly if the other person knows how to say no. When communicating with people who are not able to set boundaries, we have to second-guess them and make assumptions about what we think will make them happy, what they will or will not like or need. People who can't set boundaries often think they're being less trouble because they are accommodating and easygoing and avoid conflict, when in truth they're driving everyone else crazy trying to think for two.

Everyone needs to be able to set their own boundaries, delimiting what is and is not acceptable. As adults, "no" lets us set limits for our children and ourselves. It helps us maintain integrity. For youngsters, "no" helps them learn that their bodies belong to themselves alone and that they have the right and responsibility to protect themselves and get what they need. "No" lets children be comfortable while sleeping, eating nourishing food, and clarifying that they do not want to be touched in certain ways. Older children who are able to say no can be in control of their relationships with alcohol, drugs, and sex. Children who have not been allowed to learn healthy refusal skills are vulnerable to pressure and manipulation and are at higher risk of being bullied, being targeted, and falling into unhealthy relationships and behavior.

Saying no, like braking on a bicycle, defines our boundaries — how far we will go and how close others can come to us. Saying no keeps us from biting off more than we can chew. It helps us to be in the driver's seat and lowers stress, because we can better care for ourselves. Saying no lets us stop what we don't want and get more of what we do want. "It is not okay to say no, however," writes author Patricia Palmer, "if it is a responsibility or something you have already agreed to do. And remember, how you say 'no' makes a difference. Treat others as you like to be treated."[2]

Many people have great difficulty saying no. Why is this? If you are one of them, complete this sentence several times: "Saying no means _____."

When Mom had a group do this exercise, this is what they discovered. Saying no means rejection, selfishness, guilt, failure, weakness, stubbornness, hurting other people's feelings, not being liked by others, and risking anger. No wonder saying *no* can be such a no-no!

The next exercise was thinking about the *value* of saying no.[3] Here's what they discovered: Saying no is like giving yourself a present of honesty, freedom, relief, authority, peace, power, confidence, and integrity. It establishes boundaries. You don't feel used. "No" gives you self-definition and self-respect. It gives you time and control over your own life. It makes your "yeses" more meaningful. Parents have to say no until a child develops judgment skills and the ability to say no for themselves. Then parents need to help them build their "no" muscles.

Sometimes parents threaten their kids, saying, for example, "If you don't stop that, I'm going to spank you." A much better choice of words to stop unacceptable behavior is a simple, firm "No," or, "Stop that." As parents it is our duty to say no if our child's health or safety is at risk. Like anything else, however, "no" can be overused, rendering it ineffective. If you say no to everything, you are being too controlling. Try to say yes at least three times more often than you say no; this will give your "no" more authority. Sound serious when you say "no"; lower the tone of your voice. Look serious; saying "no" while smiling is confusing. Say no with respect and firmness. Avoid being cold or cruel. *You don't have to be mean to mean business.*

The History of "No"

In Mom's generation, and in so many others, women were raised to give away their power. She explained to me how she had an extra-difficult time learning how to say no because she so often heard the phrase "when a woman says 'no,' she really means 'yes.' " It confused her when she was young and angered her when she was older. Now we have a word for it: *gaslighting*, which means denying a person's reality as a control tactic. Kids today are taught "no means no," thanks to date-rape and child-protection education. Teach your kids that the only thing that means "yes" is the word *yes*, delivered with enthusiasm.[4] (Find more about boundaries in chapter 16, "Family Boundaries.")

Some readers may laugh at this chapter, saying, "My kids say no all the time. They're good at it." Kids do come with factory-installed refusal behavior. They shake their heads and stomp their feet and struggle against things they don't want. But my mom actually taught me the word *no*. When I was one and my two-year-old brother, Damian, wanted the toy I had in my hand, Mom sat next to me on the floor, wrapped her hand around my little fingers, and said, "No, Damian!" This was my first assertiveness lesson! It helped dry my tears and turn my sadness into strength.

Here are a few ways to set limits with your kids and model good asking and refusal skills at the same time.

- **Start with gentle "nos"** clearly founded on care.
  "No, you can't stay up another hour. I love you

and want you to be happy to see me in the morning when I wake you up!"

- **Let rules be the bad guy** so you're not always the boss. "You've reached your one-hour limit on the tablet. It's time to go play outside." Make rules together so everyone understands they're for everyone's own good.
- **Add a positive future-oriented twist.** "No, you can't watch that show; it's rated R and you will enjoy it more when you're older."
- **Address the hidden need.** "No, you can't have a cookie before dinner, but you can eat an apple if you're too hungry to wait." "Stop kicking my car seat right now! Do you need attention? I'll give you a big hug when we get home."
- **Role-play refusal skills** around peer pressure situations. Have your tween or teen try to entice you, and then model responses with a *soft no*: "That's okay, I'm good with a Coke"; a *firm no*: "Thank you, no. I don't like beer"; and a *hard no*: "No, I don't drink; I need you to respect my choice or I'm leaving."
- **Talk about the body language** that goes along with refusal. If you mean it, don't laugh as if you're kidding. Crossed arms mean business. A shaking finger or head means "no."
- **Give choices** that allow kids to practice asking and refusal skills, identifying their needs, wants, and preferences.

Asking, refusing, consenting, and agreeing are all sources of personal power. When you teach your kids asking and refusal skills, they learn to establish healthy boundaries.

9.

Dealing with Feelings

*"Feelings come and go like clouds in a windy sky. Conscious
breathing is my anchor."* – Thich Nhat Hanh

Everyone is born with a full deck of emotions. They shuffle
through us constantly, coming into play when we interact with
other people. But we don't always know how to deal with all of
our feelings. Sometimes we don't even know what the game is.
And society makes up weird rules: certain people get to have
feelings, and others don't; certain feelings are excessive or
inappropriate. But when children learn to accept and listen to all
of their feelings, they are better equipped to live their own lives
fully and freely.

What kinds of feelings did your parents express? How did they
express them? What did they do with other feelings? Whose
patterns do you tend to follow?

"Say you're sorry!" "Tell me you love me." "You should be
happy." "Don't be mad." "You don't really feel that way." It's
easy to try to force feelings on others. When parents tell kids how
to feel, though, they pressure them to give up their own emotional
reality. With you-shouldn't-feel-how-you-feel messages, kids
conclude that their feelings are unacceptable, wrong, or even
nonexistent. They conclude that they can't trust those feelings or,
perhaps, they can't trust others with their feelings.

"Un-listened-to feelings can contribute to violence, depression,
alienation from self and others, and a host of psychosomatic
illnesses," says author and psychologist Dr. Ani Liggett.[1] When
they don't know what to do with their emotions, children hide
them from themselves and others or deny them altogether. They
may become isolated in fear, worry, embarrassment, anger, or

guilt, building protective barriers around themselves. They may repress their true feelings and pretend to feel differently. Or, as they create defenses to protect their true feelings, they may come to identify with those defenses rather than their own emotions. Later on they may habitually turn to alcohol and other drugs to manage or completely numb difficult emotions.

"Safety disappears when you decide what children 'should' enjoy," writes Dorothy Corkille Briggs. "Respect for separateness proves you care." Everyone has a right to his or her own feelings. And this right must be accepted and protected. Kids have their own bodies, their own minds, their own dreams, and their own feelings. They are unique individuals, different from you. "Your way of seeing and feeling is not the only way of seeing and feeling," writes Briggs.[2]

It can be hard to accept children's feelings — especially if we have trouble accepting our own. Yet children can teach us *how* to deal with feelings. When children hurt themselves, they cry and shriek as though their whole world has fallen apart — a few minutes later, once the problem has been addressed, they're laughing. Healthy kids emote all the time: they talk and roar and cry and yell and giggle and keep their emotions *in motion*. There are no mixed messages or double meanings here. Their words (or other noises) and body language clearly let you (and everyone else!) know their emotional state at the moment. And like the weather, after the storm is over, the sun shines again, and all's well with the world. Kids don't start out with hang-ups, and parents can help kids avoid growing them in the first place.

Getting comfortable with your feelings can help you reparent yourself as you parent your child. When you accept children's emotions — whatever they may be — you help them to "own" their feelings. They conclude, "My feelings are okay, even when they're not the same as my dad's," "It's okay to be me," and "I can trust myself." Self-esteem goes up when you honor differences.

Feelings guide us through our human experience: listen to them. We all have sorrows and joys. Pay attention to the subtleties of tenderness, melancholy, reverence, and anticipation. Honor them all.

When we have feelings we can't handle, we hold our breath. When we breathe through feelings, we let them flow. Feelings that have been stuffed for a long time may become distorted and exaggerated, and we might need help allowing ourselves to accept them, to let them be. They are okay, but they are not a part of you; they are there to show you something so that you can move on. Acknowledging the pain, anger, or even hatred that might be inside you is the first step toward releasing and resolving these difficult feelings.

Understanding your *emotions* can help you *feel* better. "Feelings seem inappropriate only when they are not understood," states Claudia Black.[2] *All feelings are okay.* What you do with your feelings—your behavior—can be judged as acceptable or unacceptable.

Not talking about your feelings can create anxiety, tension, and distance. If you share your feelings openly and clearly, others don't have to rely on guesswork to know what's happening. When you express feelings, you might say, "I feel mad/glad/sad because _____," and then ask for what you want. Talking things out can release tension, help you gain perspective, and open you to the support and caring of others. *We teach children how to handle their feelings by how we handle ours.* One of the most important jobs of parenting is to notice, label, and affirm feelings.

When children get hurt, encourage them to say, "Ow!" If a physician gives a shot and it hurts, saying "Ouch!" can help release pain. When kids don't have words to express pain, they cry and fuss. Show them how to yell into a pillow, so they can express all the hurt without hurting others. The more it hurts, the harder they should yell. Tell them you can hear what they are feeling. Then encourage them to ask for what they want (a kiss, perhaps, or a Band-Aid).

My friend Laurel posted, "The other day my two-and-a-half-year-old Amanda was screaming with anger when my husband left the house in a hurry one morning. Baby Patrick was screaming at the same time. I wanted to scream, too! But I got Patrick to my breast and calmed Amanda enough to listen. I said to her, 'You're angry because daddy left and didn't say good-bye to you. Is that right?' Suddenly she stopped sobbing, and looked at me in surprise, then nodded furiously. 'I no knowed daddy is gone,' she said. The next minute she became her calm and focused self again!"[4] Louise Erdrich writes, "When you are little you do not always know when you are screaming or crying—your feelings and the sound that comes out of you are all one thing."[5] When children express emotions verbally, activity from the survival part of the brain moves to the frontal lobe, building emotional intelligence. If we help kids *talk* their feelings out, they don't have to *act* them out.

If Laurel had told her daughter to stop crying, knock it off, or get over it, Amanda would have received a different message. When we repress feelings, tension builds up in our bodies. This pressure may turn against the self in the form of psychosomatic or psychological problems, or it may be directed unconsciously against others in the family or in society. If Laurel had raised her voice and scared Amanda, the child would have felt alone in her pain, and this would have created trauma. We need to use care when expressing our own feelings, or we can harm our children: act from our frontal lobes, which are fully developed. Laurel wanted to scream, but she controlled the impulse. Instead, she acknowledged her own feelings and ordered her priorities so she could manage the pain everyone was feeling.

Feelings are private, internal experiences that inform us about our relationship to the world. Our feelings are, in fact, our interface with the world outside our bodies, and they help us make decisions and form values. We respond, normally and naturally, to everything, either with calmness or anxiety. We can react knee-jerk fashion to our every feeling, overwhelmed by emotional responses, or we can learn to take charge of our emotions and choose our responses. We need to teach our children how to act appropriately on their feelings.

Feelings follow our thoughts, or self-talk. Fearful thoughts, for example, lead to feelings of fear, which lead to a certain set of behaviors. This is true whether or not we are aware of our thoughts or beliefs. Once, while walking home at night, I noticed that my body was tense and my breath was shallow. I tuned into my thoughts and realized I'd heard stories about people being attacked and mugged in the dark. Expecting trouble, I walked faster. Once I recognized my worry, I took a deep breath and noticed my surroundings. No one was near me. I turned my thoughts to my family at home and how happy I would be to see my husband and son. I felt happy; I breathed deeply. Someone approached me, and I smiled. My moment of mindfulness created a positive connection with someone else who may have been feeling anxious.

Thoughts and feelings affect all of our decisions, no matter how mundane. When your child wants an ice cream cone, for example, and you cannot or do not want to buy one, you can

- deny your child's feelings ("You don't really want an ice cream cone"),
- manipulate his or her feelings ("You shouldn't feel that way before dinner"),
- accept and acknowledge the feelings ("You'd sure like to get a cone right now"), and then
- intervene at the thought level ("But it's too close to dinner time, and it would spoil your appetite"), or
- intervene at the behavior level ("Sorry, we can't get one right now, honey"), or even
- engage with imagination ("Dinner is coming soon, but if you could have a triple-decker another time, what flavors would you choose?").

When our family, work, and social cultures do not create space to acknowledge, much less affirm, feelings, it is generally not safe to express them. We learn when to cautiously reveal our emotions and when to keep them in check. In a winning family, we can create a culture of mindfulness in which we seek space between thoughts, feelings, and actions. This reduces reactivity and allows everyone to be who they are while at home.

There are many ways to practice mindfulness, from simply sitting and noticing your breath and thoughts, to walking and listening to your feelings, to talking about them with someone who cares about you. A good rule of thumb when dealing with kids is *talk it out so you don't have to act it out.*

Both talking and writing shift intensity from our emotional brains to our thinking brains. A journal is a wonderful tool for sorting through confusion and learning to listen to your thoughts. Writing privately releases tension and helps us learn to deal with emotions. You don't even have to make good sentences. Simply making a list of emotions you felt during the day brings clarity. Feelings often come and go without being identified, but we teach parents that *naming is taming.* What feelings did you experience? When did you feel them? Where in your body did you experience them? How did you express them? Did they remind you of anything? What thoughts were connected with the feelings? What feelings were missing? As writing brings clarity, you can identify patterns in your emotional processes that will help you change and grow. A mindfulness practice can start you on the path to becoming your own ally and best friend.

Let's dive deeper into common emotions everyone (whether parent or kid) struggles with.

Guilt and Shame

"Guilt: the gift that keeps on giving." — Erma Bombeck

Guilt has been defined as moral self-disapproval. It is a feeling we have when we know we've done something wrong. In fact, there are many levels of guilt, ranging from mild embarrassment to crippling shame. The dictionary defines *guilt* as "the fact of being responsible for an offense or wrongdoing." It is a specific state of being that can be removed by making amends. Yet when wrongs are not righted, guilt becomes a burden and can destroy self-esteem and cripple lives with anxiety. *Shame* is defined as "a painful emotion caused by a strong sense of guilt, unworthiness, or disgrace."[6] Specific guilt is concrete – you actually did something wrong. General guilt is a feeling that you did something wrong, whether or not it is factually true. The former can be remedied. The latter must be healed.

The origins of shame often precede birth and are embedded in society. For my mom, who was a good little Catholic girl, the concept of original sin — that mysterious, indelible mark of evil on her soul — devastated her and continually undermined her self-esteem. Though she had done nothing wrong, she grew up suffering a bitter, undefined, unnameable, and undeserved shame. I feel fortunate that she enabled me to construct a healthier ego, but that didn't protect me from being shamed by others. This was often such a foreign experience to me that my built-in bullshit detector didn't catch it, and I had to struggle to unravel my reactions. According to John Bradshaw, shame is one of the major destructive forces in all human life.

A general sense of guilt occurs when people do not have self-defined values and moral standards, but they subscribe unconsciously to a secondhand value system provided by parents and significant others or schools, churches, and other social institutions. Values defined by others can set up dissonance within ourselves; we want to do what we are "supposed" to do, but we don't know exactly what that is and therefore always feel like we've failed.

Our culture provides us with many sources of shame: being poor; being disabled; being a person of color; being an immigrant; having alcoholism, incest, or another dysfunction in the family; not fitting into accepted gender definitions; and having a body shape unlike an ideal. The list goes on and on, suggesting that we should feel guilty about many things for which we are not responsible.

For example, some parents feel guilty about a child's difference or disability as if it were, in some way, their own fault. If you carry around this type of guilt, acknowledge it and realize that it is perfectly normal to feel this way. Talking about it will reduce discomfort and anxiety. It will also help you avoid passing this feeling on to the child, who has to live with their ability and reality. Then let this guilt go. It gets in the way of healthy development and keeps you from acknowledging facts. If you become comfortable talking about the difference and only express your doubts and fears to trusted adults, your child's self-esteem will rise. Help them find ways to talk about themself that feel right. Disclosure to others goes a long way toward minimizing a child's chance of rejection by their peers.[7]

A dysfunctional family is a breeding ground for guilt and shame. When we live closely with others to whom we are bonded, we need a high degree of accountability and interpersonal responsibility or life becomes an emotional battle zone. Mothers and fathers, each in their own ways, often use guilt to manipulate others in order to get what they want. Disappointment is blamed on others, and children either feel guilty or resentful. Blaming and shaming create a hard-to-break cycle. If this is a cultural norm or tradition, it can be harder to build skills for communicating directly.

When children are manipulated by guilt, they learn to shame themselves. Philip Oliver-Diaz and Patricia O'Gorman write, "Unfortunately, in most addicted families, shaming and humiliation are the chief tools used for controlling children."[8] When parents are unconsciously shame-filled and lack self-esteem, they cannot give love to themselves or others. They cannot model healthy ways to express feelings, set boundaries, be intimate, or solve problems. They do not know these things themselves and therefore cannot teach them to others. Their children are deprived of bottom-line basics in life and carry shame into yet another generation.

In a family where guilt is the main operating system, there can be no such thing as unconditional love. Objects and affections that are ostensibly gifts from the heart have strings attached. Parents keep kids off balance with statements and accusations. "What's wrong with you?" "You should know better than that!" "How could you do this to me?" "You're trying to undermine me, aren't you?" "How dare you!" "Shame on you!" Sometimes it's not even that blatant. Even if they are only slightly negative, blanket statements like "You always _____" and "You never _____" instill in children a deep sense of shame and unworthiness. (Even if the statements are true, find a better way to give feedback!)

A forty-eight-year-old friend of mine revealed, "I wasted my childhood tormented with guilt and fear. I tried so hard to be good, yet I always felt bad. I tried to second-guess my mom all the time so I could avoid being blamed and criticized. I was a good little kid who grew up paralyzed by fear and guilt. If driving down the street I'd see a policeman, I'd feel an intense wave of anxiety, even though I had done nothing wrong!"

Specific guilt is a healthy thing; it's a feeling that tells us when something is wrong. Sorrow or remorse are appropriate in this case because feeling pain builds empathy and helps you take responsibility for your part and make reparations. Justice comes from fixing a mistake, learning from it, moving on, and not repeating it. Finally, forgiveness heals and completes the emotional healing. A child (or adult) can learn from this cycle: "I did a bad/stupid thing, but I am a good person and I can correct my mistakes." Justice allows everyone to be good again.

For someone who carries around a great deal of general guilt, there can be no restoration of self-esteem. If you struggle with this, here are a few ways to begin to work through and unburden yourself of guilt.

- Minimize it. Break it down. Ask yourself what specific action causes these feelings of guilt?
- Find the source. Who or what judged your behavior?
- Separate yourself from that source and judge for yourself if your behavior was actually wrong.

- Ask yourself, deep inside, what you believe, want, and choose for yourself.
- Correct the guilt-producing behavior if necessary. Make amends, or have a discussion about misunderstandings.
- Listen to your self-talk. You talk yourself into feeling guilty, so you can talk yourself out of it.
- Know that you are okay. You did the best you could given the information you had at the time.
- Forgive yourself and let go of guilt.
- Realize that what you did is not who you are.

Shame is intensified by secrecy. It's hard to identify shame because it lurks beneath the surface and speaks to us in disguised voices. Moving beyond shame is not as easy as fixing a mistake. Amends are harder, perhaps impossible, to make. And yet shame must be healed before growth can take root.

- Name and acknowledge the shame.
- Talk about it. Breaking the silence can help release its grip.
- Give yourself the gift of total acceptance — moles and warts and all.
- Again, find the judge. Acknowledge that this voice may simply be wrong. If you have actually done something to deserve judgment, reframe your shame as specific guilt and deal with it.
- Affirm that you are not perfect, but you are okay and worthwhile.
- Chose to love, and embrace yourself unconditionally just the way you are.
- Determine your own values and live by them.

The more you sift through and unravel knots of shame, the less likely you will pass shame on to your children.

Grief

"We cannot selectively numb emotions. When we numb the painful

emotions, we also numb the positive emotions." –Brené Brown

Grief is our body's way of responding to and moving beyond emotional loss. Grieving is a misunderstood and neglected growth process, and we need special care while we experience loss. When we don't know how to deal with grief, we get stuck in the loss and pain for years.

Mom tells her story: "My uncle Franz lived with my family for many years. This arrangement started with my parents' marriage; he even went with them on their honeymoon in my father's Essex! His relationship with us ended with his death when I was fourteen years old. During my childhood, he had been the love of my life and my best friend within the family. His death on the eve of my womanhood devastated me. It felt like the end of the world and I didn't know what to do with the pain. My family never spoke about it, or of him.

"Twenty-five years later I confronted my loss. A therapist suggested I create a memorial service of my own. So I set aside a full day for mourning. I draped a large box with black velvet, burned incense, and looked through old photo albums. I remembered Franz and talked to him and cried. I visited a mortuary, a cemetery, and a church, moving through and beyond the loss and pain that had gripped me for most of my life. I finally put him——and my deep wound of grief—to rest. I finally said good-bye. I finally could move on."

Every child and adult experiences losses—a lot of them. They may include the loss of loved ones or pets and losses associated with illness, moving, disability, divorce, death, abandonment, abortion, miscarriage, children leaving home, retirement, fire, war, and addiction. We are ill-prepared to deal with loss and don't always know how to help our children through painful times, even though we want to protect them. When we lack the skills to deal with heaviness, we tend to

- deny or bury our feelings. "Big boys don't cry." "Don't feel bad." "Get hold of yourself." "Suck it up." "Move on."

- replace the loss. "We'll get you another bike/pet/friend."
- grieve alone. We don't trust others with our tears and pain.
- just give it time. "Time heals all wounds."
- change the subject. We shrug off or compartmentalize our pain or avoid drawing others into the complexity of our loss.
- intellectualize. "Be thankful you have another friend." "We know how you must feel." "You just have to let things go sometimes." We pretend we have it all under control.
- keep busy. We try to forget. We focus on things we can control.

"All of this bad information causes massive pain," write John James and Frank Cherry.[9] It's massive because there is so much of it. Beginning at birth and ending at death, loss punctuates our lives. New skills, journal writing, therapy, and support groups can help us complete our own grief recovery. But we have to do better with our children.

According to the Child Mind Institute, children grieve differently than adults do. They may not know what death means. They may feel guilty, as if they caused it, or they may seem unconcerned and distracted when someone dies. All of these things are normal, as is being angry with the person or pet who passed. "While you can't protect children from loss and the pain it may cause," the institute states, "you can play a major role in helping them feel secure and cope in the healthiest way possible."[10]

By helping little ones deal with and heal small losses, we give them skills for dealing with big ones. For starters, extra attention is required to reduce stress and to promote healing. During hard times of loss, set aside special time *just to be there* with young people. Comfort them with your presence. Touch or hold them when they need it. Put yourself in their shoes. Invite them to talk.

Listen to them.

- "What happened?"
- "How did you find out?"
- "Would you tell me about it?"
- "I am sorry!"

Sometimes kids don't want to talk and just need more time alone. They might indicate this with body pain, such as headaches and stomachaches; language cannot express the strange ways our bodies can feel when we have heartache. Offer to write down their thoughts and stories if they are not able to do so themselves. Limit screen time if you can; kids need to feel things, not just distract themselves. Take more walks together if you can.

Parents can create a space for themselves and their kids to talk about their loss. At my son's pre-school, one mom was great at creating poster boards on which her kids could tape pictures and write down memories (she would write for the little ones). Kids could also simply sit in front of them and think about a person or pet who had moved on. These sorts of practices became essential during the Covid-19 pandemic, when so many families and schools lost relatives, teachers, and community members. Grieving became a practice, a part of the routine.

There is always another side to grief, which changes form as it moves through us. It takes an average of two years for life to start feeling normal again after a loss. When the storm has passed and the grieving is complete, you know it. Pay attention to incomplete grieving. It can keep coming up over and over until you give it the attention and respect it needs.

Fear and Anxiety

"Ultimately we know deeply that the other side of every fear is freedom." – Marilyn Ferguson

A lizard has two basic feelings: "I feel safe" and "I feel unsafe." When it feels safe, it enjoys basking in the sun. When it feels unsafe, it runs to hide under a rock. These basic responses are inside children and adults, as well. There are many types of fear, and fear is important. Fear events prompt us to seek safety (though being hugged by a pair of loving arms is preferable to crawling under a rock) and save our lives. But if we've experienced fear and our feelings haven't been addressed, released, or soothed, fear can turn into anxiety, which is fear we feel when we're not directly under threat.

Every child experiences worry and anxiety at several points in their development. This makes sense because they are constantly changing. Here are four things that can make a difference for a child who is afraid of a specific thing instead of generally fearful and anxious.

1. *Calm your child.* You can do this with eye contact, touch, modeled deep breaths, or food—sometimes hunger can make people edgy.

2. *Comfort your child.* Listen to their feelings and validate them. Talk things over and tell them you're in control and that everything will be okay.

3. *Offer thoughts that are helpful* from their point of view. Give them suggestions, like, "That dog is probably a nice dog when it's at home." Or, "That dog can't get to me because it's behind a fence." Choose ideas that help them focus on outcome. "If I crossed the street, it wouldn't be so scary." Deciding what you want changes your relationship to fear.

4. *Cheer them on.* Encourage your kids to have courage and do a strong thing even when they're scared. Remind them of their strengths and the coping skills that have worked before.

When I was five years old, my imagination terrified me. I could not convince myself that there were not monsters in the closet, even after turning on the lights and looking—the door had to be closed. I remember a week when I couldn't sleep in my bed because I imagined all kinds of giant colored spiders crawling under the covers. My dad took my fears seriously and helped me find a solution. Rather than arguing with my fears, saying there was no such thing as a spider the size of my fist, he tucked the covers tightly around me so they couldn't "get to me" and sang a sleepy song about turning spiders into bubbles. Another wonderful dad had his daughter draw a picture of her nightmare creatures and tape it to her bedroom window, facing outward, to ward them off. They never came back!

There are real things that kids should fear that they might not even know exist. If your child is afraid of an adult in your life, take their fear seriously. It may be a phase, or there might be something going on that you need to know about so you can protect them.

Teaching kids how to talk about and talk back to fear will help them immeasurably as they grow older. Fear prevents us from acting boldly and getting what we want from life.

Anger

"Don't hold onto anger, hurt, or pain. They steal energy and keep you from love." —Leo Buscaglia[11]

Eight-year-old Andy hits his little sister. His parent yells, "Stop that! Say you're sorry. Give her a big hug." Those orders ignore and deny Andy's feelings, demand emotionally dissonant behavior, and teach dishonest actions. He's *not* sorry and he *doesn't* feel like hugging her. But what else can a parent do in this situation, when a child hits someone?

Stop the behavior. First, make sure the child who was hit is okay, and then use this opportunity to be clear about your rules and values. "You may not hit your sister!" "We do not hit each other in this family!" "Hitting is not okay!" Realize that the hitter's behavior came from both a *feeling* and a *thought*. He hit her for a reason; he's angry about something. Help him look at his anger and turn his feelings into words. "You're mad. Where did it start and how did it get from there to wanting to hit her?" *Talking* it out can help prevent him from *acting* it out next time.

Help your child look at anger management options that don't hurt anyone. "What other things can you do when you're angry?" Help him or her brainstorm. Pound a pillow on the couch? Shake arms? Go into another room and take breaths? This makes anger a learning experience. A child finds out "My feelings are okay. I'm okay. And it's not okay to hit people." He or she learns clear boundaries and healthy ideas about dealing with anger in the future.

In our culture, there is an imbalance of anger. Boys are allowed to punch, yell, and otherwise express anger. Girls learn that it is much safer to be hurt than to express anger—not a healthy set of options. On the other hand, when boys get hurt or experience loss, they don't have good models for expressing sadness; whereas, girls often find their strength at these times. Women with cross-wired emotions may burst into tears when confronting someone in anger. Cross-wired men suffering pain and loss may express it through rage. Anger, pain, joy, and love have no gender: they are human emotions felt by everyone, and we need to teach this to our children.

Anger is a normal feeling. It identifies a problem needing a solution. We must accept it in our children as well as in ourselves. If we have experienced awkward, destructive, or violent examples of anger, we don't know how to be angry appropriately. We may express anger by hitting others, yelling, and saying terrible things. Or we may shut it down, isolating ourselves until we feel better, or turn the anger inward, making ourselves sick.

When we learn to express anger in a clean, nondamaging way, it is easier to accept in ourselves and in others, and it is easier to get to the problem that needs solving. A good first step when you feel angry is to buy time. Say to your kids, "I'm feeling angry and I need to be alone for a few minutes so I don't take it out on you. We'll deal with this later." Then get away and do something to help you restore your reason. Physical exercise, a shower, a phone call, a good cry, or writing about it may do the trick. Going off by yourself can give you a different perspective. A time-out will help you to regain your balance and perspective and model to the children how to effectively deal with anger. But definitely come back and deal with it, or it will recur again and again.

If the intensity of your anger is out of proportion to the situation, call a time-out to focus on what was triggered. Go off by yourself to take deep breaths. Deep breathing when angry literally changes our brains, switching from fight-or-flight mode into a reflective one in which we can more easily figure things out. What happened? Why? What else was going on? What's underneath it? Once you unravel your anger, you defuse the trigger. One mother told her therapist that she "lost it" when her baby cried. They focused on this problem together and discovered that she had a deep-seated belief that if her baby cried, it meant she was a bad mother. Understanding this, the mother changed her behavior.

Like other emotions, anger is typically short-lived. Research shows that the anger reflex lasts only about one second. Anger comes mixed with other feelings — fear, frustration, and love. Take, for example, the situation in which a child gets lost in a store. The mother probably feels anger, fear, love, and relief when the pair is reunited; however, her common response is to express only anger to the child. A healthier and more honest response would be to talk about the anger and then the fear, the love — and the relief.

Try this Total Truth Process.[12]

- Express the anger: "I'm angry that you wandered off."
- Express the pain and fear: "I was afraid that something bad might happen to you that would hurt you."
- Apologize: "I'm sorry that I was taking so long looking for shirts."
- Express desires: "What I want is for you to stay close enough to see me so I know you're okay. I want you to be safe and content. Maybe if I bring

along some books or toys next time it will be more fun for you."

- Express love, forgiveness, and appreciation: "I am so glad you are okay! I love you so much and don't want anything bad to happen to you." Hug and comfort the frightened child.

Many people get stuck in anger, pain, or fear. Express one feeling and then move on to another until all feelings have been addressed and released. This is an amazing process. At first do this in letter form with no intention to deliver it. Write about anger, hurt, sadness, fear, and pain. Start each section with "I." After negative feelings have been released, say what you want or wish for. The bottom line is "I love you." This is a powerful tool to use in a journal, just for yourself. You can also use this format to write a "love letter" to heal deep conflict between you and a partner or family member.[13]

Other clean tools and ideas for dealing with anger include the following:

- Deal with your anger as you would like others to deal with theirs. What does that look like?
- Learn to release anger without harming yourself or others. Rule out emotional or physical violence.
- Strike inanimate objects if you really have to hit something. Consider this: does hitting something actually work to release your anger, or does it make you more angry?
- Say absurd things. Sometimes just catching yourself acting up makes you laugh and breaks anger's hold on you.
- Bite your tongue, if you have to, to avoid a cruel tirade.
- Say one word at a time.
- Keep it short, focusing on one problem only.
- If there is no problem to solve, say your truth and then forgive and forget.

- Separate the behavior from the person. Treat the person with respect and deal with the unacceptable behavior.
- Use "I" statements.
- Don't attack innocent people who happen to be in the room. It's not fair to make your kids suffer because you're angry with your boss.
- Use active listening skills. Be curious about anger. Reflect back feelings.
- Be honest. Kids can sense your feelings. But you don't have to tell them everything. You can say, "Sweetie, I'm angry right now, but I'm not angry at you. It's my problem, and I'm working it out."
- Be truthful but not cruel.
- In a fight, act out violent feelings with safe tools, such as Nerf guns, squirt guns, or cotton balls. Set rules for battle with good boundaries. Laughter can break through and become talking.
- End on a positive note.
- If your anger is dangerous to you or others, get help.

There is a difference between anger and rage. Anger is momentary and specific. Rage is primal, unpredictable, and feels out of control.

As Marion Woodman explains, we all have rage, an intense transformative energy that builds on top of past wounds, including those inflicted upon our ancestors and even upon all humanity. Rage is deeply stored at a cellular level and can inflame anger when it flares up. Woodman suggests working through one's deepest rage with a therapist to bring it all to the surface or in a group that can help you handle and channel it.

In the absence of support, you can lock yourself in the bedroom and scream into pillows to let off steam that would otherwise harm your kids. Adding words to this physical act will intensify the release. Mom once had a special closet that served as sanctuary. I have often screamed in my car. These safe spaces help us survive the worst of times.

Listen to where your children's anger is coming from. It can be very angry-making for a child with special needs to fail activities that seem easy for others. Some may be dealing with real unfair treatment. Kids deal with real trouble and pain because so many circumstances are beyond their control. It is very important for children to be given permission to show their feelings. Reflect their anger back to them, using more nuanced words than *mad* (or *angry*), such as *frustrated, irritated, annoyed,* and *resentful*. Help kids see these on a scale of 1 to 5, 1 being calm and 5 being outraged. Help them move up and down the scale using talking, breathing, and moving. Reflect their progress. "I can see how frustrated you get when you see other children doing things that are difficult for you. It is okay to show you are feeling that way, because feelings are important. I see that just talking about it is making you unclench your fists."

When children are not able to clear problems, anger and hurt can turn into resentment, when things feel ugly and unfair. Resentment, the saying goes, is like swallowing poison and expecting the other person to die. However, resentment is a teacher. Resentment tells you what you want. Reframe your resentment in an "I want" statement, and then make that your goal.

There is always a problem to solve behind the feeling of anger. Our favorite saying is "Be curious, not furious!"

Forgiveness

"To err is human; to forgive, divine." — Alexander Pope

Will we hurt our children? Probably. Not intentionally. But we don't know everything. Being a parent means constantly forgiving yourself for getting it wrong. Sometimes you do better than you think. Sometimes what you got wrong doesn't matter. But as parents, how can we help our children understand forgiveness?

There are only two parts to it, really: asking for forgiveness and granting forgiveness.

When your child has done something wrong and feels bad about it, saying "I'm sorry" is a good start. They can ask for forgiveness. They can also ask, "Are you okay?" or, "How can I make it up to you?" Kids actually have a real genius for making things fair. Watch them be creative. *Model these words for your kids!*

When your child has been slighted or hurt, they might be lucky enough to get an apology as good as the one above. Show them how easy it is to say "I forgive you; let's put it behind us." It doesn't feel as good to have someone just say "Sorry" as they're running by. Too often, a child at school, or worse, an adult, will deny any wrongdoing and leave your kid with a yucky feeling inside. This is when forgiveness becomes more abstract. This is when you can suggest to a child that they use compassion. Ask your child, "Was the person mean, or did they make a careless mistake? Do you want to be close to that person?" If not, it may be easier to forgive and forget. If your child does want to be friends with the other person, they can ask for a better apology. That will give your child a chance to explain their hurt feelings and create empathy.

Sometimes wounds don't heal and pain gets stuck. Every grown-up has healing to do with parents, often centered on forgiveness. Forgiveness has a twofold purpose: to heal ourselves and to heal the damaged relationship. Mom's relationship with her mother had been filled with conflict for half a century. Over the years Mom had worked toward healing and forgiveness, yet she and her mom never seemed to understand each other. She finally realized, after having her own children, that pain was a two-way street. Finally, she attended a workshop where students did an exercise on forgiveness. The instructor gave Mom *orders* to let her mother off the hook! Check out what happened next.

"The next day I visited my eighty-eight-year-old mother in the nursing home. I started awkwardly saying, 'Mama, I know I was a difficult child for you, and I'm sorry. You did an okay job as a parent, and I'm okay.' Her eyes were closed. I wasn't sure she was hearing me. I thanked her for the good things she had done for me and listed a few. I hugged her whispering, 'I love you.' Silence filled the room.... I asked, 'Mama, do you have anything to say?' More silence. Finally, a feeble voice murmured, 'Forgive me.' Those were her last words. Three days later she died. Perhaps that's what she had been waiting for. It was too late to heal our relationship, but I know the experience healed me. I wish it hadn't taken me so long to make peace."

The process of forgiveness begins with courage — and a decision. Mom had to be willing to be honest with herself, see more clearly, and reframe her thinking. She learned many things: these are some of them.

- Many people overgeneralize: "This is wrong and that is wrong; therefore, everything is wrong!" They jump from a few specifics to a global catastrophe: "Everything's totally and completely awful." To reverse this process, think of someone who is "all bad." Look for the specific behavior that bothers you, and then consider all the other attributes that make up this person. You might be surprised to find some likeable qualities. The lesson? What someone does is not who he or she is.
- Separate who people *are* from what they *do*.
- When examining pain, be very specific about harmful incidents. What particular behaviors have wounded you?

For me, the relationship I needed to heal was the one with my dad. I finally made a list of all the ways he'd hurt me. When I looked it over, I noticed a pattern: all of the painful incidents were related to his ADHD, something he struggled with and was misunderstood. I was able to change the way I related to him.

- Forgiveness does not mean approval. It requires a willingness to see with new eyes — to understand

and to let go. The person who hurt you did what they did out of their own weakness. You did not deserve it. They could not teach you what they did not know. They could not give you what they did not have. Forgiveness helps you move on and find what you really need.

- When you understand that the person or people who hurt you are not awful people, but perhaps fragile and needy souls who have made painful mistakes, you are moving closer to forgiveness. When you can wish them well, you'll know that forgiveness has begun. As you peel off layers of old hurt, anger, and guilt, underneath you'll discover a beautiful, loving, more relaxed and capable you.

- After forgiveness, it is possible to repair a relationship by stating what you want to experience in the future.

People are not perfect. Talk to your children about forgiveness, empathy, and compassion. Forgiveness opens our hearts, even if we sometimes have to change or end a relationship. Letting go of blame and resentment is so important—they trap us in the past. We don't want ancient history haunting us and interfering with our present life. Forgiveness releases us from that past and lets us heal our memories and ourselves. It sets us free from prisons of pain we don't deserve.

Affection and Joy

"We can live without religion and meditation, but we cannot survive without human affection." —Dalai Lama

Love is the big one: the fundamental state of being that characterizes a winning family. This whole book is about clearing away blockades to love. Here are a few thoughts about affection and joy, two building blocks of love.

Parents who are in a constant state of stress often have trouble expressing affection to their children, but it's essential that they do. What's amazing is that this is actually a very simple skill to learn, whether or not you consider yourself an affectionate person. Here are eleven ways to build positive emotion, many of which might seem simple or corny, but *little* things create *big* bonds.

1. Say something complimentary about their body. "You have lovely long fingers, like my grandmother had," or "Your smile lights up the room." Say something complimentary about their actions. "That's impressive how you organized your Halloween candy. I like how you did that."

2. Use affectionate language and names. "When I call you Tesoro, that means you are my treasure."

3. Show that you remember what they like. "I remembered you said you liked licorice, so I saved you the black jelly beans." (Don't overdo this, or it can become heavy.)

4. Use affectionate touch that you *know* they love; for example, tousle their hair (unless they hate having their hair touched), rub their back, hold their cheeks, or stroke their arms.

5. Hug and kiss at least four times a day. Of course! Good morning and goodnight plus hello and good-bye = four!

6. Use body language. Fist bumps, high fives, and complicated secret handshakes are all expressions of connection and affection.

7. Write your love. A Post-it in a lunch box. A text that asks "How are you?" or says "I love you."

8. Make special one-on-one time. A game of cards. A trip for ice cream or to the bookstore. An extra hour spent together after bedtime.

9. Look at them with a face of love. Hold their eyes and smile. Wink. Catch their eyes when they say something funny.
10. Keep track of your affectionate expressions. Give yourself a star or check off a box each day you show your kids you love them.
11. After you build affection into your daily routine, you will feel more joy all day long.

Do you remember when you were a child and found something amazing? Or heard good news? Or did something awesome? Did you ever take your news to a parent, and they were too busy to respond? My brother did an amazing thing: he played guitar in front of a whole crowd and got them to sing along. But my dad never complimented him. It was as if he didn't notice. It broke my brother's heart. Studies show that how we respond to joy either strengthens or weakens a relationship. If you want to have a strong relationship with your kids, show enthusiasm for their joy. Even if you're not impressed by the gift of a dead bird or a high video game score, be impressed that they are proud of themselves. Find a way to compliment their achievement and success.

Gratitude

"If the only prayer you say in your entire life is 'Thank you,' that would suffice." — Meister Eckhart[14]

"Gratitude and forgiveness are deeply intertwined," says Nancy Davis Kho. "Forgiveness liberates us from dwelling over past hurts, so we can spend more time seeing the good around us and allow ourselves to feel grateful."[15] She teaches people how to write letters of gratitude, which is one of the most powerful proven turnarounds for when you are lost in self-pity.

Dissatisfaction with our modern lives — schools, politicians, prices, parking spaces — can leak into our homes and come out in our kids. Kids feel our tension and sometimes take it personally when a parent is irritated about something in the adult world or in themselves.

Feelings, including anger, fear, and resentment, are important to experience and acknowledge, but when negativity builds up, we can switch on other feelings to turn our brain into a calmer space. Gratitude is exceptionally powerful. Many studies and millions of personal experiences have shown that people who keep gratitude journals exercise more, feel healthier, take bigger strides toward their goals, and are more optimistic than those who journal about their struggles. Kids who focus on gratitude daily feel more alert, enthusiastic, and determined. They are more likely to help other kids have better moods, higher energy, and more positive attitudes toward school and families.

A practice of gratitude reduces overall tension. Focusing on the positive aspects of our children, our parents, and ourselves lowers personal and interpersonal stress. Counting our blessings increases our joy.

When we eat at Mom's house, sometimes we pause before each meal to hold hands around the table with family and guests and give thanks — for the food, for each other, for whatever is positive in our lives. At our house, we put appreciations at the top of the Monday Meeting list. Rituals such as this are special times of closeness and appreciation that build good energy in the family.

With gratitude, we focus on what we have, not on what we don't have. Sprinkle your day with thank yous. Everyone deserves to receive more of them, and they boost everyone's self-esteem.

10.

Stress Coping and Trauma Prevention

"What doesn't kill you makes you stronger."
—Ernest Hemmingway

In families, stress is part of life! A traditional mom's life with younger kids is about managing the minute-by-minute needs of a thundering herd (sometimes even one kid feels like a herd) that requires constant food, clothing, transportation, hygiene, and education for years on end. A traditional dad's life is about making money all day and missing out on all the little things. In this season of life, everyone's feeling everything, rubbing up against each other, resolving conflicts, and hopefully sharing more good times than bad. In the thick of things, families can feel like they are barely holding things together. Add past or present trauma (or any difference or dysphoria requiring extra coping skills) to the regular hassles of life with kids, and you've got a lot of stress on your plate.

How do we handle it? Cumulative stress is a killer. Stress erodes our health over the years, taking its toll in the form of disease—both mental and physical—or simply by eroding our general sense of well-being. But here's the great news for families: there are two types of stress, and one of them is actually good for you. It's called *eustress*, good stress, and it's the kind of stress that challenges you and moves you to a better place.[1]

Good and Bad Stress

Good-stress triggers include

- travel to new places,
- hard workouts and projects,
- rollercoaster rides and scary movies,
- life transitions, like weddings and divorces,
- new babies,
- new schools and new skills application,
- moving and new jobs, and
- difficult work you enjoy doing.

Good stress makes us resilient. When we are challenged, make good choices, learn, and grow, we become resilient. Living through hard times teaches us coping skills, and they get better with practice.

Another key element of good stress is its connection to relationships. The stress our kids and partners put us through raises our cortisol levels — cortisol is the stress hormone — but hugs, connection, and a shared sense of journey produce oxytocin, the trust hormone. Oxytocin lowers cortisol, so in the long run, family stress does not cause disease as much as work stress does. However, there are exceptions.

How can we tell the difference between eustress and distress? Good stress is intense and allows us to rebalance. Bad stress is prolonged, painful, and hard to shift out of. It may be caused by

- abusive relationships, in which one person always has power over another (bullying),
- hyper-alertness as the result of always losing out,
- racism, sexism, and/or anti-Semitism,
- caring for or worrying about chronically sick family members,
- heartbreak,
- financial trouble,
- divided or torn families (see chapter 30, "The Fractured Family"),
- poverty and hunger,

80

- witnessing violence, be it physical or emotional,
- toxic environments where love and caring are not expressed, and
- life without meaningful, relational experiences or affection.

We can protect ourselves from distress by consciously adding positive thoughts and experiences to existing conditions. And we can sometimes turn bad stress into good stress by reframing our troubles and cultivating a growth mindset. Even if we don't believe it at first, telling ourselves that we can get out of bad situations gives us energy. "Every cloud has a silver lining" and "I see my glass as half-full, not half-empty" are optimistic catchphrases. But optimistic thinking goes further than that. When something bad happens, "explanatory style" matters. The following three power statements activate optimism:

- "This is a temporary, not a permanent, situation."
- "This is not personal; it's something that happens to everyone in this situation."
- "This does not happen to me all the time; usually better things come to me."

Our brains are designed to be naturally pessimistic and fearful, so we have to work to change our minds. An optimistic mindset is easier to activate when it becomes habit.

It's essential for our physical and mental health that we learn to use our minds to cope with stress. When we feel we can't cope with challenges before us, our bodies go into threat mode, preparing to fight, flee, or freeze. When we feel up for challenges, our bodies go into activation mode, which sharpens decision-making and elevates energy. We seek social interaction and support, and our empathy increases. Positive emotions expand these resources, so it's crucial we build them at every opportunity.

Families can do this by building space in the home and time during the week for stress-reducing activities and rituals. When my son got to middle school, I introduced Monday Meetings, during which everyone talked about their schedules and assignments for the week. We went down a checklist and planned the week's family fun time and shared appreciations and challenges. This did wonders to reduce surprise, conflict, and emergencies and build connection and support. Other parents have made space for sacred I'm-not-to-be-provoked "serenity spots," where kids can go when they really need to take a deep breath, listen to music, receive hugs or listening, and find peace and calm.

A few coping thoughts from WholeHearted School Counseling may help you when you feel emotionally stressed.[2]

- Just because I'm thinking something does not make it true.
- This hurts, so I need to be extra kind towards myself.
- This feeling is uncomfortable, but it will pass.
- It's not that great right now, but it's not the worst thing either.
- Not everything will go my way, but I can be flexible.
- It's okay to have a not-okay day.
- I've dealt with harder situations, and I know it will get better.
- I prefer something else, but I can deal with this, too.
- I have inner strength that no one realizes I have.

Finally, here are amazing tips for shifting out of stress and into ease, or even into power.

- Take a walk, run, or swim to get your body and mind in alignment and ready to move on. Exercise is magic when it comes to stress.
- Stretch your arms and shoulders to break up neck tension. Scratch the back of your head and rub your neck. Tense muscles in your neck block blood flow to your brain.

- Stand with your feet apart and your arms raised above your head. This is the "power pose" that resets your system.
- Smile. Even just to yourself, even if you don't feel like it. This releases brain chemicals that give you confidence.

Trauma Types

Trauma occurs when we have no outlet for a shocking or stressful experience.[3] We experience two types of trauma in life. One is a traumatic event that changes everything; the other is a constant nagging that erodes our wholeness. Kellita Maloof, who creates performance experiences for women that peel away layers of pain to expose their natural radiance, calls them "boom boom trauma" and "drip drip trauma."[4] Not feeling loved is drip-drip trauma. But remember, resilience heals us. Self-care routines and nurturing rituals can foster resilience in our families and personal lives.

When you or your child experiences shock, keep it from "freezing" into trauma by doing the following:

- Shake it out—bounce; shake fingers, arms, the whole body.
- Talk it out—tell a stress story over and over (listen, listen, listen).
- Write it out—explore it from all angles, unpeeling layers.
- Dance it out—disordered exercise physically releases trauma.

Other trauma-releasing techniques using body/mind science include the following:

- EFT (Emotional Freedom Technique), or "tapping," which can defuse emotional triggers, even unconscious reactions, such as phobias.
- Pressure products, such as "ThunderShirts,"® worn by animals, or weighted blankets.

- Calming acupressure points: hold your wrist with the fingers of your other hand. Great for catching your breath when crying or hyperventilating.
- "Brain Buttons," which help calm and focus. Line up fingertips on the forehead with the pinky between the eyebrows and the index finger by the hairline, and then press and hold a few moments.
- The Havening Technique, which involves soothingly stroking down the face and upper arms. This comes naturally to many parents and is a powerful primal type of touch that soothes stress *instantly* and prevents stressors from hardening into trauma.

You Come First

"Kids' needs are best met by grownups whose needs are met," writes Jean Illsley Clarke.[5] Children and parents alike need love, support, and nourishment. If you're running on empty, you have nothing to give.

Imagine self-esteem as a cyclical triangle (like a recycling symbol) of self-compassion, self-care, and self-love. These are like the legs of a sturdy table of self-esteem. We talk a lot in this book about accepting and being affectionate and kind to oneself. It's important to support self-care and create healthy boundaries when kids get older, so you don't become sick and weak as you age.

There are times when we need to put our own needs on hold, especially in years when we care for babies and young children. It's easy to lose sight of our own care when we have growing active kids. But when we recognize what we're missing, we can find many ways to nurture our lives. Reading books like this is self-care. Exercise of any kind helps. We can make sure we get the nutrition we need as we serve foods our children want. Scheduling time amid the busyness to keep relationships strong — with friends, family, and especially your partner — will keep you healthy. If you're able to, it's important to nurture and enrich the relationship where your family started; that love enriches your children.

Things You Love to Do

Our emotional state can change faster than the weather. Like a checking account, we can be flush one day and overdrawn the next. We need to keep ourselves out of emotional debt by making deposits of self-esteem and self-care. It's important that you take good care of yourself, because you can't give what you haven't got.

If you've never tracked your mood or your self-esteem, try it for a week or a month. What causes good feelings and what causes bad ones? Start to recognize your triggers and supports. You deserve to have fun and enjoy life. It's important to be happy. When you are good to yourself, you feel good about yourself.

Positive emotions expand health, wealth, and well-being. As my coffee cup states, "If mama ain't happy, ain't nobody happy!" (This is true of papas, too.) Emotions are contagious. As your home becomes more positive for you, it becomes more nourishing for your children, creating a win-win environment—a home sweet home.

At the end of every workshop, Mom would assign homework. "The best homework you'll ever get!" she'd say. "Make a list of twenty things you love to do. Some are things you'd do alone, some with your children, some with your spouse, partner, or friend. Then cross off any that are not good for you!" Everyone would laugh. "Be aware, as you write, of when you last did those things."

What's on your list? Every day, do at least one of those things for yourself. Notice what happens. Take very good care of yourself—because your children count on you to take good care of them! There are some great ideas in appendix D, 100 Sources of Joy.

11.

The Power of Words

"Healthy families remind each other of their goodness; unhealthy families remind each other of their failings." — Matthew Fox[1]

While on a family picnic in the mountains, my twelve-year-old brother, Damian, asked, "Mom, can I climb that mountain?" She gave him her okay, and off he went.

A little later, my seven-year-old brother, Felix, asked, "Mom, can I climb the mountain?"

"No. You're too clumsy," she replied. I still remember the look on her face (oops) and the look on his (darn).

I tried to soothe him. "Come on, Felix, let's see if we can catch a fish in that stream," I suggested, thinking I could watch over him in case he tripped or fell. I was about eleven.

Back home, Felix began to drop, spill, bump into, and fall over things. He was probably thinking, "That all-knowing person who is my mom thinks I'm clumsy; therefore, I must be clumsy." It was a self-fulfilling prophecy. He became a walking disaster. Whenever he poured milk, it ended up all over the counter.

Feeling guilty, Mom was careful not to make an issue out of it, but simply encouraged him to clean things up. In a couple of weeks, Felix returned to "normal." Years later, when Mom was writing this book, she remembered this painful experience. "I wish I could have eaten my words," she said. Trying to figure out what she might have done differently, she replayed the incident in her mind and thought of how she might have undone her clumsy words. She could have simply said, "Felix, that was a clumsy thing for ME to say, and I'm sorry," and given him a hug. Then she could have called Damian over and asked him to take Felix with him or suggested we all go. That experience taught Mom the positive and negative power of words.

The language parents and teachers choose, and the way they use it, can curse or uplift a child, or even change their destiny. Words have the power to lift others up or put them down. Word choices build or shred self-esteem.

Words that damage self-esteem are uttered without respect. They can be spoken in a nasty tone of voice and can be condescending, cruel, or just plain careless. Sometimes as parents, when we feel we are not being heard, we "turn up the volume," raising our voices, sharpening our tone, and pulling out stronger words in hopes of improving listening ability on the other end. More often than not, these strategies are counterproductive. They help turn people — especially kids — into losers. And they help turn people against us. If your parents spoke to you this way, start listening to your own words and the tone of your voice. Think about who it was who said those things to you. Remember how you felt hearing those words and how they shaped your behavior. Those old patterns may still be operating in your life.

Fortunately, once you have awareness, you have a choice. You can choose to go on automatic and do to your kids what was done to you (even though you hated it), or you can choose to become the kind of parent you would like to have had. You can *react*, knee-jerk fashion, and put down your kids, only to regret it later; or you can choose to *respond*, instead, with care and wisdom, and be proud of your parenting moment.

When you next catch yourself about to react, stop! Bite your tongue if you have to. Take a deep belly breath and let it out slowly. Maybe walk into another room. If you wait sixty seconds, you can collect yourself enough to respond without hurting your child. Pause to evaluate your thoughts and feelings and the consequences of possible actions. Think about the positive outcome you want to accomplish and how to bring it about. When you *react*, others are likely to react as well. When you *respond*, others tend to listen and cooperate. Think about the difference.

Listen to yourself over the course of a day. Notice the words coming out of your mouth. What effect do they have on others? What effect do they have on you? Do you really want to say those things? Someone once told me they never gossiped — they would never say something behind someone's back that they wouldn't say to their face. Do you? This applies to your kids and to other adults. If you are separating or divorced, it's especially important that you don't bad-mouth a co-parent to your kids. If you need to talk about your struggles, talk to a friend or a therapist.

There are times we need to bite our tongues to stop a nasty comment from slipping out. In fact, a bit of scar tissue on the tip of the tongue can be a badge of honor for parents. It means you cared enough to stop and take time to cool off so you could talk about a problem later. After the fact, it's easier to describe what everyone was feeling and what you want to be different.

Living with a family requires us to interact with and respond to others. Whether we do so negatively or positively, we will notice the results.

Self-Esteem Shredders

Killer statements are the most damaging. They should never be used. Examples are

- "You make me sick."
- "You were a mistake."
- "I'm going to leave you!"
- "I wish you had been a boy/girl."
- "I wish you had never been born."
- "If I didn't have you, I could have had a career."
- "No son/daughter of mine is gay."
- "I wish you were more like your brother/sister."
- "You are such a loser. You'll never amount to anything."

Killer statements are deadly — psychologically and physically. Do not use them — ever. Verbal abuse prompts a child (or adult) to question who they are and feel inadequate, stupid, and worthless.

It is a control tactic to maintain power over another person by defining them in a bad light. When a parent does that to a child, it demeans and weakens their self-esteem, putting them at risk for self-harm.

Nonverbally abusive *cold behaviors* include rejection, battery/abuse, constant ignoring, and acting or speaking as if the child were not there when he or she is present. The latter happens often to severely handicapped children. These behaviors send damning and damaging messages as much as verbal abuse does.

Crooked communication sounds positive at first, but has a negative damaging twist (like left-handed compliments do). Like greeting cards that look cute and funny on the outside, yet are cutting and hurtful on the inside, such statements are often sarcastic, insincere, or patronizing. An occasional sarcastic joke to another adult is one thing, but "stingers" are verbally abusive judgments your child will take as the truth.

- "You're pretty good at math—for a girl."
- "Oh, you *never* make mistakes."
- "You always know the answer, don't you, smarty pants."
- "Oh, that's just like you."

Crooked communication is confusing and painful; it erodes self-esteem.

Negative ways of dealing with negative behavior include criticism, put-downs, ridicule, name-calling, blaming, and rejection. Often these are delivered in *you statements*. [2]

You Statements

You statements are so common, we think they're not problematic, but they are. Listen to the TV, your family, or the people at your job for one day and count how many times you hear things like

- "You can't do anything right."
- "What's wrong with you?"
- "How could you be so stupid?"

- "You always get into trouble."
- "When are you going to grow up?"

You statements are sometimes delivered in a nasty tone of voice and are often exaggerated ("you *always* _____" and "you *never* _____"). Related to external force (and punishment), you statements attack the whole person. They focus on *who you are* (things you can't change) rather than on *what you do* (things that can be changed). You statements are always negatively focused, pointing out what is *not* wanted, instead of talking about what *is* wanted. And, finally, you statements focus on the past, which can't be changed. "You were late yesterday; you were late last week; in fact, you were *born late!*"

Many of us were raised on you statements; they're a commonly accepted tactic of mainstream parenting. Take a moment and return to your childhood. Do you remember times when people spoke to you that way? What did they say to you? How did they say it? What did you feel about yourself? About them? What conclusions did you draw? How did those incidents affect your relationship with the person(s) involved?

You statements feel like attacks, and when we feel attacked, we want to protect and defend ourselves and tune out those painful words. You statements, therefore, can effectively impair a child's hearing. A child cannot understand how the people who claim to love them can hurt them in this way. It's no wonder behavior doesn't change. Instead of being able to respond appropriately, kids lock into fear and self-protection, compliance or defiance.

A parent's intent to deal with and change behavior is understandable. The negative methods used to achieve it just don't work. You statements don't teach children what it is that you *do* want. The child has to second-guess what might please and satisfy the authority figure. Children are not mind readers, and they are set up for failure when adults expect them to be.

If you tell children they are bad, that's what they believe they are, and that's probably what they will become. Children hear, "I'm no good." "I can't do anything right." "I'm worthless." "I'm not lovable." They draw conclusions, not only about themselves, but also about the parent: "I can't trust you." "You don't care about me." This leads to anger, withdrawal, and rejection. They don't realize they are being emotionally abused. The self-esteem of both parent and child is damaged, and the relationship between the two may be harmed.

Note: All sentences with a second person pronoun are not you statements. It's fine to say, "You did a good job!" "You need to finish putting away the dishes," or "You must be proud of yourself."

If you were brought up hearing negative messages, you have probably caught yourself saying things to your children that you swore you would never say. It is hard to change behavior, especially habitual ways of acting and speaking, but it can be done. It begins with awareness, and then continues with commitment and work. You try, you succeed, you fail, you try again. Yes, it takes effort. But the payoff for you and your children will be tremendous.

Many destructive patterns keep repeating themselves simply because we don't know of better ways to deal with problems. It is crucial that we expand our options. In the days when extended families were the rule and not the exception, kids had many role models. We could see how Uncle John played with his kids and how Aunt Judy solved problems with hers. Today, with smaller families, we may be unaware of many options available to us because we just don't see them. Below are a few positive approaches.

Self-Esteem Builders

Words that build self-esteem are spoken with respect for the other person and with care about what is going on inside them. They are encouraging and invite people to become winners. The tone of voice is "clean" and intentionally devoid of negative emotion. A loving touch—a pat on the back, a hug—often accompanies the words. This is positive feedback. Feedback can feed the spirit, validate others, and make people want to win. Two types of positive feedback build self-esteem: affirmation for *being* and affirmation for *doing*.

Positive strokes for being are nourishing and life-giving.[3] Read the following statements and be aware of the feelings they evoke.

- "You are special and unique."
- "You are important to me."
- "I like/love you!"
- "I believe in you."
- "You've got a great sense of humor."
- "I'm glad you're here."

Nonverbally, these are expressed by an attitude of respect and enjoyment, outward signs of affection, taking children seriously, spending time with children, and really listening. We do not recommend directly praising intelligence when a task is at hand: that can backfire. Intelligence is a collection of strengths: notice them when you see them, and teach them when you don't.

Rewards for doing recognize effort or improvement with appreciation. Sincere feedback encourages children to do things well.

- "Fantastic!"
- "I see what you're saying/doing there."
- "You've got this handled."
- "Atta girl/boy!"
- "It looks like you did your best."
- "Keep up the good work."
- "Go ahead — try it."
- "Look at the progress you've made."
- See appendix A for more ideas.

Too many children, and too many husbands and wives, feel unappreciated. Kind and respectful words like *please* and *thank you*, pats on the back, and detailed appreciation both sweeten life and prevent burnout. It's good to acknowledge and celebrate accomplishments, but for building self-esteem in kids, it's even more important to give positive strokes for the effort they are

making.
- "You worked hard at this."
- "I can see you really care about this."
- "Wow, what a great try."

Praise and Compliments

The Self-Esteem Movement during the 1990s, when this book was originally published, did much to repair deep wounds in children of the 1950s who felt unappreciated by their parents. But there was a backlash when some people were thought to have become entitled, lazy, incapable adults.

Carol Dweck performed a ten-year study comparing "person praise" to "process praise."[4] She discovered that praising innate characteristics, such as intelligence, promotes a fixed mindset in kids, whereas praising their efforts promotes a growth mindset. In the study, children who were told they were smart didn't try as hard as others to solve problems and didn't do as well in what teachers call "productive struggle." This fascinating discovery helped refine the way we build self-esteem. Sadly, the public failed to incorporate nuanced understanding and stopped focusing on how important self-esteem was for kids. Depression in children rose.

Everyone needs more appreciation than they're getting: turn this around. Give others — and yourself — more appreciation than you think is necessary. Watch how things change.

Many kids and adults have difficulty with compliments, so they flip one back ("I like yours, too.") or shrug it off ("This old thing?"). They don't know what to do with praise. It's really very simple: see a compliment as a gift and just say thank you. If you trust a person's sincerity, all you have to do is take a deep breath and let it in.

Compliments, like feedback, are always more effective when they are descriptive and specific. "I like how you help your brother" gives more useful information than "you're such a good boy." Don't be afraid to show your enthusiasm. "This painting is really coming along. The colors make me feel really alive. Look at the attention you're putting into the details: that shows real craftsmanship."

There are many ways to feed the spirit with compliments. One dad put a positive statement in his daughter's school bag when he made her lunch. He discovered that she papered the back of her bedroom door with them!

In addition to complimenting your child, tell others you're proud of them. When your praise gets back to them, it will have increased in value. (But don't only praise them behind their backs, give them direct encouragement.)

What about you? To enhance your own self-esteem, take notes when your kids or peers say positive things to or about you, and place them where you'll see them often. Or put them in an in-case-of-emergency notebook, so you can reread those strokes when you need a lift.

Respect and caring are keys to dealing with negative behavior positively. We can challenge unacceptable or inappropriate behavior by giving children feedback and explaining what they are not seeing. A parent coach I admire taught me the rule of thumb "praise in public; criticize in private." (We prefer *feedback*, rather than *criticism* — see chapter 12, "How Parenting Responses Affect Self-Esteem.") It really worked to build trust between my child and myself. As a parent volunteer, I saw classrooms where teachers used this amazing strategy, and their classes were bonded and focused. When teachers shamed children in the classroom, kids disconnected.

When we explain to kids the problems with negative behavior, it's crucial we state the positive behavior we expect. When you go a little further and ask what support kids need to be able to get there from here, you invite them to become winners.

As parents, we must set reasonable and healthy limits for our children. The most effective way for us to deal with inappropriate behavior is to *separate the behavior from the person.* They are okay; their behavior is not. Be very clear: "I love you, but I do not like

94

what you did!" We cannot change who we are, but we can change our behavior.

I Statements

Using *I statements* is an effective way to deal with undesirable behavior. The model is "I feel _____ when you _____ because _____, and what I want is _____." For example:

- "I feel mad when you leave your shoes on the living room floor because they make the room look messy, and I work hard to keep it nice for everyone. What I want is for you to put them under your bed."
- "I feel disappointed when you lie to me about your homework. It's your responsibility to do it, and I'm only trying to help you build good skills. I expect you to tell me the truth, good or bad."
- "I feel hurt when you use language like that when you talk about girls. I was a girl, and what you may think about women when you're grown up worries me. I want you to never use that word again, and I want you to encourage your friends to find a new favorite word."

I statements are specific, focusing on the behavior, not on the person. They clearly state what it is that you *do* want. With I statements, children learn cause-and-effect relationships (Mom feels _____ because I did _____) and build judgment skills.[5]

Substitution

Another successful way to deal with negative behavior is with *substitution*. Stop the behavior you don't want, and then encourage the behavior you do want. "Don't do _____; do _____ instead." For example:

- "Don't hit your sister; hit a pillow or your punching bag, instead."
- "Don't use my toothbrush; go find your own."

- "Don't pull the cat's tail; pet her nicely, like this."
  Even better,
- "Don't do _____; figure out a better way to do it
  instead."

With substitution, we stop the undesirable behavior and lead the child to more acceptable behavior.

Tune in and Talk Back

Sometimes criticism comes from within. Automatic negative thoughts can really mess up kids. Automatic negative thoughts, or "ANTs," as ADD psychologist Daniel Amen calls them,[6] tell kids they are lying (mind-reading), they'll never change (always/never thinking), they're going to fail (fortune-telling), or they're bad (labeling). We need to talk back to these thoughts because they're not true and they hurt our kids. Learn to recognize ANTs and teach your kids about them, too.

Talk back to ANTs! "Wait—give the kid a chance." "Maybe there's more to this story." "That's not true because I saw them succeed at _____." Engage kids in the process. Once, I noticed my thoughts were scaring me, and I told my son, "My thoughts are telling me I can't trust you to turn your homework in. Do you want to help me talk back to them?" We had fun and became closer, and guess what? My thoughts were wrong. (See chapter 21, "Monkey Talk.")

Turn-About Statements

When you decide to change your ways, you need to break old habits. It's easier to do if you have a few helpful tricks. One good tool is the *turn-about statement*. Turn-about statements can ease the transition from who you used to be to who you are becoming.

Here's how they work. If criticism taught you to say "that's the way I am," or "I can't help it if I'm _____," or "I'm the kind of person who _____," turn those words around so they can no longer trap you in the past. Instead, say "in the past I _____, but now I _____." Parents, here's one you can try right now: "*I used to* criticize my kids a lot, but now I'm learning to give them feedback instead!"

The next time you hear negative words slip out, stop yourself — bite your tongue. Say, "Cancel!" or "I'm sorry! I didn't mean to say that!" or "Let me say that differently!" Engage others in this exciting and heroic process. Talk it over with your kids or spouse. You might say, "I just realized that I've been using the same words that hurt me when I was little, and I don't want to do that anymore. The next time you hear me say that, please remind me." Then you can establish a signal, like "Cancel," or "Replay," or "Ouch, Dad, try again!" After a while, you'll automatically censor your hurtful words. Be patient with yourself. Keep encouraging and supporting yourself. Success, it has been said, is picking yourself up one time more than you fall down.

Halting criticism is an extremely important step toward building kids' self-esteem. It cannot be overstated that parental criticism causes many social problems. Equally important is increasing positive strokes — appreciation, compliments, and support. A woman in one of my workshops told me that after her oldest children went off to college, she paid special attention to her youngest daughter, who suffered from low self-esteem. For two years she focused only on the positive. If she couldn't say anything positive, she said nothing at all. "It worked," she reported proudly. With self-esteem repaired and strengthened, the daughter went off to college with a confidence the mom never thought possible.

It's never too late to begin. As we decrease negative and increase positive attention, we increase satisfaction and joy for the whole family. Imagine how your life would be different if you had received from your parents only love and support. The Golden Rule of Parenting is *"Do unto your children as you wish your parents had done unto you!"*

12.

How Parenting Responses Affect Self-Esteem

"I have yet to find the man, however exalted his station, who did not do better work and put forth greater effort under a spirit of approval than under a spirit of criticism." — Charles Schwab

For better or worse, adults constantly influence the self-esteem of children — whether they realize it or not — whether they intend it or not. The words they use fall into four basic types of responses. Nurturing and structuring responses increase self-esteem; marshmallowing and criticizing responses tear it down.[1] Let's play a game and see if you can tell the difference between them. Which response is which?

Responses Game

Twelve-year-old Jennie says, "I want to sleep at Janet's tonight. Her parents won't be there, but her sixteen-year-old brother will." Her parents may say,

1. "You'd like to have fun with your friend tonight. Invite her to come here for the night."
2. "No. Unless her parents are home, you may not spend the night there."
3. "Well, I don't like the idea, but I guess just this one time wouldn't hurt."
4. "No! Of course not! What would people think of us? And don't you know what sixteen-year-old boys are after?"

Judith says, "My husband is away on business, and the baby is driving me up the wall." Her friend may say,

1. "You're in a difficult situation, Judith. Ask for help—you need it. The baby needs a mother who is not up the wall. You'll both be better off when you start taking care of yourself."

2. "Call someone for help. Find a church or agency that offers child care. Take care of yourself and your baby."

3. "Poor thing. There just isn't any good help available these days. I hope you make it."

4. "If you were a better mother, you wouldn't have that problem!"

Eight-year-old Ryan won't clean his room and says, "I hate you, Mom." His mother's response could be,

5. "Ryan [touching him], I know you don't want to clean your room and you're mad at me. That's okay. I still love you. Let's both clean our rooms at the same time, and when we finish, we'll go outside and play."

6. "We're all part of the family, Ryan, and we all have chores to do. Cleaning your room is an important way of being part of our team."

7. "Fine! Whatever! No, wait, don't hate me. Is it really too hard for you? Poor thing. Do you want me to do it for you? When you're bigger you'll be able to do something by yourself."

8. "How dare you feel that way! After all I do for you? Get in your room right now and don't come out until it's perfect! And just wait until your father gets home!"

Did you guess which was which? I bet you did. Let's take a closer look.

Nurturing Responses

If you guessed that all number-one options were nurturing, you're right. Based on respect, love, and support, nurturing responses encourage self-responsibility. Parents invite children to get their needs met and offer help in doing so. They believe their kids are winners with the capacity to grow, and they give them permission to succeed. Nurturing responses include I statements and affectionate touch.

Structuring Responses

All number twos were structuring responses. Also based on respect, structuring responses protect, set limits, and demand performance: "I know you can do it!" Parents expect and encourage children to be capable and responsible. They encourage them to ask for what they need and want, thereby empowering them.

Nurturing and structuring responses work well together. The underlying message for both is, "You are a valuable person, and I encourage and promote your growth." This promotes cooperation, empowerment, win-win situations, and high self-esteem.

Marshmallowing Responses

Threes were all over the map, weren't they? Look at what marshmallowing responses have in common: they grant freedom without requiring accountability or responsibility in return. Based on a judgment that children are weak and inadequate, marshmallowing responses disempower while sounding supportive. They invite dependence and codependence and encourage failure by blaming other people, the situation, or fate for a problem. You statements are commonly used: "Why don't you quit?" "You poor thing, there's nothing you can do." "I'll do it for you."

When kids have special needs, parents can get really trapped in marshmallowing responses. They know their children have a hard time with something, so they're often unsure how or when to step in. It's hard to see your child as being limited, and it's easy to push too hard or not enough. But if you find yourself viewing your child as fragile or incompetent or thinking they have endured enough punishment, watch out for marshmallowing responses. They mix up kids and can lead to behavioral problems.

Criticizing Responses

All of the number fours were . . . yep, criticizing responses. They are easy to spot. Based on disrespect, criticizing responses encourage children to fail. Ridicule, put-downs, blaming, faultfinding, comparing, and labeling are common. You statements are often global: "You always _____" and "You never _____." Humor is cruel; touch is hurtful or punishing.

"Every time I get in trouble," a junior high school student wanted to say to a critical parent, "you remind me of everything I've ever done wrong in my life. I'm not too sure what kind of person I am, but you're convincing me I'm bad."[2]

Marshmallowing and criticizing responses damage self-esteem. They result in anger and resentment, passivity and powerlessness, hopelessness and hurt, and dependence and depression.

Changing Response Styles

Which response styles did your parents generally use? Are you glad they treated you that way? Which style do you mostly use? How do you feel about treating your children that way? Many parents find themselves doing to their kids what they swore they'd never do—and then feeling guilty about it.

It is possible to change your response style. When you let go of damaging behavior learned from your family and society, your self-esteem will go up, and so will everyone else's. It's not easy to change habits, but you can do it if you really want to. You will thank yourself a thousand times over; so will your children—and your grandchildren.

During a workshop, one mom described her experience. She

yelled at her son, "I'm going to beat you!" And then she stopped herself, realizing that she didn't want to beat him, and added, "With a sock . . . with your dad's smelly sock!" She beamed with pride while telling her story. In a follow-up letter, she wrote, "I'm really excited with the changes in our lives. I really AM becoming the parent I wish I'd had."

Here are some specific strategies for switching into the habit of healthy response styles.

Change your focus. Instead of always catching your kids being "bad," catch them being good: it's a universal truth that *what you look for, you find*. Once you look for the things they're doing right, you'll be surprised at what neat kids they are. Appreciate, encourage, and support positive behavior.

We all need strokes. People prefer positive feedback, but they'd rather get negative attention than nothing at all. You might find that your kids behave badly so that they don't feel ignored. Use this technique to make them more interested in showing you the qualities and behaviors you want and need from them.

Expect the best. Kids want to live up to our expectations, unless those expectations are unrealistic or impossible. Expectations of perfection lead to disappointment and despair. Marshmallowing and criticizing parents expect the worst—and they get it. Nurturing and structuring parents communicate high standards simply and clearly, and they encourage, support, and coach their children toward reaching them.

Do you believe that kids are worthless and a bother? If so, you will expect that, look for that, and get that. If, on the other hand, you believe that kids are valuable resources with lots of potential, you will expect, look for, and get that.

Give up blaming and faultfinding. Criticizing parents look for what's wrong, find it, and then put down their child in order to feel one-up and superior. But no one likes to be put down, ridiculed, humiliated, or blamed. Criticism leads to resentment and anger or passivity and dependency. It results in powerlessness and discouragement. Mom's brother once told her that whenever he talked, as a child, he was criticized, so he just stopped talking. "Our family didn't know how to say nice things to each other," he said. When criticism is the culture, everyone's self-esteem suffers.

Nurturing and structuring parents avoid blaming and faultfinding. Instead, they think in terms of responsibility. *Respons-ibility* means "the ability to respond." Children need to be encouraged to assume responsibility for their behaviors and their consequences. When a mistake is made, it's not the end of the world — it just needs to be fixed. It's easier for children to assume responsibility when they understand that mistakes are opportunities for learning, not for receiving ridicule and shame.

One day, I found a broken jar in the kitchen. I could have yelled and blamed someone. Instead, I asked who knew about the breakage. I needed to be sure there was no broken glass to cut bare feet. When I questioned my children, I found out that it had been broken when my son removed it from the dishwasher; somehow, he hadn't noticed. So together we checked out the machine and removed the remaining broken glass. We both *responded* to the situation — assumed *responsibility* for it — and resolved the problem together, without damaging anyone's self-esteem (or foot).

Some people believe that criticism is good for kids. "Life is going to be hard on them, so I want to teach them how to take it." What kids learn, however, is not to trust you. In spite of what our parents, ancestors, friends, or associates believe or might have believed, our job as parents is to provide nurturing and structure, not criticism. We see the results of our parenting responses every day. If we use criticism to control behavior or any sort of pain, the effects are temporary, and it is not necessary. If we make a commitment to ourselves and our children to make our responses nurturing, our children, in turn, will respond by being more motivated to connect with us and each other and become better, more responsible people. Nurturing and structuring responses teach kids how to nurture and structure themselves.

Criticism vs. Feedback

Fortunately, criticism has an opposite response that gets better results. Did you notice that nurturing and structuring responses include feedback? The difference between criticism and feedback is that criticism blames, and feedback does not assign fault.

Criticism, typically delivered in you statements ("You did this wrong." "You just don't get it."), puts others on the defensive, and for good reason. It feels like an attack. On the other hand, feedback can feel like a gift. And it builds self-esteem. The child observes acceptance, respect, and caring and concludes, "Mom/Dad cares about me enough to tell me this and encourage me to be better. Obviously, I am important. I am worthwhile." Everyone's self-esteem is enhanced. Neutral language and an encouraging approach allow the receiver to hear what is being said, and the desired change in behavior is more likely to happen.

Feedback's underlying message is one of acceptance, valuing, and inspiration. Feedback changes others through guidance, encouragement, and support and can be a caring gift to others. It is given as a suggestion — something important for others to consider — rather than an order. Feedback works by motivating others to be good and desire to correct a situation. See appendix B for a helpful chart. The difference between the two responses is that critical communication (criticism) blames, and no-fault communication (feedback) does not assign fault.

The "hook" with criticism is that it continues long after words are spoken. Criticism delivers emotional pain, which repeats like a broken record, often lasting years. If you're having trouble changing your response style, pause and listen to your own negative self-talk. You may be able to identify the voices of important people who criticized you years ago. Are you hearing "You're too fat to wear that" every time you get dressed? Do you hear the echo of "You can't do anything right!" when you make a mistake? Fortunately, negative self-talk can be interrupted and corrected (see chapter 21, "Monkey Talk"). Keep reading!

13.

Proactive Parenting: Have a Vision

"Example is not the main thing in influencing others. It is the only thing." — Albert Schweitzer[1]

In families, people belong to and with each other in a primal, sacred, undeniable way. Our histories and futures are linked, for better or worse. Families are where we are made, where we first find our power. Maybe no one has told you this, but as a parent, you are a king, a queen, a president. You are an important leader with tremendous power. With this power you can create health, happiness, and high self-value in your family, building your children into strong, caring citizens.

I love horses. One day while riding, I had an epiphany about how I could work better with my three-year-old son. I came up with the following six basic components to leadership that work in any situation:

1. **Have vision, direction, goals.** If I am riding a horse, I have to have an idea of where I am going. The horse does not know the grand plan, but it's important that I do.

2. **Communicate the message.** I must let the horse know what I want by heading it toward my goal. Parents are teachers who must clearly communicate to their children what it is they want.

3. **Keep focused.** It's important to keep sight of my vision — my goal is to go out the gate and onto the

trail. I need to focus on what I do want, not on what I don't want. Otherwise, we could end up wandering all over the barnyard.

4. **Consider the needs of others.** Success is more likely if I consider the needs of the horse. If it's very thirsty, I can almost count on having a power struggle unless I allow it to get a drink as we cross a stream. Once the horse gets a drink, we can continue on our way. When people are sensitive to and respectful of each other's needs, they can usually both come out winning.

5. **Support the desired progress.** As the horse moves in the desired direction, I encourage and support its progress up and over the hills by talking to it, keeping contact with my legs, and keeping a firm hand on the reins. I give it a pat to reward its efforts. Likewise, with children. We don't wait until a toddler speaks clearly in complete sentences to cheer; we get excited about each understandable word and phrase.

6. **Expect success and get it.** I fully expect that we will get to where we're going, and we will. Your expectations that your children are healthy and responsible will nudge them along that path.

Turns out, these are all components of proactive leadership. Proactive leaders describe what is wanted in advance and guide the way to it. Most of life's problems can be anticipated and avoided. Proactive leadership (also known as prevention) moves children away from trouble and danger and redirects them to better, safer activities.

Unfortunately, the more common style of leadership is reactive. Reactive leadership feels easy and natural, especially if it has become habitual, yet it actually creates more difficulty and stress. Many parents don't know what they *do* want from their children and therefore don't guide or encourage them. My stepmother used to scold us for our innocent actions. She'd lay into us and leave us emotionally devastated. I remember many times thinking all was well, and then she'd start scolding. "You shouldn't have done that! What were you thinking?" Having been raised by my mom, who had figured out how to be a proactive parent when I was an infant, we were stunned and confused by our stepmother and always on the defensive.

In our blended family, anxiety and fear became a way of life. I once saw my little brother walk past some toys on the bottom stair. My stepmom reacted by yelling, "Why on *earth* didn't you take those things upstairs?" I wanted to point out the obvious: he had not been asked to do that, had not thought of it, and had not been taught to do that. I wanted to say, "He can't read your mind." But I didn't want to offend her. I was afraid of her. I didn't want to make her mad at me, too. Later, I comforted him. She spoke this way to her own kids, but they had learned to shield themselves and tune her out. I wish my stepmother had been able to spend more time riding horses.

Examples of Leadership Styles

Reactive parents often have their own anxieties to deal with. Unable to cope with the clanging inside their heads, they resort to threats, force, criticism, humiliation, ridicule, and punishment, which create negative feelings in both their children and themselves. Self-esteem plunges on all sides in familiar mainstream adult practices that make kids wrong. What they don't know is that clearly communicating what they want in advance makes cooperation more likely, life much easier on themselves, and kids more successful.

Proactive leadership identifies dangers lurking in the world and gives kids permission, encouragement, and support to resist those pressures. Look at the examples on the next page, and see what they tell you about your own style of leadership.

Proactive Leadership	Reactive Leadership
Childproofs a home as baby becomes a toddler.	Changes nothing and constantly says no.
Removes broken glass from the yard before a foot is cut.	Removes broken glass from the foot.
Lets a child know that you must leave in 15 minutes, and then sets a timer for 10 minutes.	Waits until it's time to leave, and then gets angry because the child is not ready.
Tells children you're going to a restaurant and explains desired behavior.	Takes unprepared children to a restaurant, and then threatens never to take them again.
Says to teen, "I hope you'll always let me know where you are and when you'll be back; call if you're late."	Does not discuss plans and expectations in advance, and then yells at the teen who arrives home late.

The Language of Leadership

The essence of leadership can be heard in the language leaders use. Listen to yourself, and other parents, and you will find many examples of proactive and reactive leadership. What works better?

Proactive Leadership (Looks toward the future)	Reactive Leadership (Focuses on the past)
"I want you to____."	"Why did you ____?"
"Next time, please ____."	"Why didn't you ____?"
"Why don't you try ____?"	"You shouldn't have ____."

108

Reactive leaders reinforce unwanted behavior by focusing on the past, which cannot be changed. Proactive leaders acknowledge what happened in the past, confront inappropriate behavior in the present, and guide toward desired outcomes in the future. There is no need for criticism, much less punishment. They offer another chance. Ask a child, "How can you do it better next time?" This guides and encourages them toward desired behavior.

Think, for a moment, about the leadership style of your parents. Was it proactive or reactive? How did it feel to you? How did it affect your self-esteem? What do you want for your children? Being proactive is so fundamental that the very first page in our book *The Bullying Antidote* talks about Foresight vs. Hindsight. As a prevention psychologist, Mom loves to say, "An ounce of foresight is worth twenty pounds of hindsight!" With a little foresight, we can prevent the anxiety, trauma, and toxicity that drive our children away when they grow older.

Re-Visioning Your Family

Vision is the basis of good leadership. Knowing the direction you want to take is the first step. The Haudenosaunee (Iroquois) culture, which organized a confederacy of first nations centuries before America was "discovered," is guided by the Seventh Generation Principle. This philosophy considers the benefits of every decision as far as seven generations into the future. This long-range vision guides their daily actions and lives.

What vision do you have for your family five years from now? Ten years? Twenty years? Keep the vision broad, not "I want my son or daughter to be a doctor." Focus on qualities and values— not specific goals—that will enhance your lives and, down the road, those of your heirs. Knowing what you want is always the first step to getting it.

Ask yourself this: In what ways do you want your family to be like the family you grew up in? How do you want your family to be different? You have the power to not only create a vision, but also live it. Find and create meaning by clarifying your values.

What were the important qualities of the family of your childhood? What was valued?

Consider working the following values, or characteristics, into your vision — or leaving them behind:

performance • perfection • work • being "good" • possessions • being who you are • adventure • conformity • obedience • trust • authority • conflict avoidance • clean house • friendships • travel • spontaneity • rules • fun • daily love • choices • acceptance • being obedient • thinking for yourself • openness and honesty • cleanliness • looking attractive • being "nice" • religion • spirituality • faith • intellect • expressiveness • connectedness • integrity • family unity • taking care of yourself • safety • pleasing each other • pleasing parents • sense of humor • being social • isolation • hiding pain • having no pain • playfulness • respect • responsibility • self-protection • encouragement • discouragement • risk • taking care of others • belonging • denial • being there for each other • forever love • laughter • conversation • vacation • service • community
• what else? _____

Which of these feel like health and happiness to you? Which describe the values or characteristics of your family of origin? Which do not? Which do you now choose for your own family?

When I look at this list and compare my two families, I see how strongly my mother's vision — a family of laughter, love, connectedness, authenticity, choices, spirituality, and encouragement — clashed with my stepmother's — a family of obedience, conformity, unity, religion, being nice, and hiding pain. I feel fortunate that both women had visions of belonging (although it was conditional in my dad's family), cooperation, community connection, and family travel. I felt safer in one than in the other. My own family values focus on freedom, responsibility, creativity, openness, playfulness, integrity, and service to community.

Being in a family, or in a close relationship with any

110

community, leads us to examine our values. I was confused until I had an important insight. I realized that if I trusted outside voices more than my inner voice when values clashed, I would teach my children values I didn't believe in, which would create confusion and conflict (see chapter 22, "Who's Pulling Your Strings?"). As a peaceful mom, I didn't like how the culture pushed toy guns and violent video games. But on the other hand, I thought squirt gun fights were really fun! In the end, I realized what was the most important thing to me was that we had awareness about the toys that came into the house. I said yes to water and nerf gun toys, but no to the sounds of gunfire in the house. And I said yes to long discussions in which my son could choose his own values.

Once you have your own vision of what a winning family means to you, take a small step every day in that direction. Believe in your vision, and then communicate it. When we were young, my mom told me I would grow up to be a "beautiful, strong woman." She said to her sons, "Someday you'll grow up to be wonderful, gentle men." Maybe without even realizing it at the time, she was planting seeds of her vision. Now, as adults, we are all sensitive and strong in our own ways. She taught us by example, as well.

Talk about your vision with your partner and kids. Encourage them to share their dreams and visions, and listen. ("If I could give the world the best present, I'd give it ____.") Inspire, encourage, and support them in growing into the future they want. Celebrate each little step of progress.

What about morality? What is your personal code of ethics? We must teach our children right from wrong. Everyone needs basic values and manners in order to get along with others. Teach your kids kindness, respect, and honesty. Teach them the Golden Rule: *Do unto others as you would have others do unto you.* And do good unto yourself. What we model is what we teach best — and what our children tend to become. When we live our lives from our highest values, we bring peace and compassion to our families, communities, and the world.

14.

Parenting Leadership Styles

"To revere power above everything else is to be willing to sacrifice everything else to power." — Marilyn French[1]

Were you raised with strict rules? Were the politics rigid? Was one parent a tyrant? If you never experienced flexibility and freedom growing up, your parents employed an autocratic leadership style, keeping and overusing power. Were you raised without rules? Did you do whatever you wanted? Were you confused a lot? Were your parents absent? If you grew up with little guidance or few limits, your parents were permissive; they relinquished their power or didn't know they had it. Or maybe you were raised by adults who balanced rules and limits with freedom and choice? If so, your parents shared power in a democratic leadership style.

There are different way parents can use power. They can be overbearing, they can abdicate, or they can find a balance between the two.

MOST	CONTROL/STRUCTURE/GUIDANCE	LEAST

<----------------------------------->

AUTOCRATIC	DEMOCRATIC	PERMISSIVE

Most people grew up in a mix of autocratic and permissive styles. It's very common for one parent to be autocratic and the other to be permissive, or for both parents to swing between extremes. We call this "Ping-Pong Parenting." Often children who dislike their parents' style vow that they will bring up their own children differently. Many swing from one extreme to the other, creating a new family with just as many problems, only different ones. They commonly swing from the autocratic to the permissive style. The leadership style parents use reflects their own self-esteem and affects the self-esteem of their children.

With love, all parenting styles work out okay, and families recover from hardships and stick together somehow. But when love is lacking or uncommunicated — often because of self-esteem issues or trauma — extreme parenting styles hurt kids. The autocratic style, without love and support, becomes *abuse.* The permissive style, without love and support, becomes *neglect.*

What we are talking about here is power. Many people don't know how to use their personal power correctly. Without a strong sense of self, people take control of others or let others make their decisions for them. Both of these imbalances lead to codependency and passive-aggressive behavior. In a family with balanced power, everyone is mindful of their role and responsibility. In a democratic family, everyone has a voice.

Reflect on how your parents' leadership style affected you. Did you like being in your family? Was their style good for you or did it make things hard? What kind of a relationship do you now have with your parents? Is that what you want to have with your children when they are grown?

There is a chart of all of these leadership styles in appendix C.

Autocratic (Authoritarian) Leadership Style

Authoritarian leadership style means one person is in charge.

Characteristics of Parents

Autocratic, or drill-sergeant, parents impose their will through a rigid structure that allows little flexibility or freedom. They tend to

- overuse or abuse power,
- impose rigid rules,
- take total control over and responsibility for all decisions,
- take charge of other people's lives without respecting their boundaries,
- believe that their way is the only right way,
- withhold information,
- be out of touch with feelings (or shut them down),
- disregard/diminish the opinions and feelings of others ("You're too sensitive." "You shouldn't feel that way."),
- deny or twist the feelings of others ("You don't really feel that." "That's nonsense."),
- deny the reality of others (gaslighting),
- use pressure and punishment to force compliance,
- be right at all times,
- never apologize, and/or
- hurt others, intentionally or unintentionally.

Autocratic parents demand "respect," which sometimes translates as "fear." They may say, "Children should be seen and not heard," or, "A child's will must be broken." Autocratic parents generally feel

- superior,
- distrustful of others,
- burdened with responsibility,
- lonely,
- anxious, with a need to control,
- depressed and reactive, and/or
- low in self-esteem.

Military families often have autocratic leaders, since the military is based on a chain of authority, and that structure makes parents feel safe. Fundamentally religious families often believe in the divine dominion of man over wife and parents over children. Parents who are teachers, bosses, coaches, or other leadership types can bring their autocratic roles home, unaware that they have a choice to be gentler. Sometimes, parents who are just plain stressed out default to autocratic behaviors, barking orders.

Sometimes parents don't realize they are abusing their power. One father said, "I didn't realize the impact of my voice on a child. But then I saw another guy, a 6-foot-tall man, yelling at a child 3 feet tall. It was just plain bullying. The power differential really hit me. A lot of times men feel vulnerable inside but don't realize how they look to others." Again, there's nothing wrong with being powerful, but it is the duty of the powerful to be caring to the powerless. This makes a healthy society.

Characteristics of Children

There are severe consequences to the self-esteem of a child in an authoritarian family structure. Placed in a one-down, inferior position to their parents (even when grown), children with autocratic parents work hard second-guessing, trying to figure out how to please their parents to avoid getting punished. They don't have a chance to develop their own power and thus may

- want to be told what to do—or resent being told what to do,
- lack a sense of personal responsibility,
- distrust their feelings because they've been told those feelings are wrong,
- lack imagination and creativity,
- become self-rejecting and lonely,
- become compliant and withdrawing (accepting powerlessness)—or become defiant and rebellious (fighting for power),
- withdraw by moving or running away, breaking ties with the family, and/or
- bully others.

Children who are not allowed to make their own choices often rebel outwardly. Eating disorders and oppositional behavior are both symptoms of kids trying to have some control over their own bodies. One young mother reported that she rebelled against her autocratic parents by getting pregnant and keeping her baby, in spite of the fact that they wanted her to have an abortion. Another woman got back at her father by marrying the "wrong" man — guess who suffered? An older woman finally dealt with her autocratic parents by moving to another country. The authoritarian leadership style may work for a period of time, but in the long-term, it disconnects people and creates misery. In politics, this style is called fascism.

In an autocratic family configuration, children tend to feel afraid and guilty, yet they don't know what to do with their feelings, which are ignored or denied by their parents. The may also feel

- powerless and out of control,
- submissive and dependent,
- hostile and angry,
- distrusting and helpless,
- self-rejecting,
- lonely, with low self-esteem,
- anxious, and/or
- depressed.

Yet children need limits, and it is necessary for parents to be strict at times. Let's look at what happens without those things.

Permissive Leadership Style

Permissive leadership style means no one is really in charge.

Characteristics of Parents

In a permissive family, there is *too much* freedom. Parents abdicate power. Permissive parents may be too busy, under the effects of drugs or alcohol, mentally or physically ill, or simply disinterested. Kids in these families miss out on the security and safety of rules, limits, and structure. If rules exist, they always change, which causes confusion and chaos. Permissive parents tend to

116

- believe they have no rights,
- condone everything their children do,
- lack interest in their children or what they do,
- be physically or emotionally absent and uninvolved, and/or
- neglect their children's need for healthy development.

These parents often feel

- hopeless or discouraged,
- confused,
- angry,
- powerless and out of control over their lives,
- disrespected,
- overwhelmed,
- low in self-esteem, and/or
- their own needs aren't met.

Characteristics of Children

In permissive families, children

- don't learn boundaries,
- have trouble with limits (while at the same time crave them),
- lack self-discipline and responsibility (or may have had to assume too much responsibility too soon),
- may take on an unhealthy role reversal with parents,
- are often on their own before they are ready,
- think they have the right to do exactly as they wish,
- have little awareness of social responsibility,
- may become violent toward their parents, and/or
- may later seek highly structured groups, cults, or institutions.

Children in these families often feel

- powerless and out of control,
- unsafe,
- unloved,
- confused and discouraged,
- dependent,
- unable to cope with routine, and/or
- low in self-esteem.

Surrounded by confusion and inconsistency, these children can't ever fully trust their parents. If they do, their trust is broken again and again.

A husband and wife attending one of our workshops realized that he was autocratic and she was permissive. The more he swung one way, the more his wife swung the other. This was confusing to their children and difficult for the whole family. Insight into their conflict gave this couple an opportunity to create a more consistent environment for their kids.

When you meet children who have a high level of self-esteem and a sense of personal power, you can be sure their parents gave them both structure and freedom. Read more about parenting leadership styles in our book *The Bullying Antidote.*

Add love to both autocratic and permissive styles, and they become more caring and less damaging. Love is the baseline for mental health and successful family life. Love is a "whole other" dimension of parenting. Love enhances each leadership style, making it healthier for the family. But there is another style that allows for maximum love.

Democratic (Authoritative) Leadership Style

Democratic leadership means being in charge but sharing power.

Characteristics of Parents

Democratic families are based on respect. Everyone's needs are considered important. Parents share power with each other and with their children. They offer choices and treat children as capable, worthwhile human beings who are able to think for

118

themselves and make good decisions. They demonstrate good boundaries, allowing each member of the family to feel like a sovereign being, in charge of themself. Parents who use a democratic leadership style teach responsibility and allow freedom. In these families, frequent meetings and discussions with clear ground rules allow everyone to develop their own abilities to offer problems and solutions and make decisions, rules, and plans. There is a balance of power among caregivers: no one person is solely the boss.

Democratic parents

- are in charge of themselves and the family,
- provide structure, but allow flexibility and freedom,
- give children limited choices appropriate to their ages,
- invite and encourage children to participate in planning and decision-making, yet enforce rules of respect,
- encourage children to learn from mistakes and fix them, and
- teach responsibility by giving it.

Starting from an attitude of cooperation with their children, democratic parents function as managers, counselors, and coaches. This style — when based on love — is the framework for a winning family.

Parents who use a democratic leadership style

- are in charge, yet flexible,
- feel respectful and respected, loving and loved,
- trust their children and themselves,
- are sensitive to needs, and
- have high self-esteem.

Characteristics of Children

Feeling like part of a team in which everyone is important, these children are eager to cooperate. They

119

- respect rules,
- are self-disciplined and responsible,
- understand cause-and-effect relationships, and
- are capable and self-determining.

By making choices and decisions, children raised in democratic family structures learn to direct their own lives and become good social leaders. Throughout their lives, they tend to have friendly relationships with their parents characterized by mutual respect, and they share power, easy affection, and a sense of equality.

In these families, children know they are responsible for themselves and their behavior. They feel

- valued and heard,
- trusted and respected,
- worthwhile and important, and
- self-confident and self-respecting.

Democratic parents share power with their children, creating relationships based on mutual empowerment instead of mutual victimization. This empowerment is necessary for mental health, for making dreams come true, and for your children's and your own self-esteem.

In our democratic society, where people must be able to make many decisions, think for themselves, and vote for leaders, this family style is the training ground. As we teach children that they can choose to be who they want to be and do what they want to do with their lives, we empower them to build their own cathedrals on good foundations.

Mom grew up in an autocratic family; therefore, she learned only this restrictive parenting style, and she "naturally" employed it when her children were little. However, she wrote, "As they [my kids] grew and became able to think, communicate, and be more responsible, I found that they were ready and willing to assume more and more responsibility for themselves, and that I, in turn, could 'loosen up.' I gradually let go of my need to be in control all the time and learned to share power. In the grocery store, for example, I'd pick out three boxes of acceptable cereal and let one of my children select one. When they were older, I'd have them read the labels and select the healthiest items. As I trusted them more, they became more trustworthy; as they became more trustworthy, I trusted them more. Shifting from external control and influence to motivation from within, I gradually developed a democratic leadership style. We became a team."

After having worked on this book as a young adult, I was eager to share power with my own child . . . but it took a while. The first year of his life I had to do *everything* for him, from lifting his head to chewing his food. When children are little, we have complete responsibility for their care and protection. As they grow and develop, we can gradually turn over responsibility to and share power with them, guiding and protecting them as necessary. One thing I learned is that a flexible leadership style grounded in democracy can fluctuate with circumstances. For example, in an emergency, "Fire!" is a complete sentence and an order to act. However, when playing at a park, it's time to be permissive— because kids are safe and know their boundaries.

15.

Parenting and Empowerment

"When you give away some of the light from the candle by lighting another person's candle, there isn't less light because you've given some away — there's more. When everybody grows, there isn't less of anybody, there's more of — and for — everybody."
— Kaleel Jamison[1]

Healthy parenting is nothing if not a process of empowerment. As we help to raise our children's self-esteem, we also increase their personal power. When we encourage them to be confident, self-reliant, self-directed, and responsible individuals, we are giving them power. For better or worse, patterns of power by which we live, and that our children copy, will profoundly affect their entire lives and the lives of those around them. As parents, we have much to gain by learning to share power with our children.

Mom taught and encouraged us kids to ride bicycles. There was a rush of pride and power — and a tinge of surprise — as we each yelled back to her, "I'm doing it!" Nearly twenty years after she gave her oldest son, Damian, one last push on his wobbly two-wheeler, he spent an afternoon looking for the perfect bike for her. He taught and encouraged her to use it, giving back that same encouraging push. The icing on the cake came when we all went bike touring in Europe — Mom, on her special bike, kept up with us kids. Each of us was able to push our own pedals and pull our own weight for many days and zillions of kilometers (or so it seemed). It was an empowering experience packed with cherished memories.

My younger brother, Felix, taught Mom things she would

never have learned on her own. "When I'd ask him to fix something for me," she says, "he'd show me how to do it. Under his guidance, I've become a veritable whiz on a computer! Later, while discussing the process of empowerment with him, he laughed, 'Yeah, Mom, we had a wimp rehabilitation program for you!' Over and over, the power I gave my sons came back to me." And, of course, Mom raised me to believe in myself and in my talents. Because of her, I have always been employed as a resourceful artist and writer, learning and developing expression and communication skills.

As a mom, she encouraged us kids to use our personal power. And our personal power has always enriched her and many others as we followed in her footsteps as teachers, thinkers, problem solvers, connectors, and even visionaries. Because of her, we all have the power to live healthy and effective lives.

Mom writes, "When I was a child myself, however, I was told, and thus believed, that my purpose in life was to be a nice little girl. When I grew up, I found I was a very nice lady. By being 'nice,' I avoided situations that called for much power and yielded to others to avoid power struggles. I was acutely aware of my isolation and lack of support and had little sense of my own personal power.

"My children have taught me differently. Through the conflict-ridden process of being a mother and 'just a housewife,' I became aware of my awesome power and responsibility: to give life, to nurture, and to shape young beliefs and behaviors.

"When I studied psychology in graduate school, I began to recognize a common thread through my courses and my own experience. Everyone needs to feel confident, to feel competent, to have a sense of power. I spent the next twelve years or so unraveling the fabric of my own beliefs and behaviors and letting go of those that held me back. Bit by bit, I began to reweave the pieces. The new attitudes, skills, and habits have formed a cloak of power that is all my own."

Power comes from the Latin word *poder*, meaning "to be able."

Everyone needs to be able and capable and have a sense of personal power. At the heart of personal power is the knowledge that you are in charge of your life — that you have the ultimate responsibility for how you live it. When you accept more and more responsibility for your own self and behavior, you gain personal power. Connecting and collaborating with others can expand that power.

Power comes in many forms. We talk about buying power, staying power, power lunches, political power, power dressing, and a thing called clout. Certain roles — president, principal, policeman, parent — have power inherent in the job description. Success, in the United States, is commonly measured by power in the form of money, status, or control and influence over others. With this kind of thinking, power is a pie without enough slices to go around.

Power Associations

Power means different things to different people. Some positive associations include the following:
- having choices
- making a difference
- bringing about change
- influencing others
- responsibility
- expressing one's uniqueness

Such associations make people desire power. But sometimes the word makes people nervous because of its many negative associations.
- domination and oppression
- violence and abuse
- patriarchy and sexism
- rape and incest
- racism and slavery
- militarism and war
- manipulation, exploitation, and seduction

124

- dishonesty and secretiveness
- burdensome responsibility for others

Power can be intoxicating and lead people to do inhumane things to others. Power can corrupt and destroy lives, or it can create peace and understanding. It's all about how we use it.

Power Games

The simplest video games involve players killing or being killed, activating survival-level thinking: in order for one person to win, the other has to lose. The concept "I want you to lose so that I can win" is deeply woven into the fabric of how we think and who we are and has been humanity's operating norm for about seven thousand years. But this up-down, win-lose model of power is not "normal human behavior."

We simply cannot have healthy relationships if people are always on guard or attacking and counterattacking. We cannot have a win-win family if it's normal to make others wrong so that we can be right. We cannot have healthy children if they receive unhealthy messages and operate from a distorted value system.

Let's explore the difference between the two types of power games we can play.

- **Power Taking.** People who lack a sense of personal power often try to get it at another's expense. They dominate and disempower others. They may use any means, including violence, to gain control. Spurred by me-versus-you thinking, they put others down so that they can feel one up on them. Always competing with others, they think they are okay if they are better than, stronger than, or smarter than others. Trying to feel good at someone else's expense is unsustainable. When one person wins, sometimes it's the relationship that loses.
- **Power Sharing.** Based on respect, caring, compassion, and support, people share power with each other. Cooperative, mutually nurturing partnerships enhance

and expand everyone's personal power. As people share power, power increases.

Riane Eisler, founder of the Center for Partnership Systems, argues that for approximately 30,000 years, partnership was the norm.[2] In fact, biological science gives us abundant evidence of partnership among all ecological systems, from fungi in the soil sharing nutrients between trees to our own microbiome giving us vitality. Our culture's focus on the classic power-struggle model constantly emphasizes examples of control drama, poor impulse control, and problems solved with violence.

When we view competitive power in up-down/win-lose terms, powerful kids, wives, or husbands may appear to be a personal threat to a power holder. Aware of only two options, parents (or siblings) not wanting to lose, will fight to keep others from winning. Everyone feels the stress of competition.

When we move beyond the dominant/submissive definition of power, we discover that giving kids a sense of their own power does not take it away from mom and dad, or mom and mom, or dad and dad, or other grown-ups in the family. Power sharing lies at the heart of families in which people are for, not against, each other. Just as a democratic society honors the rights of all citizens, a winning family honors the rights of every member.

The Four Dimensions of Power

Imagine four people together in a room, each representing one stop on the spectrum of power. Pat Powerless is helpless, dependent, insecure, and uninformed. Parker Powerful is confident, capable, and in control and takes risks. Elliot Empowering is supportive, encouraging, and challenging. Drew Dominating is overpowering, manipulative, arrogant, and pushy. Who would be attracted to each other? What would each one's spouse be like? Who would be drawn together? Who would avoid each other? Do any of them sound like your own secret identity? Who would you be attracted to?

We have all been affected or hurt in some way by an

overpowering person—a parent, teacher, friend, boss, or even a stranger. The object of this person's unconscious game is to gain power at another's expense. Some common tactics include

belittling • diminishing • dismissing • demoralizing • discouraging • changing rules • withholding support • intimidating • keeping secrets • arguing • name-calling or labeling • gaslighting (denying someone's reality) • ignoring • blocking, weakening, or destroying connections.

Divide and conquer is an ancient strategy used around the world. In US society, we have been fragmented from family and friends, from ethnic roots, from communities and neighborhoods, and from Mother Earth. In our quest for individuality, competition, and progress, we have become separated from other ethnic groups, believing that their well-being directly threatens our own. Constantly on the move, many people feel alienated, disconnected, and lonely.

Gabor Maté writes and speaks about how trauma comes from disconnection. Naomi Klein illustrates how governments and corporations destabilize communities by creating a traumatizing experience that destroys connection and strength, so they can come in and restructure societies for their own advantage.[3]

Reconnecting and Mending

We can gain power by turning to others to share our common experience. As we connect with others, we can increase our personal and collective power while simultaneously healing ourselves.

In a Mexican barrio, a rural worker gathered together women living in the same area. Although they lived very close to one another, they didn't know each other at all. As they sewed together, they discovered they had things in common. Each one was being battered. They realized that they were not alone or crazy or at fault.

They decided to do something to stop the abuse. Each woman got a whistle. They pledged that if any of them were abused, they, or one of their kids, would blow the whistle. The other women would immediately gather around her house in a circle banging on pots and pans. "That simple and empowering action began to transform the cycle of abuse in the barrio and change the relationships fostered among the women, within other relationships, and in how they saw themselves and their own power."[4] That single action—telling their truth—led them out of isolation and into empowerment.

If we have been divided from ourselves—our bodies, minds, emotions, spirituality—we can regain our power by reclaiming the missing pieces. Acknowledging and reclaiming our negative and abused parts, and talking about and/or writing about them, helps us accept and forgive ourselves. We become integrated, whole, and strong.

As we accept, embrace, and send love into our childhood wounds, we can heal and transform our lives. In honoring, supporting, and having compassion for ourselves and others, we can tap into our deepest power. This source of strength gives us the courage to meet life's challenges.

Violence: The Abuse of Power

Understanding power dynamics is crucial for a safer world. A 1992 study revealed that, of all the industrialized nations, the United States was the most violent, and since then, police violence has increased (disproportionately so against black Americans). Worldwide, women and children are the primary victims of violence, and men are the primary perpetrators. Conditioned to accept violence and trained to commit violence, men have difficulty talking about how it affects them—as perpetrators or as targets, when they are victims of child abuse, rape, or war.

Violence is the number-one health hazard in this country, more threatening than cancer, heart disease, or even automobiles. Here are some 2020 statistics.[5]

- Terrorism is on the rise worldwide, with far-right extremism on the rise in the United States and beyond.
- One in three women worldwide suffer physical or sexual abuse by an intimate partner.
- Since 1963, four times more teens have been killed by guns at home than soldiers killed in all wars since then combined.
- Over 60 percent of women have experienced violence online (and 6 percent of men).
- Mass shootings are now so common that many aren't even reported in the news.

Every family has to deal with violence in some form or another, within the home, among extended family, in the community, or on the news. Children raised in violent homes learn violence as a way of life, doing unto others what was done unto them or what their parents did to each other, unless they find safety in which to heal and make new choices. Many boys raised in violent households become perpetrators, while their sisters learn to accept abuse as normal.

Violence of all kinds is reaching epidemic proportions in US families, and it does not stay within families. Childhood maltreatment roughly doubles the probability that an individual engages in many types of crime.[6] Because violence creates ripples, domestic violence is not a private family problem. It affects all levels of society.

Violence has become so widespread in our society that we have come to accept it as normal, but it *not* normal. In fact, America is below average compared to other developed countries, according to the International Peace Index.[7]

Raising children with positivity will not protect them from all bullying and violence, but it absolutely builds resilience and instills a respectful and compassionate moral code, plus a sense of empathy and justice.

If you live in an abusive home, be responsible for your own

safety and that of your children. You must find someone to talk to. You must get help. Visualize what you want for yourself, and muster your courage to make a change.

Timing is important. Protect yourself and your kids from harm. *This is your right and your responsibility.*

If you were raised in an abusive family, instead of repeating past mistakes, learn from them. Remember what it was like for you. Instead of wounding your children, heal yourself. You didn't deserve abuse; neither do your kids. Seek information. Get help. Find supports. Believe in yourself. Be smart as you build your inner strength and skills. Develop a vision of hope. You can move away from past destructive patterns and create a positive healthy future for yourself and your beloved children.

Gender and Power

Although aspects of both masculinity and femininity are beautiful, most cultures encode gender with negative human qualities that can apply to any person. Anyone can be dominating, superior, and controlling; anyone can be passive, inferior, and obliging. But society tells us that to be masculine is to be powerful, and to be feminine is to be powerless. Toxic cultural definitions of power have locked us into unhealthy win-lose power struggles and are a blueprint for dysfunctional families.

When boys acted in dominating ways, parents traditionally said, "Boys will be boys," and let them escape consequences. In recent women's marches, we've seen proudly displayed on t-shirts and posters a new vision for male children: "Boys will be Good Humans."

Meanwhile, when women are put on a pedestal, they are set up to disappoint others and to "deserve" punishment. In 1996, Anthony Bouza, the former chief of police of Minneapolis, spoke up at a National Conference on Violence: "For centuries women have been raised to accept their fate as victims and therefore to think and act like victims. If they were abused, they were led to believe that they somehow 'deserved' it. But those days have got to end for all women." According to Bouza, police and the criminal justice system "must abandon their convenient myths of male authority and power"[8] and treat women differently. (In 2020, this same police department's actions showed the world how brutal the myth of white male authority and power is when the murder of George Floyd sparked Black Lives Matter demonstrations around the world.) *Respect* is an empty word if it does not mean sharing power. In winning families, men and women have equal importance and dignity, and everyone's work and contributions are valued and appreciated. When women are valued and empowered, they are not victims of crime.

Healthier expectations have been placed on adult males at other times and in cultures in which the word *power* is associated with service. Author Paula Gunn Allen discusses images of male power in her indigenous tradition.[9] A man, if he's a mature adult, nurtures life. He performs rituals that help things grow, he helps raise the kids, and he protects the people. His entire life is aimed toward balance and cooperation. The ideal of manhood is the same as the ideal of womanhood: to be autonomous, self-directing, and responsible for the spiritual, social, and material life of all those with whom you live.

Their language did not, perhaps, encode unhealthy stereotypes as does English, in which the word *virtue* has the same Latin root as the word *virile*. Worldwide, women are judged on their virtue or lack of it—a standard set by men.

The US women's movement has done much to challenge attitudes toward sex roles and blur lines between gender-based power roles. Today more and more men are rethinking and challenging restrictive cultural definitions of manhood. Realizing that family economic security is not the only, or even the most important, domain, they are rediscovering their innate capacity to bond with and nurture their children. Men are tapping into freeze-dried parts of themselves and making new choices. Men are also learning to be better friends and important resources for each other. More couples strive for relationships in which partners share power rather than fight for it.

In this millennium, an even more enormous shift is taking place, going far beyond gender definitions and stereotypes. Same-sex marriage is socially accepted, as is gender fluidity. Parents seek gender-neutral names for their children, something about which Mom and her generation couldn't even talk and for which my generation longed. Mainstream societal changes are redefining masculinity, femininity, and equality.

Family Empowerment

When this book was first written, the term "family friendly" was new. Breastfeeding in public was taboo. Rarely were there crayons on tables for kids in restaurants. Restrooms had no place to change diapers. Since then, parents working together have educated[10] and politicized. They lobby for the concerns and well-being of millions of families in the United States. Working together, they have learned how to shape a unified voice and a vision of empowerment for families. T. Berry Brazelton, pediatrician, author, and cochair of Parent Action, states, "I want to empower young parents to get in there and get what they need. I want to fight for parent power. Our culture is in grave danger and it's because we're not paying enough attention to strengthening our families."[11] This parenting icon has made an enormous difference for family well-being.

The study of positive psychology has led to a new worldwide focus on well-being. We now have data indicating which societal structures support family and child wellness and which ones don't. Several countries have let go of the idea of Gross Domestic Product in favor of Gross Domestic Happiness. For the fifth year in a row, Finland is the world's happiest country, according to the World Happiness Report, and the United States has moved up to sixteenth place.[12]

The family unit is a basic societal building block. Traditionally, it has been a source of identity, strength, and stability for individual members and the community at large. If a family is a battleground for personal power struggles, everyone suffers. On the other hand, when family members feel a sense of personal power, they don't have to fight each other. Co-parents can empower each other in egalitarian relationships. They can empower their children with words and actions, by offering them choices, and by encouraging them to be strong and smart. Empowering parents teach kids

- to be respectful of themselves and others,
- to be responsible for their behaviors,
- to create and respect boundaries,
- to be assertive,
- to be sensitive,
- to be nonviolent,
- to be kind and protective,
- to avoid danger, but fight their battles, and
- to get their needs met so no one is victimized.

We can raise our sons to be sensitive and strong men who are not abusive. We can raise our daughters to be strong women who will not be battered. We teach these things best when we honor these qualities in our families and model them in our own relationships.

People with high self-esteem, who respect and value themselves and others, do not tolerate abuse. They know they don't deserve it. Parents have the power to create supportive and peaceful families where people are for, not against, each other.

16.

Family Boundaries

"Good fences make good neighbors."
—Robert Frost

What are personal boundaries, and why are they important? Do boundaries belong in families? "Boundaries," one child explained, "are the imaginary lines that separate us from each other so we don't get mixed up." Boundaries are about what you believe you deserve and what you are willing to put up with.

Boundaries are important for a strong sense of self. Infants don't see themselves as being independent beings until they are nearly a year old, and, unless trauma intervenes, they don't see themselves as being separate beings from their mother until they are nearly two. A two-year-old really struggles with what's "mine" (everything) and what's not. All our lives, we define and refine what is "me" and what is "not me."

We learn about ourselves by observing boundaries. We may become uncomfortable when someone stands too close, uses our things, or speaks in a way that bothers us. We may be surprised when others react to mannerisms and habits that feel normal to us. Our ability to set and respect boundaries defines our self-esteem, and vice versa.

There are three types of boundaries: *rigid, permeable,* and *flexible*. Rigid and permeable boundaries are formed automatically or unconsciously; flexible boundaries are learned consciously. We learn all types from our parents and can pass on all types to our kids—it's our choice.

- People who have **rigid boundaries** easily communicate "no." They need to be in charge of everything, and they feel vulnerable if they are not. Often people with rigid boundaries threaten or control others. They are hard to be around. About 18 percent of people are like this, so they're not unusual.[1]

- People who can't say no, or whose "no" is weak or disregarded, have **permeable boundaries**. They allow, even invite, others to make choices and decisions for them. They are unable to be in charge of their own time and/or space. These are people who don't set limits, and if they do, they don't guard them. They often feel resentful, afraid, or shut down.
- People with **flexible boundaries** are able to talk about and negotiate feelings and agreements so that things feel fair. With strong boundaries that aren't rigid, they have good mental and emotional health and positive energy. Their well-developed sense of self and relationship skills make them the easiest type of people to get along with. These people can choose whether to hold strong boundaries or open up.

Unhealthy boundaries negatively affect lives. They require more time and energy than healthy ones. People who don't tend to their boundaries feel they don't get the respect they deserve and often suffer mental and emotional distress. We take care of ourselves by communicating our needs, which creates boundaries. We need assertiveness skills to do this.

In autocratic systems, be they in families, communities, or governments, boundaries are set by one person or defined by an inflexible set of beliefs. In fundamentalist systems, men set boundaries for women and children. Fathers and male leaders, and their traditions and laws, dictate what women can and can't do. In these systems, a low-status man often has the right to make more choices than a high-status woman.

Democratic systems acknowledge that each person is endowed with inalienable human rights, even children. But with rights come responsibilities. We have to take care of ourselves and make good choices.

Examining Boundaries

We can examine our boundaries and update them at any time by making different choices. As parents, we can ask ourselves questions, such as,

- How much do I do for our children?
- Do I have the time to myself that I need?
- Am I available to others as much as I need to be?
- What do I believe about setting boundaries around my personal time and space?
- Do others respect my boundaries?
- Am I comfortable with the boundaries of others?

The path of parenting is the path of losing and then rebuilding your own boundaries, so this work is great to do with your kids as they grow. As you edit your boundaries, you can teach your children to define theirs. "It's your job to clear your place now."

Kids need to explore the world and learn about life. Keeping in mind children's ages and development, a parent's job is to guide them while they discover limits, work within them, and advance beyond them. Toddlers, for example, need to touch. They explore the world with their fingers and hands. Mom, instead of saying no all the time to my brother and I (her first two babies), put special things out of reach and allowed us to touch other nice things with only one finger. The One Finger Touch satisfied our need to reach out and explore without the risk of breakage, and, as tiny kids who didn't understand much, we learned self-control and respect in one fell swoop.

Boundary Issues

Here are patterns that have to do with permeable boundaries. They mainly pertain to women, due to patriarchal cultural patterns, but they can be a problem for anyone struggling with codependency (see chapter 24, Internal Barriers to Self-Esteem).

Self-Sacrifice

In many cultures, women are expected to be caretakers and

end up focusing on everyone's needs but their own. Women have been taught to expect and hope that by doing enough caretaking, their turn will come automatically; but, somehow, it rarely does. Women are still led to believe that taking care of themselves is selfish. "I almost denied myself out of existence," confessed a woman who was raised to be self-negating. Many people become long-suffering martyrs and doormats, watching life pass them by, doing what's expected of them. Without a connection to their own creativity, meaning, or drive, they become emotionally bankrupt, unable to connect with strong people, and they burn out on life long before it's over.

Those who never stand up for their rights or preferences can be annoying and a burden to others. For example, a friend's visiting grandmother was invited to tour San Francisco in a convertible. They urged her to sit in the front passenger seat, where she could enjoy the view without too much wind. Her adult grandchildren would sit in the back and enjoy the ride. But she refused to take the front seat, insisting that she was being treated too well. Consequently, the car's top stayed up; exciting vistas flew by, viewed through tiny windows; and no one had a good time. Her commitment to self-sacrifice made everyone suffer.

The opposite of self-sacrifice is self-care. After having two babies eleven months apart, Mom wished someone had told her to take care of herself and make time for exercise and rest. "I wish someone had given me permission to play more," she recalls. "I wish someone had told me that nap time for baby is 'me time' for mom." Mothers have to take care of themselves so that they can take care of others. Self-care is primary, since you can't give what you haven't got.

"Kids' needs are best met by grown-ups whose needs are met," writes Jean Illsley Clarke. Yet, there are times when we need to put our own needs on hold, especially when we have young children. One of the challenges of parenting is to do for our kids *and* for ourselves. We need to strike a healthy balance in which no one loses. Healthy boundaries turn self-sacrifice into self-care.

Self-care means taking care of your body, your space, and your possessions — and every child needs to learn these things. But it also means taking care of your time. You need time for yourself, and you also need time for your interests and your relationships. Friends, extended family, and your spouse all support you, and relationships with them need to be nurtured. When kids come along, it's easy for parents to fall out of touch with each other. Here's a quick recipe for creating nice boundaries around partner relationship time and communication.

- **Daily check-ins:** Set a timer for five minutes and take turns talking about your day or what's on your mind *with no interruptions.*
- **Weekly check-ins:** Schedule two hours per week to circle back to the daily issues and take turns listening about deeper issues. This can also be problem-solving time.
- **Playdates and romance:** Weekly, if possible, but no less than monthly, do something fun that reconnects you with the joy that brought you together.

Love that exists between parents showers down on children. Being in the presence of two people who truly love and support each other has a powerful positive effect on the family.

When you are good to yourself, you *feel* good about yourself. *Take good care of yourself, because your children are counting on you to take good care of them!*

People Pleasing

Many people are taught to spend their lives trying to please others. They avoid saying no, for fear of upsetting others. They want everyone to like them and enjoy being with them. It's a wonderful thing to care for and help others. The world works best when everyone does that. But people pleasers who constantly put the needs of others above their own can suffer from low self-esteem.

As a senior in high school, Mom was voted "most cheerful" in a class of three hundred girls. "Wanting to be pleasing so that everyone would like me, I wore a permanent smile, which actually had little to do with cheer," she says. "I was shocked in graduate school to learn that, statistically, one out of eight people would not like me (or anyone else)!" Struggling with this new reality, she learned that little girls are socialized to want to be liked by others, while boys are socialized to look for respect. She realized that if being liked were most important, people would do anything to achieve it—even things that were against their principles. It's a vulnerable position that invites manipulation.

After giving this a lot of thought, she decided that she would rather have people respect her than like her. She stopped reflexively smiling. She lowered her voice and started learning assertiveness skills. She began to respect herself more, and others began to respect her more. Her self-esteem rose many notches as definitions of what pleased *her* changed.

The flip side of people pleasing is pleasing yourself. If you're not pleased, it's hard to hear compliments. People said our wedding day was the best ever, but for a long time I was troubled by all the things that went wrong. Then I realized I wasn't able to let in all the compliments, and it diminished them to respond, "Yes, but the flowers were wilted," or, "Yes, but my husband forgot his pants." After our first anniversary, I decided to focus on the day's joy and love.

Scratch the surface of a people pleaser, and you may find someone who is never pleased themself. If you're a people pleaser, start focusing on your own pleasure. Give yourself a present every day: a bath, a flower, a moment with a good book, a foot rub with nice lotion, or a call to a friend.

It's important to teach our preteen daughters and sons about the dangers of people pleasing. When you lack the inner strength to set boundaries around sex, you can lose track of yourself in troubling ways.

Over- and Underresponsibility

When babies are born, parents have total responsibility for their survival and well-being. As kids grow and are able to do things for themselves, parents must turn over to them more responsibility — from feeding themselves to driving themselves.

If this transfer does not occur, and parents carry more responsibility than is necessary or appropriate, children lose opportunities to grow, develop, and expand. Do you run the risk of becoming a helicopter parent? What's causing that? Women who believe that mothering is their only role may hold on to caretaking responsibility longer than necessary and deprive their children of self-responsibility. Parents who don't let their children fail and succeed on their own will struggle with uncomfortable family boundaries as their kids become adults. Parents who carry too much responsibility may feel burdened and be perceived as controllers. Blame and anger may result, with a drop in everyone's self-esteem.

Assumption of too much responsibility can be particularly heavy for parents whose children have special needs. All too often parents continue to do things that a child was capable of taking over long ago. Your child is whole and complete. Share with them the vision that they will be able to take over responsibilities in their own life, even if they will always need extra support.

We can't remind ourselves often enough that every person is first and foremost responsible for himself or herself. The task of the parent shifts from having total responsibility over infants to having almost no responsibility over them as adults. This gradual letting-go process, in harmony with a child's developmental stages, occurs over a fifteen- to twenty-five-year period and includes thousands of boundary adjustments.

We teach children responsibility by teaching ourselves not to do things for them that they can do for themselves. Each time they gain a skill, your load gets lighter. Praise their contribution. Learn to delegate. But always acknowledge that they may do things differently.

As kids learn to do more things for themselves, their competence and confidence increase. As children assume more responsibility for their behavior and lives, parents can relax protectiveness, increase trust, and breathe a sigh of relief as their responsibility diminishes. Then parents can refocus and get on with other important areas in their lives.

Boundaries and Consent

Life in a family is always changing, and we need to constantly negotiate. Small children will barge into our rooms and teenagers will lock us out of theirs. Having a dialogue about changing boundaries creates love and respect. Parents often complain, "Boundaries are always pushed!" Indeed, this is true. This is normal and natural. As kids grow, they test limits, and parents need to constantly assess and reevaluate them. When a family talks about boundaries, and everyone is allowed to have them, there tends to be more respect and less conflict. We need to set and then enforce boundaries (I keep the bathroom door closed when I go) and loosen them when needed (I can step out of my comfort zone if it means being closer to my family). We need to set and then enforce our boundaries: "When the bathroom/bedroom door is closed, you must knock and ask permission to enter." Loosen them when needed: "You can do number one when I'm in the shower if it's an emergency."

As a young mom, I felt exhausted and unappreciated when my son's friends thundered into the kitchen, wolfed down snacks, and then ran off to play, leaving me with a mess. Without knowing it or meaning to, they walked all over my boundaries. I wanted them to be respectful of the kitchen being a space of nourishment in many ways. I finally spoke up and told them my expectations: "I work hard to make you healthy food you like. When you're done, I'd like . . ."

One of the boys interrupted and asked, "You'd like us to clear our places?"

I smiled and nodded, and then added, "I'd also like for us to all

141

talk together when we eat together." They liked that idea so much that they began bringing me conversation topics. I added one more thing: "Also, when you leave the kitchen, I'd like you to say, 'Thank you, Mama K, for that lovely meal.' " They did just what I asked for and appreciated the guidance. The other moms were astonished to hear those words come out of their sons' mouths at their own houses!

Some boundaries do need to be firm and inviolable. Worldwide, too many women and children suffer sexual violation, bullying, and violence. One thing that's changing is awareness of consent. When I was a teen and a college student, date rape was rampant. This changed with educational interventions, but when targeted education ended, campus rape got worse again. Now, as we understand more about sexuality, legal questions addressing consent are changing from "Did she explicitly say *no*?" to "Did she explicitly say *yes*?"

Strict, spoken agreements around physical violence keep everyone safe. Teach your daughters and sons that "Can I give you a kiss?" are the sweetest six words and any violent behavior means a relationship has to end. Because if it happens once, it can happen again, and abuse is not the path to happiness.

Setting boundaries in the family can cause anger, rejection, and pain. Popular wisdom teaches that "you are not responsible for other people's feelings," "you don't owe them anything," and "you don't need to respond." But setting boundaries in a healthy way does not include ghosting, flaming, or saying whatever you want. Especially in a family where you want relationships to change, but you want to keep them. Is it possible to set boundaries in a way that doesn't hurt? It is. Here are few approaches.

- If you need to talk about feelings that may hurt the listener, say, "I need to get these feelings out. Please understand that I'm not saying them to hurt you, but they may, and I'm sorry about that. I care about you, and I need you to hear this."
- Make it clear to others that this is not about them. "I'm

facing a challenge with dad/junior/grandma right now, but we're grown-ups, and we can work it out."

- Use opportunities to set boundaries to teach your needs. "I didn't ask for this, so it's a surprise. I do like chocolate cake, but I don't really like surprises. Next time, please tell me you want to get me a cake, and I'll be ready for it and feel happy!"

Setting boundaries in a hurtful way can cause unintended harm that may go on for years. Separations are part of life, but they don't have to be awful. We need to help our kids figure out how to create good friendships, how to maintain good relationships — and how to leave relationships.

- Be as kind as you can. "I so enjoyed getting to know you, and I appreciate that you care about me. But I don't see this working out and we need to end it."
- Be as clear as you can. "I won't be calling you anymore, and please don't contact me. Maybe we can set a date for some time down the road so we can connect and reflect and get closure."
- Understand it's a process. "What steps do we need to take to sort ourselves out?"

Welcoming the idea of boundaries into family conversations can feel awkward at first, but, one by one, each person will recognize their own sovereignty and respect that of others more. Improved relationships are worth the effort.

17.

Discipline without Damage

"SAY 'Yes' to the feelings even as you say 'no" to the behavior."
— Patty Wipfler, Hand in Hand Parenting

Punishment doesn't work.

My mom figured this out when my brother and I were about six and seven. I remember her being so upset with me that she sent me to her room to wait for my dad to come home and give me a "bare-bottomed spanking." ("Wait 'til your father gets home" was a common threat back then, unfairly making daddies the bad guys.) I remember watching the bedside clock flip over numbers, minute by agonizing minute, terrified of what would happen at 6:00. When he finally entered the room, I was already crying. I lay across his lap — usually a place of comfort — waiting for the pain to come. When it finally came, it stung my butt and numbed my heart.

That day, things changed between us. I was a wreck for weeks afterward. I lost trust in both of my parents and learned to fear adults. My parents were shaken by their collusion in this bizarre and ineffective ritual and later apologized. No one remembers what I must have done to deserve it. My dad gave up both spanking and smoking that year, when he became conscious of the effects his choices had on his children.

Idiomatic Parenting

Violence toward children is encoded in our language. Perhaps you recognize some of the following common phrases that damage the mental health of both children and adults.

Spare the rod and spoil the child. People who misunderstand this biblical concept[1] use it to justify the misconception that you have to inflict pain on your kids to make them good. This notion could not be further from the truth. Hitting a child harms a child.

Biblical scholars give us insight into this damaging statement, opening our eyes. Shepherds in earlier times had two tools, a staff and a rod. The staff, with a curved hook on the end, was used to pull in sheep when they went the wrong way. The rod was used to guide the sheep in the desired direction. No shepherd would ever use a rod to hit a sheep.

Knowing this, the idiom rings true. If children are not guided — or if they are misguided — their healthy development will be spoiled, and they will have problems that hold them back.

You can spoil an infant by holding it too much or by responding to its cries is another harmful idea. In fact, the opposite is true. If no one responds to a baby's needs, the child misses out on crucial brain development triggered by bonding. A baby must never, *ever* be punished. Children can develop problems if their every whim is indulged, but a child can not, absolutely NOT, be spoiled by too much love! A *lack* of love and guidance creates problems. It is tragic that well-intentioned parents do so much damage. And it is sad that cultural trends and norms often justify child abuse and neglect.

A carrot and a stick. Another common cultural metaphor people use to justify getting good behavior from kids is "use a carrot and a stick." Someone drew a cartoon in the mid-1800s depicting a boy who wins a donkey race by suspending a bunch of carrots in front of his mount's nose instead of hitting it with a stick. Politicians combined the images to convey the tactical use of rewards and punishment to control a military outcome. Many parents believe this is what discipline means.

Did your parents ever say the following things? If not, you've certainly heard them somewhere else.

- *"I'm going to teach you a lesson."* More often than not, the lessons children learn from punishment are not at all what the parents had hoped to teach.
- *"I'll show you who's boss."* Even though parents do need

145

to be in charge, this statement mixes domination and revenge.

- *"This hurts me more than it hurts you,"* and, *"This is for you own good,"* are common attempts to justify spanking.

Different cultures have their own sayings about spankings. Stacey Patton, author of the highly recommended *Spare the Kids,* connects the cultural tradition of corporal punishment in black homes to racial violence in America, defining the relationship between "whuppings" and school failure, crime, and the prison system.[2] Many black parents justify spanking because their parents did it "to prepare them for life," but this exhibits an explicit trauma pattern of internalized racism.

The Pitfalls of Punishment

"The floggings will continue until morale improves."
— Anonymous

Beliefs behind punishment are that children are bad and parents can make them good by making them feel bad. Growing up Catholic, Mom was taught to pray every week for God to take away her original sin. She was raised to feel awful about herself. In the United States, the prison system expanded and proliferated based on a false belief that black men were inherently criminal. Punishment dynamics backfire. When we feel bad, it's easier to do bad things. The punishment system is based on external control, using the negative emotions fear, anger, disappointment, and guilt to control behavior. In families, punishment pitfalls include the following:

- Parents assume they are responsible for their children's behavior. When kids misbehave, parents feel guilty and ask themselves, "Where did I go wrong?"
- Parents make all the rules and decisions and expect compliance and obedience, which leads to resistance, rebellion, and toxic relationships.

146

- Children are not allowed to make decisions or define their own standards of behavior.
- Parents use negative emotional strategies to enforce their will — yelling, ridicule, criticism, blame, put-downs, labeling — all of which damage self-esteem and trust.
- Behavior controlled by an authority figure lasts only while that person is present.

A thirty-four-year-old client of Mom's vividly remembered the time her parents sent her down to the bottom stair in the basement to finish her dinner after she complained that she couldn't chew the meat left on her plate because it was too gristly. When asked what she learned from that, the woman said, "I learned that my parents didn't believe me, even if I was telling the truth. I also learned that I was less important than their 'clean your plate' rule, and I hated them for humiliating me."

Parents use punishment with good intentions, but their goodness becomes twisted, since the only point of punishment is to force submission or to retaliate for perceived wrongs. Unwanted behavior may stop, but the consequences are heavy. When children are deliberately hurt by parents, whom they trust, love, and depend on, they receive a powerful negative message: *I don't deserve love or care.*

Children learn about themselves by observing how they are treated and then drawing conclusions. Children who are mistreated may conclude that

- they are not okay; they are bad,
- they don't deserve love; they deserve hate,
- their parents don't love them; they hate them,
- their parents are bad and cruel,
- they deserve to be punished,
- they cannot trust their parents or anyone else,
- it is okay to hurt people, and
- the world is not a safe place.

When these conclusions become their truth — when they believe that they deserve bad things — they may create punishing relationships for themselves and others throughout their lives. When they believe that they are bad, they feel shame, and their sense of self-worth is shattered.

Think back to a time when you were punished as a child. What were your feelings toward your parent(s)? What did you learn? How did you feel about yourself?

Children learn fear, distrust, and hatred when parents vow "to teach them a lesson." When parents use force and violence, they teach children to be either violent themselves or victims. When parents "make them behave," they raise children who are passive and fearful or passive aggressive. When people are blamed and punished, they feel as if they have been attacked or violated. They may react by

- being defensive,
- making excuses,
- protecting themselves,
- withdrawing,
- being afraid,
- giving in (complying),
- becoming defiant,
- becoming a perfectionist ("If I were perfect, I might be okay."), and/or
- lying, cheating, or covering up.

Rewards and Motivation

On the surface, rewarding children for their behavior may not seem to be as potentially damaging as punishment, but it can produce similar results. Children who are manipulated form a poor sense of self. They look to and depend on others (external validation) for a sense of worth. They learn to "perform" to win their parents' attention and approval. They learn to become people pleasers, trusting others more than they trust themselves. After a time, they resent rewards as much as punishments.

With reward, as with punishment, children focus on trying to please those who have power over them. Kids feel manipulated when parents use bribes and scoldings. A carrot-and-stick approach is an external motivation. So is just a carrot. The idea of positive parenting is to help kids find their own internal motivation.

When my son was young, we had to try a few different things before we figured out mornings. At first I was the one who put on his shoes before we rushed out the door for preschool. When he got a little older, I'd give him a gold star if he put his shoes on himself. But it got to the point where he would only do it for the star, and then he wanted bigger rewards.

Then I remembered process praise — encouraging small steps toward the goal. "Hooray, you got your shoes on. I see you're almost ready," celebrates self-responsibility and shows that you care. Reflecting small achievements back to kids helps them to feel intrinsically good about themselves. Tomorrow they may tell themselves the same thing: "Good for me, I'm almost ready."

Everything (except violence) in moderation can be fine. All kids are different, and if rewards work, children can help decide what they will be and even learn how to reward themselves. The ultimate goal is for them *to want to* get dressed, practice piano, or keep their room clean without requiring parents' time or energy. I used to motivate myself to clean my room with the reward of practicing piano: How weird is that?

Discipline Is a Noun

"Your goal in disciplining your child is actually to help him develop self-discipline — meaning to assume responsibility for his actions, including making amends and avoiding a repeat — whether the authority figure is present or not."— Laura Markham, *Peaceful Parent, Happy Kids: How to Stop Yelling and Start Connecting*

The word *discipline* is commonly misunderstood. When we ask parents what comes to mind when they hear that word, they list punishment, force, and hitting. In some family cultures, discipline becomes synonymous with punishment. Yet the word *discipline* has the same root as the word *disciple,* meaning pupil or learner. A discipline is a highly personal practice — think of learning how to play the piano, training for sports, or practicing religious observance. Discipline is about following a path.

Traditionally, parents and teachers use discipline to enforce rules compliance. Kids do need to learn how to work and play by the rules, and parents can help them do that. Self-discipline skills can help kids follow rules set by others as well as follow their own pursuits.

In the family, instead of having rules, we can keep agreements. Agreements are ideas that groups of people create through trial and error, providing a baseline that guides everyone's actions equally. By focusing on agreements, we help children develop their inner guidance system so that they eventually function responsibly by themselves. Using our positive parenting tools effectively, we teach our children *self*-discipline.

The entire idea that children need to be disciplined in order to behave well is a power-over approach. Consider this: when we use the word *discipline* as a verb, we mean *control.* "I have to discipline him to get good behavior." "I have to discipline myself to eat right." Having and using power responsibly means only using *discipline* as a noun. We use and have discipline. We do not *do* discipline.

Guidance, however, is absolutely necessary, using a rod (encouraging), a staff (limiting), and a carrot (focusing on a positive outcome). Guidance focuses on engagement and learning, not punishment. Guidance works as well as, if not better than, short-term discipline, protecting children from hurting themselves and others. In the long run, guidance builds trust and self-reliance.

Teaching Good Behavior

"It is easier to control than to teach. Teaching requires time, planning, and patience, but it lasts longer, gives clearer direction, and builds a foundation for a system of value."
— Dr. Stephen Glenn[3]

150

Once parents decide that they want children to be self-disciplined, they must discipline themselves to change old punishing patterns of behavior and to model new behaviors. Once parents decide that they do not need to control — that they can trust children to learn from the consequences of their behavior — they can give up punishment and discipline and all the associated feelings of distrust and resentment. They can move from an autocratic to a more democratic leadership style. With a proactive guidance approach,

- children are responsible for their own behavior,
- children are allowed to make their own decisions and learn from successes and mistakes,
- children learn from reality, rather than societal conditioning.

Proactive parenting focuses on the whole child, not only on their behavior. The goal is to teach *self*-discipline, *self*-direction, and *self*-responsibility. Since parents won't always be around to tell children what to do, they help children develop the ability to think, to judge, and to make decisions on their own. Parents must also model the behaviors they want to see in their children. Example and love are the best teachers.

"We can't teach children to behave better by making them feel worse. When children feel better, they behave better." —Pam Leo

Natural and Logical Consequences

People who grow up in rural settings learn a lot about life from nature. If you plant and take care of your garden, there will be a harvest. If you don't milk the cow, she will dry up. Natural consequences are a natural occurrence. The connections are direct and clear.

Individuals in families, neighborhoods, and communities function as parts of interdependent systems and are accountable to each other. Extended families provide diverse role models, and there is a sense of connection even between all adults and children. For individuals today, however, this lifestyle is the exception, not the rule.

Today, children spend less time with adults than they do with the media. Most television programs and games do not teach natural consequences, such as the pain, burials, and rebuilding that happen *after* a story ends. Children miss learning about life's cause-effect and action-reaction cycles. Removed from lessons about natural consequences, we must rely on logical consequences to help children learn these skills.

Logical consequences[4] are structured situations based on mutual rights and mutual respect that permit children to learn from social-order reality. Consequences must be related, respectful, and reasonable and *never* put your kids in danger. Cause-effect thinking skills empower children to see relationships and make wise judgments. Kids will, for example, more easily understand that smoking causes cancer, diet and lifestyle affect health, and uncontrolled spending leads to financial trouble. They learn to think for themselves.

If children do not know what is expected of them, they may be confused by consequences. It's important that children see the connection between cause and effect. When children know what behavior is expected and don't comply with the rules, they learn from the consequences of misbehavior. When they know what is expected and do comply with the rules, they are rewarded with a sense of accomplishment, importance, and greater self-esteem.

For example, one day, when I was young, my brother and I started fighting in the back seat of the car. Mom was distracted and irritated and could have yelled, "You're going to lose your allowance!" "You're grounded!" or some other threat of punishment. Instead, she pulled the car off the road and turned off the engine. Very soon we stopped and asked, "What happened, Mom?" She softly explained that she couldn't drive with so much noise because it distracted her; she would have to wait until we quieted down. It worked like a charm — for about two miles. After a few repeats, we got the point. This was nonviolent discipline.

152

When I was an adult and had the same problem, I used the opportunity to teach. I pulled over and asked my son and his friends, "What's going on?" I explained the same thing, but added, "Do you need help working it out, or can you do it yourself?" This was pure guidance, with no discipline. We can't blame kids for *making* trouble when they are *having* trouble.

Parents in my generation often fell into the helicopter-parenting trap, taking care of kids more than was necessary. More stressed out than adults in previous generations because of income inequality, fear of letting kids play outdoors, and pressure to work 24/7, it was often "easier to do it ourselves" than to give our children the time and guidance needed to help them learn to take care of themselves.

Rescue Behavior

It is easy to interrupt the important process of learning from consequences. When we rescue others, they miss out on important lessons. The undesirable behavior is therefore likely to be repeated. Here are a few examples:

	Morning	Money
Action	Child turns off alarm.	Child spends money without anticipating future.
Result	Oversleeps; misses school bus.	Wants money for activity; has no money.
Logical consequence	Child must walk, bike, or take city bus; is late for school.	Child misses activity or has to earn extra money.
Rescue action	Parent drives child to school.	Parent gives child money.

153

The choice to *not* rescue takes a strong commitment to help children learn about life from their own behaviors and their consequences. Balance the age and maturity level of the child and the situation. Limiting rescue behavior must also be done with dignity and respect, love and firmness. The art of parenting— including wisdom and good judgment—is finding balance.

Parents who have children with special needs struggle more to draw this line; no amount of encouragement, for example, can help a blind child suddenly see, but with persistent coaching, a child with ADHD can build habits that help them with their difficulties. If kids are to become self-sufficient, allowing them to learn from consequences can be a gift. An adult friend with Down's syndrome described his childhood: "All my life, my mom got me up, got me dressed, did everything. I never made a mistake. Then I moved into my group home and didn't have anyone to take care of me anymore. I made a lot of mistakes, but that's okay, because I learned how to take care of myself. I still am. And that feels good." Mistakes, or undesired results, are learning opportunities that give feedback about how to do something differently the next time. Don't rob children of those opportunities.

There are times, however, when every parent needs to rescue a child. Sometimes situations occur that are damaging or too difficult for a child to handle. A bullied or abused child needs extra resources and support.

There may be times when grown-ups need to be rescued, too. Sometimes life deals us a hard blow, and we need help when we're down and out. People get stronger by asking for help and support, and when they do, they find strength to move on. The problem occurs when rescuing becomes a way of life, by either always looking to others to take charge and solve problems, or always rescuing others. These behavior patterns disempower, weaken, and create low self-esteem and dependency, so we need to make sure we don't teach our kids to give up.

Coach, Don't Control

Children are often energetic and mischievous. They express their individuality and aliveness. If they want to do something outrageous and it doesn't hurt them, think twice before automatically saying no. Kids need freedom to be who they are. All normal kids act out once in a while; they are constantly changing and testing their environment. Allow them self-expression, but also set limits.

Mom made up a funny name for us — Boobledink — that expressed mild displeasure when something unpleasant happened without serious consequences. When my brother poked a finger in the icing of a birthday cake, she said, "You Boobledink," with partly serious displeasure. It made her point and was so much better than using hurtful labels such as *bad, brat,* or *stupid.* We still call ourselves Boobledink when we're forgetful or do something dumb. It helps us laugh at ourselves.

It's important to be aware of the degree of seriousness of the mischief. If it's serious, it should be dealt with, but there is wisdom in letting little things slide sometimes. *Choose your battles carefully.*

It's also important to look for the cause of undesirable behavior and deal with it. Misbehavior is a signal that something isn't right. A child may be tired, hungry, or reacting to something in their diet. A teen may be struggling with hormones. Something discouraging may have happened at school or with friends. They may be feeling sad or powerless. Get to the underlying feelings. *Help a kid talk it out, so they don't have to act it out.*

Parents who want a family in which everyone feels like a winner see themselves as positive, encouraging coaches who correct when it is necessary and give praise when it is deserved. Kids need attention and feedback so they will be aware that they are fulfilling your expectations. Parents who are coaches get positive results.

Coaches expect the best in their players and communicate that sentiment to their team. They believe in them and inspire them to greatness. Team members don't want to disappoint the coach, or each other, so they do their best.

Coaches are teachers who explain how to do things better. One dad, for example, observed his daughter using a hammer. Seeing her clumsy technique, he stopped her, took the hammer, and showed her the correct way to use it. Giving the hammer back to her, he asked her to try it the new way. As she hammered more effectively, Dad celebrated her success.

Look for opportunities to share your knowledge and your skills. You know so much, and your children have so much to learn. Teaching kids what you know empowers them and sets up positive contact. Let them find their own opportunities to learn, as well. You'll be surprised what they teach you!

Good coaches spend time correcting undesirable and unacceptable behavior, and do so without discouraging or demoralizing players. In *The One-Minute Manager*, Kenneth Blanchard and Spencer Johnson[5] outline this simple plan for managing troubles on a team.

5. Let them know you want them to learn and grow and you will correct them at times. (Correcting them does not mean you don't like them or that you're rejecting them; it means there's a better way. It's feedback.)

6. Correct behavior while it's happening, or as soon as you are aware of it. Deal with problems in private.

7. In private, tell them that what they did was not acceptable. Describe the behavior, being specific, firm, and kind.

8. Tell them what you think and feel about that behavior, being clear, but not angry.

9. Pause and let it soak in.

10. Touch them, smile, or say kind words to show that they have not been rejected and you are on their

side. Tell them you value them, but the specific behavior is unacceptable.

11. Forgive and forget it. It's over. Move on!

Expect to experience more emotions when dealing with children in your family than you do when dealing with grown-ups who are unrelated. Add plenty of hugs, reassurance, and caring statements as needed. We must deal with unacceptable behavior — in our kids, spouses, friends, and ourselves. How we do this makes a difference. If we do so in a firm caring way, with a sense of humor, we will make a difference in the self-esteem of our children and ourselves.

Getting Good Behavior

The whole point of punishment/discipline/guidance is to promote behavior you want. Our philosophy is always to take the proactive approach and only correct when necessary. There are so many ways to work with kids (and adults) to get the outcome you want. Here are a few healthy options.

- **Keep kids informed.** If a child knows what to look forward to, he or she can be more prepared for it. Talk about future events and behavior expectations. "At a dinner party, everyone puts their napkin on their lap and asks to be excused."
- **Focus** on what happens after your child accomplishes something they don't want to do. Try this formula: "After ____, then ____." "After you get your pajamas on, then we'll have time to cuddle and read a good story." Build in a reward.
- **Suggest.** "It might be a good idea to ____." A serious look and a low voice will let them know you mean it.
- **Ask** for a favor or a change in behavior. "Can you please lower your voice right now? Thanks."

- **Offer an alternative** activity or location. "It's not okay to be so wild in the living room; go play in the yard."
- **Say no.** "No, you may not do that. It's dangerous."
- **Plan ahead.** Keep a toy or book up your sleeve in case of an emergency or a long wait.
- **Communicate clearly** what you want and how important it is to you. Eye contact and a gentle touch helps the message get across.
- **Remove the temptation.** Separate the kid from the problem.
- **Substitute.** If a child is heading for trouble, head him or her off with something more interesting. If a toddler has found something dangerous, take it away while presenting something that's safe.
- **Team up.** Try "ten-minute pick-up," making a game out of picking up toys. Race against the clock.
- **Ignore small misbehaviors.** It may be wise to overlook some things — to do nothing — especially if you or your kid is having a bad day. Or check in: "Are you tired?"
- **Use nonverbal signals.** Mom got tired of reminding her young ones to buckle up their safety belts, so she tried a new technique: she'd tap us on the knee. We quickly got the message.
- **Distract them.** Divert energy. On car rides when we kids were thirsty and there was no water handy, Mom told us to lick our lips. It didn't work, but we stopped whining!
- **Make believe.** "Your teddy bear is lonesome for you and wants you to come to bed."
- **Outsmart them.** While walking with my little nephew, he complained of being tired. I suggested we run instead! It was fun, and we got there faster.

- **Become a detective.** Figure out what's behind the undesirable behavior. Check, for example, their nutrition, whether they have food allergies, or if they are tired or upset about something. Figure out what your children need. Help kids find a better way than misbehaving to get their needs met.
- **Write notes.** I jotted down chores for my kids to do after school. After establishing this form of communication, it became routine.
- **Take turns.** Say, "First we'll do what I want, then we'll do what you want." In this way, everyone wins.
- **Signal.** Advance notice is fair and makes good sense while driving and parenting. Announcing that you have to leave in ten minutes allows kids to shift gears and complete what they're doing. Setting a timer can help make kids aware of time limits.
- **Relax your standards.** Instead of expecting a perfectly made bed, for example, realize that some ideals are not worth daily battles. Pulling up blankets was a compromise that worked for me. One way to deal with a messy bedroom is to close the door!
- **Break down** a large task into manageable pieces; encourage small steps. Celebrate progress.
- **State your expectations explicitly.** Instead of saying, "Clean your room," say, "Pick up the toys on the floor, make your bed, and put away your clothes." Then say, "Tell me when you're done."
- **Let children know your limits.** When Mom announced, "Pajama time!" and no one moved, she'd begin to count slowly to three. We knew she meant it and moved by the time she got to "th . . ."

- **Say nothing.** Sometimes it's best to bite your tongue, for example, when you're in a bad mood and know your words could hurt them.
- **Lead by example.** Kids learn almost everything that way. *Do as I say, not as I do* doesn't work!
- **Use words that empower.** Instead of saying, "You can't go out until ____," say, "You may go out when ____." Rather than, "Because I said so," teach them, "Because when I did that, something bad happened." Moving from words of control to words of empowerment leads to cooperation rather than resistance.
- **Be playful.** Perhaps you have turned a toddler's spoon into an airplane full of food. I once overdramatized great disgust and nausea on finding dirty underwear in the bathroom and found it to be quite effective. When Mom noticed our untied shoelaces on a walk with us, she'd try to step on them.
- **Appreciate** and cheer your children's efforts and their successes. See appendix A for some great ideas.

There are many ways to get what we want. The methods above avoid direct confrontation and punishment. You can get things done more easily if you avoid power struggles. Self-esteem will remain intact and healthy!

"If I keep from commanding people, they behave themselves. If I keep from preaching at people, they improve themselves. If I keep from imposing on people, they become themselves."

— Lao Tsu

18.

Problem Solving

"To the questions of your life, you are the only answer. To the problems of your life, you are the only solution." —Jo Coudert[1]

I remember Mom telling me about her childhood in an immigrant family focused on work and survival. "When my brothers teased me, I ran to my mother wanting protection for me and punishment for them. When I had a misunderstanding with my friends, I would not play with them again—or at least not until we forgot about it. I ran away from and avoided problems because I never learned how to face conflicts and get through them. I was unprepared for the challenges of the world and was afraid of them."

The Stair of Love and Peace

As a mother, Mom didn't want us kids pulling her into the middle of every argument we had. She wanted to empower us to solve our own problems. She had a friend with many adopted children who suggested she designate one step on our staircase as the "Stair of Love and Peace." When Damian and I bickered—and we bickered a lot—she or Dad would make us sit there until we worked through our problems.

I hated it. Having to sit next to my tormentor without protection made me feel angry and vulnerable. Damian felt the same way. A lightbulb popped on when we realized we had something in common, and we found the power to agree, temporarily, on a truce. "Mom, we're good," we'd say. "Can we go play now?"

The Stair of Love and Peace would have worked better for us if Mom or Dad had used it to actually teach us problem-solving skills. Instead, I learned how to stuff down my emotions and let go of my problems — until they surfaced again. I always felt like I was giving something up. But maybe that's what it takes to make peace.

My brother and I met again on that stairway as teenagers, when we needed to learn how to get real with each other. Our family had changed so much since Dad remarried, and Damian was being teased, insulted, and shunned. He apologized for bullying me when we were younger. Now it was happening to him, but by adults. We craved love and peace and decided to find them with each other. The Stair became a metaphor for the safe place we could create together. We finally began developing connection and collaboration, but our problems were harder to solve now.

Our childhood home had become a constant clash of rage we didn't understand. Our stressed-out, anxious stepmother always thought we were lying, did not trust us, and constantly accused someone of something in the most hurtful way. We were completely out of our depth and out of control. We solved our problems by acting out in ways we thought our parents might understand — shouting, threatening, and running away (behaviors we had never before considered). We were desperate to be listened to. We pleaded for solutions, but the grown-ups' skills were limited. In the end, we could only escape.

Our acting out was a symptom of the real problems our parents refused to discuss or deal with. The stress was unbearable, and they added to it by trying to control us with name-calling, angry tirades, teasing, and punishment. We didn't mind having limitations (which were always completely out of proportion to the problems), but the rough and loveless ways they were delivered left scars. After having been a parent, I know how much love there is in putting food on a table and giving rides to school, but my stepmother, like Mom's mom, did not know the language of emotional nourishment, of which teens need *a lot* in the best of times. My father was out of our reach, his rare moments at home occupied by our stepmom's needs and troubles.

When I was a parent, we did not have or need a Stair of Love and Peace. Instead, I kept an ear open for the inevitable conflicts that arise when kids play. Typically, kids would work things out themselves, or come to me for help if they couldn't. But sometimes, with certain kids, I'd step in, de-escalate the situation, and then teach. Teach, teach, teach. Kids need a lot of practice taking steps to solve problems. When parents guide kids toward solving problems, instead of solving problems for kids or letting them flounder, children begin to gain the skills, experience, and confidence to get through tough situations.

Problems and conflicts are natural life events. Everyone has them, all the time. We don't choose our hassles, but we must choose how we want to react to and deal with them. Some strategies intensify a problem and cause distance, distress, and low self-esteem. Other strategies de-escalate conflict and bring about resolution, closeness, and joy. Without skills and confidence, every problem is a crisis. With skills and confidence, problems become challenges through which we grow.

It is not your job to fix all of your children's problems, especially as they grow older, but it is your job to give support and guidance. Solving problems for others can deprive them of the opportunity to gain competence, confidence, and personal power. What's more, our solutions may not be the best ones for others. Encourage children to solve problems in their own way before stepping in with ideas.

My son's preschool teacher had a great way of explaining problem solving. "Grown-ups get so intellectual about things. But it's really simple with kids. You get in the elevator, push 'B,' and go to the bottom floor."[2] Down at the bottom, where the only way to go is up, you need to figure out *who needs what.* Another way to put it is *whose problem is this?*

Whose Problem Is This?

We need to teach our children that when they have a problem, they are responsible for creating a solution. Children need to learn to deal with disappointment, loss, and pain so that they know they can survive these things. It can be difficult for us, as parents, to watch them struggle; we want to take away pain. But children who have been overprotected will be incapacitated and overwhelmed by the first big problem they have to handle on their own. Kids who don't know how to deal with failure, disappointment, or loss are at risk.

We need to encourage and support children through their struggles — and believe in them. ("I've seen you solve some tough problems; I know you can get through this one, too.") We need to allow them to experience their own mistakes and failures and help them discover the joy of overcoming. Problems themselves don't necessarily overwhelm kids, but self-doubt and lack of skills do.

On the other hand, sometimes children have problems that are more than they can deal with. My son had a friend whose rigid emotions escalated beyond what other kids could deal with on their own. My brothers and I were out of our depth with our verbally and emotionally abusive parents. Children everywhere, and too often, face even worse problems and need protection. (We talk about that more in our book *The Bullying Antidote*.) It is crucial that we build strength in children whenever we can. One of the best ways to teach problem solving is to model it.

We need to share our own struggles with our children. If we pretend to have it together all the time, they may conclude that something is wrong with them for having problems. When we share our mistakes, our losses, our failures, our sorrows, and how we deal with them, our kids understand that we, too, experience disappointment, that we, too, are human. And they learn new ways of coping.

When Kids *Are* the Problem

The more positive attention you give your kids, the more you fill their basic human need for safety, love, belonging, attention, and self-esteem and the fewer problems you will have. If you ignore their needs, misbehavior and problems may result. There are always reasons — thoughts and feelings — underneath problems and misbehavior. Listen for signals that indicate something is wrong. *Behavior is an expression of how children feel about themselves.* To help resolve a problem, and the behavior it causes, we must play detective and figure out what's really going on from the child's point of view.

When there's a problem, make time to sort it out. Sit with them on a Stair of Love and Peace. Take time out before bedtime or after school, or drop what you're doing if things are emotionally on fire. Build time into your family schedule to listen to each other and keep communication channels open. In dealing with family problems, believe that there is a solution and work to find it. Listen to each other to understand the situation clearly, and have the courage and be willing to make necessary changes. When all involved parties assume responsibility for a problem and its resolution, there's hope for a positive outcome.

Barriers to Problem Solving

Problems get worse if we don't solve them or if we try to solve them in ways that make them worse. Below are common strategies for coping with problems that *don't* help.

- **Denial.** Putting problems aside for a little while may help us cope, but we can't get through our problems if our heads are in the sand.
- **Drugs.** Sometimes alcohol and recreational drugs can give us new perspective, and sometimes prescription drugs can sort out serious situations. But it is also true that they can make things worse. Substance abuse is a serious family problem.
- **Distraction.** "Changing the channel" is an excellent coping strategy that reduces stress, but avoidance doesn't solve problems.
- **Gunny-sacking.** Storing up problems, anger, and pain gets us from one moment to the next, but

unexpressed negative feelings can make us sick, or they can explode harmfully.

- **Blaming.** Problem solving is about taking responsibility. Faultfinding shuts down this process. Blaming puts people on the defensive and places attention on the conflict, not the solution.
- **Rejection.** Cutting people off may appear to solve a problem, but important relationships can be damaged or lost. Time away is okay, but if you really care about someone, be clear that you are rejecting the problem, not them.
- **Fighting/withdrawing.** Both are natural hard-wired responses that can be productive (getting out feelings/having a time-out) — but they can get out of control. Set limits on both or problems will continue.
- **Personal attacks.** Name-calling and you statements hurt each other's feelings, escalate conflicts, and harm the relationship.
- **Rationalization**. This strategy intellectualizes pain to avoid feeling it. Some problems can't be explained away, and trying to do so only perpetuates a problem.
- **Defeatism.** If you believe there's nothing you can do to solve a problem, you feel powerless to do anything and remain stuck in a helpless position.

These are all win-lose strategies, by which one wins by proving that one person is right and the other is wrong. No one likes to lose; no one likes to be made wrong. An emotionally charged power struggle that is not met with problem-solving strategies can only escalate, and it can even become a lose-lose situation. Everyone's self-esteem is at stake: "If I don't win, I'm not okay; therefore, I must win." The problem may appear, at times, to be settled, but it never really is. Sooner or later, relationships with unsolved problems weaken and die. When facing a problem, it helps to examine the underlying goal. Do you want to win at the other person's expense? Or do you want to resolve it to everyone's satisfaction? What do you need, and what do you want?

The strategies listed above are mainstream and very common, but ultimately painful, and they keep us emotionally or physically stuck in one place. None of them proactively change a situation. To cope with and resolve problems, we must give them attention. *We must attend to the needs that aren't being met.*

Win-Win Solutions

It is possible, more often than not, to solve problems in a way that no one loses. Win-win solutions take time, energy, and self-discipline. Sometimes we have to bite our tongues so they don't get us into trouble. Win-win problem solving calls for direct, honest, and assertive communication and the willingness to really listen and understand each other. This approach is not easy, but it's worth it. Increased respect, intimacy, and enhanced self-esteem are the payoffs.

Families trapped by using behaviors listed above can benefit from Non-Violent Communication (NVC) training. This four-step problem-solving process calls for

1. listening without reacting to the problem,
2. identifying the needs of each person in the problem,
3. brainstorming solutions together, and
4. choosing a solution that works for everyone.

It may take a few tries, but NVC can be a miraculous process the first time you crack the code — and once you're adept, it makes everything so much easier!

The goal of all win-win strategies is to resolve a conflict so that both parties are satisfied. The focus is on the solution: "What will we do about it?" The underlying attitude is respect for oneself and for the other. And the operating principle is listening, to make sure everyone is heard. Win-win strategies work best when there is a commitment to caring. Everyone in a conflict must accept responsibility for the problem and be committed to resolving it without damaging the relationship.

Stepping Stones to Problem Solving

These steps do not have to go in order, and not all of them are needed but all are helpful.

- **Believe that your problem is solvable.** Be positive, hopeful, and expect good things to come of it.
- **Determine ownership.** Whose problem is it? Everyone is responsible for solving his or her own problems. Don't solve kids' problems for them unless they are in danger or overwhelmed.
- **Dissect the problem.** While running on a trail, my four-year-old nephew fell down. He howled at the top of his voice. I asked where he hurt. "All over!" he cried. Then I asked if his chin hurt. "No." His knees? "No." His stomach? "No." We narrowed the pain down to sore hands. Then I knew where to put the healing kisses.
- **Don't try to figure out who's right and who's wrong** until all facts are out. If a judgment is made too early, someone will feel that they were not allowed to make their point, and the conflict will continue. Quick judgment gets in the way of understanding.
- **Put the problem in a chair.** Stand outside of it together, so it doesn't feel personal.
- **Evaluate the importance of the problem.** Tell how important it is: "This isn't very important, but I'd like to talk about it," or, "This is very important to me, and I really need to work it out."
- **Speak in terms of "I want" or "I feel,"** rather than "you did this" or "you didn't do that." I statements often resolve problems (see chapter 11, "The Power of Words").

- **Listen to feelings.** Receptivity to how someone feels often unlocks a situation, and the solution becomes more apparent.
- **Use active listening skills.** Try to understand another point of view, another way of seeing a situation (see chapter 7, "Listening Skills").
- **Express your beliefs, values, and opinions as your *point of view*,** not as The Truth. This can be difficult in extremely religious autocratic families, but truth is something we all must discover for ourselves.
- **Read between the lines.** Try to figure out what's going on underneath words. Fear? Anger? Sadness? A struggle for power? Protection? Address that.
- **Be sensitive to timing.** Use good judgment about when to talk. If you are unsure, ask, "Is this a good time to talk?" Allow enough time for discussion, and speak to people when they are relaxed. Also, discuss important matters after a meal: families have seven times as many fights before dinner than they do afterward.
- **Respond to the other person;** don't just react. A response comes from a centered place. A reaction is something out of your control. The difference between reaction and response is about ten seconds. Counting to ten before answering can assure you are in control.
- **Ask for what you want.** "I just want you to listen while I tell you what I feel." "Can you sit down next to me?" "Please don't look straight at me while I say this; I feel too scared." "Would it be all right if we held hands while we talked?" "Can you look at my face while I talk to you?" Don't require compliance, but do ask.

- **Be willing to make changes.** It's hard to accept, but negotiation can only happen if *both* parties are willing to give something up in order to reach a mutually satisfying result. Conflicts resolve more quickly if priorities are understood.
- **Always learn from mistakes** and figure out how to do things better the next time.
- **Take time out if things get tense.** Take a break to cool down. When our brains go into danger mode, it takes a full half hour to switch off alarms. Do something physical to release tension. Agree to continue at a designated time.
- **Examine all assumptions.** "Do you mean ____?" "Are you saying ____?" "Am I understanding this right?"
- **Repeat back what you think you hear.** It might take a few tries before you get it right.
- **Look for the lesson behind the problem.** Figure out how you can avoid it in the future by learning from it.
- **Keep focused on the here and now.** Pulling up ancient history muddles things.
- **Apologize** for any name-calling, unkindness, or unfair action.
- **Forgive others their mistakes** and ask forgiveness for your own. Agree to let heated words be forgotten.
- **Keep a sense of humor** — especially by laughing at yourself.
- **Rule out violence.** "Use your words," said the nursery-school teacher, "not your feet, teeth, or spit." Violence does not solve conflict, and if you use it, you have a lot of cleaning up afterward.
- **Get help** if you have trouble resolving problems. Family mediation or counseling can help before

problems get so far out of hand that relationships are lost and children are hurt.

Problem-Solving Steps

"You may not be responsible for being down, but you are responsible for getting up." — Jesse Jackson[3]

For many people, problems are stumbling blocks — unwanted challenges, anxiety, and stress. With a shift in attitude and new skills, however, they can become stepping-stones to deeper understanding and better relationships. The following problem-solving process can be used in any situation, whether it is inter- or intrapersonal.

1. **Identify and define the problem or conflict.** What is really the problem? What exactly is wrong? Identify the problem without blaming. Be aware of everyone's feelings and needs.

2. **Brainstorm for possible solutions.** Express and record all ideas as fast as you think of them. Sometimes the craziest, wildest ideas become the best ones after a little adjustment. No judgment or discussion should be allowed while brainstorming. This can be an enjoyable process.

3. **Evaluate the alternatives.** Look at the consequences of each choice. Would it solve the problem or make it worse? Work together to find a solution acceptable to all parties. Give and take is necessary for a win-win solution.

4. **Choose the best solution.** All parties in the conflict need to find and agree to this solution. They must be committed to following through.

5. **Implement the solution.** What changes need to be made? Who will do what? When will they do it? For how long? In some situations it may help to informally write

out an agreement and sign it to avoid confusion. Decide when to evaluate how it's working.

6. **Follow-up evaluation.** Assess the results. Is the situation better, worse, or the same? If it is better, do you want to extend the contract? If worse, consider another solution from the brainstorming session and implement it. Be persistent until the problem is resolved.

When we know we can get through conflicts without losing, we have no need to avoid or withdraw from them. When we acquire the skills and experience to resolve touchy situations, our confidence grows, as does our self-esteem. The more we learn, the more knowledge and skills we have to teach our children.

"Every problem comes with a gift." — Richard Bach[4]

19. Touch Is Vital

"Emotional CPR: one hug, one deep breath. Repeat."
– Felix Baum[1]

"The tickle monster is coming! You'd better get to bed!" I remember the way Mom or Dad could send us running with a crook of their finger. This is a great memory for me. Daddy's *cosquillas* ("tickles") were just right—enough pressure to make me giggle, but not so hard that they hurt. He'd stop when I said, "Stop." But I'd ask for more. This playful touch game was a fun bonding ritual, like his foot squeezes and shoulder rides. So were Mom's back rubs and head scratches. Mom and Dad always had a hand I could hold and a neck I could hug.

Touch is vital to life. As physical beings, we need caresses, cuddles, and strokes as much as we need food and water. Babies who are fed and changed can still die from touch deprivation. A scientist from the National Institute of Health discovered that a lack of touch and pleasure during the formative years of life is the principal cause of human violence. He observed that individuals and societies that experience and promote physical pleasure are peaceful societies. The two exist in one's life in inverse proportion: "As either violence or pleasure goes up, the other goes down."[2]

We learned about touch from our parents. If they cuddled and hugged us a lot, we learned to enjoy touch. If they didn't touch us at all, we learned either to crave physical contact or to physically close ourselves off to others. If they punished and abused us—touched us violently—we probably learned to fear and avoid touch or punish and abuse others.

For persons who have been abused, it makes sense that healing should come through the same modality. If, for example, abuse was verbal, positive loving words can be very healing. If abuse was physical, healing can be facilitated through respectful, appropriate, loving touch. Touch can be a cruel and damaging violation of another person or a nourishing gift of love and pleasure for those we care for.

We need to be careful when talking to our kids about "good touch" and "bad touch." Natalie Cherrix, a domestic violence specialist, teaches "touches are better categorized as safe and unsafe touches."[3] Keep this in mind as you read about unhealthy and healthy touch.

Unhealthy Touch

Each year thousands of children are paralyzed, physically deformed, mentally damaged, and killed through unhealthy touch. Ninety percent of abuse is committed by known, trusted people. Sexual and physical abuse are devastating to a child's self-esteem.

Sexual child abuse refers to any inappropriate sexual exposure or touch between an adult and a child. It is inappropriate because the child does not understand the nature of the request and is coerced through threats or deception. The current political obsession with pedophilia indicates a deep confusion about sexual abuse, which is more prevalent than we ever wanted to believe. But we can prevent it with education and emotional support.

An abusive father, brother, friend, or uncle may tell a younger girl or boy that his affection is normal, or an expression of love, encouraging victims to keep secrets, thereby making them feel guilty. But it is, in fact, criminal for an adult to take advantage of a child's innocence, needs, or fears in this way. Inappropriate touch by an adult is devastating to the child and to the parent-child relationship.[4] Incest has been taboo in cultures around the world for good reason, although, in many, sexual abuse of children has been normalized in the form of child marriage. But as many as 40 percent of abused children are victims of older or more powerful children. The book *I Said No!*, by Kimberly King, is a terrific resource for parents and kids who want to learn more about being safe together.[5] It is important to explicitly point out to children that unsafe touches can feel good. This does not mean children are to blame or they should not tell an adult about the abuse.[6]

We discussed corporal punishment in previous chapters. Severe physical punishment—hitting (with hands, fists, or objects), pinching, burning (with cigarettes, for example)—is literally torture. It has caused unspeakable harm to individuals and widespread social violence.

Cycles of Abuse

Lee Harvey Oswald, Charles Manson, and Adolf Hitler were all victims of physical and emotional child abuse. All abusive parents were abused as children or taught that the abuse of children was normal. These patterns repeat generation after generation unless we take on the task of stopping them.

Many of us who were abused as children deny it. Our parents were very important to us; we depended on them for survival. We needed to believe they were good, and, therefore, we denied the abuse or made up excuses for our parents' behavior. "I deserved what I got." "It was my fault." "I had it coming." We concluded that *we were bad*, or else they wouldn't have treated us that way. Childhood abuse and neglect leaves us with an inner emptiness that we may try to fill by means of food, alcohol, drugs, sex, work, or money. These things don't fill the hole, but they frequently become addictions.

When abuse occurs in families, parents usually have some of the following attributes:

History of battering. Parents have learned that beating is the "right way" to discipline children. Quick to anger, they may have poor impulse control. Perhaps they learned those behaviors from their own parents, who may have been abused as well. A pattern of emotional or verbal battering may be prevalent.

Distorted view of the child. Parents may believe that a child is basically bad and therefore deserves punishment. They may also believe that about themselves. It's easy to *be* bad when you believe you're a bad person. Parents may justify abusive treatment, claiming it is necessary to prevent evil behavior from developing. A better way to get kids to be good is to believe that they *are* good—and help them believe that about themselves.

Unrealistic expectations. Parents may have expectations of the child—and perhaps of themselves—that are too high or impossible. They don't realize that children are immature. They may expect behavior that is developmentally impossible. A six-month-old, for example, cannot be potty trained. Young children are not always respectful and considerate of their parents. Nor can kids be expected to understand things like adults or behave like adults. Not understanding this, parents may inflict severe punishment for minimal infractions.

Expectation that a child fills their own needs. A mother, for example, who wants her daughter to love her as her own mother didn't, is asking for the wrong thing. Kids do not exist to satisfy their parents' needs. It's the other way around. It is important to remember who is the grown-up and that children need love and guidance. Parents who were not loved as children must care for their own wounded inner child. In becoming aware of their own unmet needs, they can begin to fulfill them; then they won't (unconsciously) expect others to parent them. Pam Leo says, "It takes the same amount of time and attention to meet children's emotional needs as it does to deal with behaviors caused by their unmet emotional needs."[7]

Lack of warmth. Parents may not actually like their children. They may be unaware, unable, or unwilling to relate to and meet their children's emotional needs. For example, a mother may have felt unloved and therefore married for love, but found loneliness instead. She and her child may give up hope for acceptance and love. Yet, hope is a spark. *Love* is a verb. If you practice acceptance and caring, love will kindle.

Negative focus. A parent seldom notices or mentions good qualities in a child, but rather is always catching him or her being "bad." The parent may withhold a privilege or love or isolate the child to teach a lesson. Regardless of the child's efforts to please, the parent will find something to criticize. The child will rarely receive praise. Yet, kids need appreciation and encouragement, just as parents do. Try flipping the focus to find one likable or endearing quality about a child — a cute smile, perhaps — and then another, and another. Say out loud that you like the child. The quality of the interaction will automatically improve.

Poor communication skills. Parents don't know how to really listen to their children. They don't put themselves in their children's shoes or see things from their kids' point of view. *Seeing from another's perspective* is an important skill that can be learned. Learning to really listen and to feel empathy and compassion can begin to transform a negative relationship (see chapter 7, "Listening Skills").

Overuse or abuse of power. Perpetrators of violence often have a deep sense of powerlessness. Instead of enhancing their own personal power, they overpower others. Such parents believe that children must be taught "who is the boss" and should not be allowed to get away with anything. They are righteous about discipline and punishment. They may imagine that children are trying to anger or hurt them, often taking things personally and retaliating violently. ("I'll show you to talk back to me!") Adults who lack self-discipline are dangerous disciplinarians.

Overpunishment. Parents may not be aware of the limits beyond which punishment becomes abuse. For example, to sit a young child in a corner for five minutes may not be damaging. To do it for an hour is abuse. Children have a different sense of time. Many parents don't realize how fragile a child's body is. Shaking a child can cause mental retardation, permanent brain damage, and death. Striking a child's body is physically and psychologically dangerous. One "good slap" on the cheek of a small child can bruise the brain and cause permanent retardation. (For better ways to discipline, see chapter 12, "How Parenting Responses Affect Self-Esteem," and chapter 17, "Discipline Without Damage.")

Isolation. An abusive or battering family has few close friends, family supports, and social activities. Family members feel alienated and do not know where to turn for help. One way to begin is with a phone call. Suggest a cup of tea or a walk in the park with someone. Visit a Parents Anonymous meeting in your area. No one needs to be alone!

When abuse occurs, damage results. Adults who didn't learn to control damaging impulses when they were children must learn now. Parents who are afraid of hurting a child have reached a turning point. The next step is to take time out to cool off and get away from the dangerous situation. Ask for help. Call the national toll-free number for Childhelp, a crisis/referral line: 1-800-422-4453 (1-800-4-A-Child). *Child abuse is 100 percent preventable!*

What can you do if you witness a parent abusing a child? Try one of these statements.

- "I know you want to do the right thing, but this is not good for your child."
- "I know this is a tough time/age for you, but this is not good for your child."
- "Perhaps you were raised this way, but this is not good for your child."
- "I know it's hard to be a good parent sometimes, but . . ."
- "You are the most important person in your child's life, and they need you to help, not hurt, them."
- "I'm a mom/dad, too. Is there anything I can do to help?"

Then you might offer a suggestion and support for that person and the child.

Get "In Touch"

Many of us don't want to remember the abuse because it was so bad; we may have needed to forget what was done to us. Many of us minimize the abuse: "It wasn't all that bad." "I was never hospitalized." "It could have been worse." Many of us hold in the old anger, afraid that we might explode and hurt someone we love or hurt ourselves.

People don't generally wake up in the morning saying, "I think I'll whomp my kid today." As the day goes on and stress builds, something or someone pushes a button that triggers a reaction. It's important to learn about your buttons and triggers — and how to defuse them. What happened just before you "lost it"? Magnify that moment; unravel it. *You can choose to react differently.* What can you do to prevent it from happening again? If you need help doing this, get it. You may realize you are not responding to the child — but to something that happened to *you* as a child.

One dad decided he wasn't ever going to hit his kid again. He established a house rule for himself: *hug instead of hit.* When this man was tempted to smack his kid, he would continue his arm movement, but instead of hitting, he would surround the child in a big embrace. He would then explain that the behavior that angered him was unacceptable, but that his child was very, very much loved!

Another mom told us that, even though she had decided to not spank her daughter when stressed out, she found herself acting automatically. "I slapped her on her bare bottom once and was shaken to see how hard I had hit her. My handprint stayed on her bottom! My husband and I talked about this and agreed on a few rules: 1) we wouldn't hit her, and she wouldn't hit us, either; 2) when her dad and I were angry, we'd say, "I love you. I don't like what you just did. I still love you and will always love you."

Mom remembers a time many years ago when she got very angry about a mess in the living room. When she tried to figure out why she got so angry, she realized that she was taking it personally — the mess sabotaged her self-image as a perfect housewife. Giving this a great deal of thought, she decided that she did not really believe in or want the impossible standards she set up for herself and others, but she did want to feel good about herself — and her kids. She eased her standards of cleanliness to allow everyone to be more comfortable, relaxed, and happy. Us kids? We never minded the dirt. She was okay no matter what.

Years later, she told us that when she wanted to punish us, she learned to stop and think: is a messy house a good enough reason to spank my kids? Her mother had thought it was, but Mom chose differently. Our house was rarely perfect, but our self-esteem was healthy. (My stepmother never hit us either, but our feelings seemed less important than a clean house.)

Parents need to get in touch with bottled up anger. We all have anger, and for good reason. A family friend's story illuminates how anger and annoyance can so easily surprise us.

"A battered child myself, I had no awareness of the incredible anger stored inside me until a month or so after my daughter was born. Having been raised with impatience, demands, and punishments, my instinctive behavior was to lash out when her needs conflicted with my limits. While in my mind I saw only love for her, I continued to hurt the most precious being in my life.

"When she was one and a half, I made a conscious commitment to become the person I knew I could be, which brought me, two years later, to the realization that violation and violence had been passed down the line of women in our family, and that if I did not stop the pattern, the battering tendency would continue with my daughter. I took responsibility for making that change. It's now been twenty years, and we have created a loving, accepting, respectful, and caring relationship. A long time coming, it has definitely been worth the effort."

Our parents raised us the only way they knew how, and we learned to parent from them. Take time to remember not only what they did to you, but also the effect their actions had on you and your relationship with them. Remember how their words and actions affected your self-esteem. For the sake of your child, let those memories return so you can see them in your mind.

The good news is if you are reading this book, you have survived your parents' mistakes! Just as, somehow, they survived theirs. All parents mess up, but children can be remarkably resilient. Blaming our parents keeps us stuck in the past. It's healthier to work through our problems (therapy may be helpful), choose our own path, and then forgive them and ourselves. *Learn from their mistakes, and don't repeat them.* Create the future you deserve and desire for yourself and your family. Only you can change the course of your personal history. You absolutely have the power to do it. And if you need help, get it.

The biblical saying, "The sins of the father are visited upon the third and fourth generation," is absolutely true when it comes to family abuse. Children who are rejected tend to become rejecting parents. Children who are loved grow up to nurture others. Let this be the last violent generation. Call it quits for violence in your family. Begin, instead, a cycle of healthy touch.

Healthy Touch

Some children suffer touch disorders created by their parents through neglect (insufficient touch), battering (painful touch), and incest (inappropriate and violating touch). If you experienced any of these, you need to heal yourself as you parent your child.

Premature or disabled infants can experience touch neglect when spending time in an incubator or because of physical deformities. Studies show that parents of differently formed children or those with special needs use less touch initially. Physical therapists often need to work with these children to combat their "tactile defensiveness," or resistance to touch.

The kind of touch we need on a daily basis is warm, affectionate, casual, and nonsexual. When we understand this neurological requirement, we clear confusion and separate the two in our minds. Touch as an affectionate gesture is an art worth learning.

Massage and other bodywork accelerate the healing of abuse trauma in adults. Learning to touch our kids in healthy ways is the other piece of the puzzle.

A group of nurses in New Zealand worked with parents who were at risk of abusing their children because abusive touch was the only touch they had learned. Every week these parents attended a lecture on child rearing, had a cup of tea, and did the following exercise to practice the art of touch in a new, healthy, loving way.[8] It's important to establish that the person receiving this attention is in charge and gives feedback, such as *more, harder, softer,* and *stop.* Remember, the purpose is to inflict pleasure, not pain. Treat your own children and spouse to this adapted New Zealand "Weather Report."

- **Snowflakes:** Tap fingertips lightly on the other person's head, shoulders, and back, like falling snow.
- **Raindrops:** Tap fingertips simultaneously and with greater intensity.
- **Thunderclaps:** With cupped palms, clap hands across the person's back and shoulders. This makes a good noise; be careful not to slap.
- **Eye of the Tornado:** Circle thumbs across the person's shoulders and down either side of the spine using your fingertips to anchor the motion.
- **Tidal Wave:** Slide hands in long strokes up and down the person's arms and across the back. Sound effects can be fun here.
- **Calm after the Storm:** Rest hands on the shoulders and breathe deeply. Slowly lift the hands to about half an inch above the skin and hold them there. Step back slowly — it may feel to the other person as if your hands are still there.[9]

The nurses found a similar exercise to be a great success. One mother reported that she stifled an urge to hit her baby and massaged his back, instead — with wonderful results. Nurturing touch is an enjoyable, relaxing, and self-esteem-enhancing gift — both to give and to receive.

One child had difficulty getting to sleep; his mom tried this massage technique, and "he turned into Jell-O and was out." Another turned this into a geography lesson. Before bed, she gave her twin what they called the "US Weather Report," with snowstorms in the northeast, earthquakes in California, and so on, until the storms stopped and the sun came out. And a dad stated, "My ten-year-old boys love it and do it to each other . . . and to me!" This ritual might even make your kids eager to go to bed.

Peaceful Touch, a program from Sweden, incorporates massage in the classroom. Teaching kindness and consent, this calming and relaxing routine improves concentration and reduces conflict.

In another unusual school program, a professional acupressurist worked on twenty-three special education students with remarkable results: every child showed significant gains in cognitive, motor, and social/emotional skills and physical health.

In other classrooms, students are taught how to adjust pressure points that block energy and hold tension in the body. When they say, "Push my buttons," to a classmate, they get a little massage. Parents and teachers alike report immediate improvement in behavior and self-esteem.[10]

Touch can be almost magically therapeutic for kids. Barbara told us about clashes with her nine-year-old daughter who had recently entered "the age of contradiction." In order to mend the rift and ease the tension between them, she made a concerted effort to do more touching. Over the next several months, she patted her daughter on the shoulders and back, hugged her more often, and held her hand on walks. "As I increased the amount of physical contact, her acting out and resentment decreased. Eventually, the turbulent nines disappeared, and the daughter blossomed into a fun and happy ten-year-old child." My husband and I had the same results while raising my son. At the age when boys usually withdraw from their mothers, I gave him his space, but his dad made it clear that healthy, supportive touch was part of our family's well-being. Daily hugs and kisses helped him know that he was connected, not alone, as he grew through his challenging teen years.

"The way we treat the child, the child treats the world." —Pam Leo

20.

Beliefs and Believing

"Speak to your children as if they are the wisest, kindest, most beautiful and magical humans on Earth, for what they believe is what they will become." – Brooke Hampton

Beliefs are so important, and so powerful, that people will die for them. We witnessed this during the pandemic, and it has been true throughout time. Our beliefs are like a computer's operating system, shaping who we are and what we do. They form our attitudes, which shape our feelings. On a day-to-day basis, we respond to life with those feelings, unaware that they have deep roots in our beliefs.

What we believe deeply and profoundly affects who we are and what we get out of life. From our earliest decisions, we create a subconscious map that we use all our lives—even after it's outdated. As adults, we struggle against limiting beliefs, core beliefs, and unconscious beliefs.

A child raised by fearful parents and one who experiences trauma may form the core belief that "the world is not a safe place." A child who is teased for crying may come to believe "I cannot show my feelings." These beliefs can cause illness and unhappiness in adulthood. Our core beliefs shape expectations, attitudes, biases, and self-talk, which, in turn, shape our decisions and actions and, in many ways, create our personal reality. Often limiting, and sometimes devastating, these beliefs are hard to uncover—but we can't change them unless we do.

What were your earliest "truths"? What were your family's beliefs? What were the household rules? Did your parents make you feel like you mattered? Did you learn to equate making

184

money with ruthless people? Were you taught that women are second class? Many people find it easier to spend a lifetime living out hand-me-down outdated beliefs than to uncover and examine their own life program. But if we don't do the work of weeding out old beliefs that no longer serve our goals, we can't develop and grow. As parents, we need to be sure the beliefs we pass on to our children will work for them in the world they are growing into. Prince Charles used to say to his boys, "Well, it was like that for me, so it's going to be like that for you." Prince Harry thought about this and concluded, "That doesn't make sense. Just because you suffered doesn't mean that your kids have to suffer. In fact, quite the opposite — if you suffered, do everything you can to make sure that whatever negative experiences you had, that you can make it right for your kids."[1]

Tune into your beliefs. They bubble up all the time, in every situation. We just need to notice them. You can also interview yourself. Start with the following questions:

- *What do I believe about life?* Is it a rat race we must endure, or is the universe a friendly place? Is life a bowl of cherries, or is it just the pits? Is life to be enjoyed or endured? Do you believe you can't have everything, or you can have it all?
- *What do I believe about children?* Are they senseless little monsters, a burden to their parents? Or are they exuberant beings full of life, to be cherished and guided?
- *What do I believe about parenting?* Do you believe it is a mother's duty to serve her family and a father's to earn money? Or do parents face a challenge to balance caregiving and breadwinning in the way that's most fulfilling to each of them?

Unconscious Beliefs

Sometimes we may say we believe something, but still act the opposite of our beliefs. Our unconscious minds are incredibly powerful. Unable to distinguish between fact and fiction, it will do anything and everything it can to confirm our unconscious beliefs, adopting a multitude of *biases*, which are tendencies, inclinations, and prejudices that can shortcut reason.

When you recognize a negative belief, unpack it. Parents who believe that kids are monsters *expect* trouble. Irritation, anger, and readiness to use punishment reflect in their *attitude*. When a child does something parents consider "bad," their *bias* says, "It's just like him or her to do that," and they reinforce the negative *behavior* with this judgment. The kid's *self-talk* then says, "Mom expects me to be a holy terror" — and she or he becomes one. Kids don't want to disappoint their parents!

On the other hand, parents who believe kids are precious gifts reinforce positive behavior with their positivity bias. When kids do something "bad," these parents believe the kid made an error and want to correct their behavior. Parents clarify expectations for better conduct. Again, kids don't want to disappoint.

Dimensions of Belief

Our kids are great at helping us become aware of our biases and old beliefs. When we become aware of our beliefs, we need to ask ourselves, do we want them to come true? Do they enhance our life? What assumptions, expectations, attitudes, judgments, mind-chatter, and behavior do they create?

Assumptions can really make a mess of a family. My stepmother once saw wineglasses on the table when my friends and I had a dinner party before a school dance. Later that week, I heard her shouting at my dad about how I had gone out "drinking and carousing" with my friends. I don't know where she got her belief that I used alcohol, but it never occurred to her to ask me about it — the truth was that we were drinking grape juice! She always expected the worst from my brothers and me, and I never knew why.

Expectations are the most powerful forces in human relations. People naturally try to live up to their own expectations, often set by others. It's important to have high expectations for our kids, but it's also important that they be reasonable and realistic. Impossible expectations for children are highly damaging if children feel they are constantly disappointing their parents. A child concludes, "I'm inadequate; something's wrong with me," when, in fact, it's the parents' expectations that are at fault. Expecting too little of children can also be damaging, leaving kids feeling unmotivated and parents feeling exasperated. Helping kids set high expectations for themselves, especially kids with physical or mental differences, is the sweet spot. Ask your kids questions like, "If you were to do your best, what would the results be?" and, "How can I help you make that happen?" Everyone feels better when they set high and attainable expectations for themselves, because our expectations affect our attitudes.

Attitudes are habits of thought that connect with our emotions and behaviors. When someone has a "bad attitude," they feel negative or pessimistic and drive away people and opportunities. Someone with a "good attitude" is open to positive things. Attitudes are like beliefs that tell us how to feel about things. They change, depending on our experiences, and sometimes it's easier to change an attitude than a belief. When you recognize, in yourself or your family members, attitudes of suspicion, recklessness, disrespect, contempt, hostility, inflexibility, pessimism, selfishness, stubbornness, condescension, sarcasm or cynicism, defeatism, and defensiveness, you don't have to challenge these head on. Instead, ask what it would take to create an attitude of acceptance, calm, caution, openness, flexibility, optimism, resilience, empathy, patience, sincerity, curiosity, cooperativeness, confidence, collaboration, or anything else that will create a more positive experience. Our attitudes color our everyday judgments.

Judgment is often thought of as synonymous with prejudice or prejudgment, but having good judgment related to critical thinking is essential to having a good life. Making a judgment is making a decision about how we feel about something. Unfortunately, many of our judgments are based on outdated beliefs, unrealistic expectations, unforgiving attitudes, or implicit bias. We judge others based on their jobs, taste in clothing, and facial expressions. We judge people based on gender and race. When interacting with others, we need to be mindful of differences between our own beliefs and those of the person before us. Often the most judgmental people are the most insecure, wishing to boost their own self-esteem with comparison. We can become aware of our judgments by listening to our self-talk and mind-chatter.

Self-Talk is a term for the inner voice that comments on our lives throughout the day: the background noise. It combines conscious thoughts and unconscious beliefs, trying to explain what's happening with us. Self-talk can be beneficial if our minds are trained to be cheerful and supportive, or damaging when it becomes critical (see chapter 21, "Monkey Talk"). Self-talk guides our behavior.

Behavior is when our thoughts turn into action. We drive recklessly when we're worrying about being late. We make bunny pancakes because we think they will make our kids happy. We raise our voices when we think we're under threat. We always behave as if our beliefs are true. Our reality, or, in other words, the truth we live, is a result of our beliefs. When we see our kids misbehaving, our best action as parents is to slow them down and see what they are thinking. Then we can dig deeper and see what they believe. Children gain most of their basic programming during their first two years, and intense experiences later hardwire their basic core beliefs. Their behaviors and attitudes are based on the reality we, as parents, have shown them, which they have simply accepted as fact, and which will become their "truth." Good parenting helps our kids choose better beliefs before negative ones become entrenched. Choosing better beliefs of our own allows us to grow and be our best selves.

We can work to change our behaviors, but we can slip back

into old patterns if our core beliefs remain the same. I used to struggle with binge eating and could control it for a while, but it always snuck back. The impulse didn't leave me until I got down to a core belief about scarcity that had been passed down by my parents — who were raised in the Depression — and perhaps by my grandparents, who grew up impoverished. Trying to change behavior without examining beliefs is like correcting an error on a printed computer document over and over, instead of correcting the digital document first. I had to reprogram my mind to realize that putting food I didn't need into my body would not fix the problems experienced by past generations.

Behaviors and Beliefs

Most parenting books focus on getting kids to behave. In our experience, when you see a child as a human being struggling with their beliefs, behaviors become clues to their development. Our main job as parents is to help our kids develop a healthy sense of self.

Here are some ways to help kids form healthy core beliefs that don't limit them.

- *The placebo effect.* One-fourth to one-third of patients show improvement when given placebos by their physicians. Even though the pill has no active ingredients, the placebo effect is powerful because patients believe they are being cured. An example of this in children's culture is Dumbo's magic feather.
- *Let them experiment.* I was careful not to pass on limiting cultural beliefs to my son about gender, letting him form his own judgments. One night at dinner he announced, "Girls are vegetarians; boys eat meat." That's what he'd observed. His dad made a point of supporting Meatless Mondays after that.

- *Don't label or judge.* When I heard my sister-in-law tell my niece, "You're not a good artist. Your sister is the artist," I was quick to praise both children's drawings in front of the mom, seeing talent and possibility in them both. I knew how a careless statement could harm a creative spirit.

The easiest way to change children's behavior is to change their beliefs about themselves. If you believe kids are okay and treat them accordingly, they conclude that they must be okay, and they become okay. If you believe kids are smart and capable, and you expect them to use intelligence, they work harder to develop their skills, because they don't want to disappoint you.

When we look for things that prove we're right and validate our beliefs, it's called *selective perception.* "If I believe that kids are bad," my mom reasoned, "I look for things that prove I'm right. And, voilá, whatever I look for, I find." Parents who focus on the negative filter out all the fun and delightful things their kids do. At a school gathering, I watched a mom observe her daughter clear a table. She said to her friends, within her daughter's earshot, "That's not like her." Her daughter's good behavior didn't fit her stated belief that her daughter was a brat. The teacher said, so all the kids could hear her, "All the kids in this class are helpful and kind." For better or worse, parents reinforce the behavior that proves we're right. Kids repeat the behavior we reinforce and expect. *What we believe is what we get.* But too many parents *would rather be right than happy.*

According to Cognitive Behavioral Therapy (CBT), unlocking our experiences is as easy as ABC.

- A stands for an Activating Event (sometimes called a trigger) that starts the problem,
- B is for Beliefs, in the form of thoughts that occur to you next, and
- C is for Consequences, or feelings you have and actions you take according to those Beliefs.

190

Beliefs vs. Reality

Parents, teachers, television, the Internet, friends, peers, education, religion, and propaganda all shape our beliefs. Most of them work beyond our awareness. Some of these beliefs — our truths — may not be true at all. Or they may have been true in the past, even helping us survive, but are no longer relevant. So it's important to reexamine beliefs. Are they really true or just one way of looking at things?

When my stepmom saw wineglasses on the table the night of my school dance, that **activating** event led her to **believe** my friends and I had been drinking wine, and her thoughts ran away with her. The **consequence** was a terrible relationship between us. I was horrified that she thought the worst of me. Later, when I had real problems, I did not trust her to help. Unfortunately, it is very common for parents to act on untrue beliefs about children.

Parents, grandparents, and greats might say, "If it was good enough for me, it's good enough for you," and, "I turned out okay." But the truth is, it wasn't good for you, and it is not good for your children.

Parents often base their beliefs about their children on experiences they had as kids. When they voice negative beliefs, they create expectations that kids will either rebel against or live up to — or more precisely, live *down* to. Parents need to guard against *self-fulfilling prophecies.* Never predict a child will turn out to be a criminal relative — *especially if you enjoy being right.* You might feel smug, but the child will think they're no good, the relative will be disappointed, and everyone will be miserable. In some cultures, this is called a curse.

You get in life what you believe you deserve. Whether you believe you can or believe you can't, you're right. Give your children positive beliefs. If you tell them that they matter, they should expect great things of themselves, and they will certainly create fulfilling relationships and achievements.

191

21.

Monkey Talk

"All that we are is the result of what we have thought."
—The Buddha[1]

Buddhist thought refers to the monkey brain as the source of negative mind chatter. Other models contrast the evolved monkey brain—the part of the brain evolved for empathy and understanding—with the primal lizard brain, from which fight-or-flight impulses arise. Whatever you call it, our brains are biased toward negativity and fear, but they all have potential for reflection as well.

I taped a cartoon anteater on the back of our kitchen door, which long ago I fashioned out of construction paper to teach myself something. It's surrounded by paper ants, each labeled with a name. I made it the day I learned about ANTs (Automatic Negative Thoughts) from Daniel Amen.[2] This simple display helps me tune into my mind chatter and get a grip on my noisy mental zoo. (See it in appendix E.)

Self-talk plants in the unconscious that which grows during our lives. We encourage or discourage, lift up or put down, and empower or victimize ourselves. The quality of our self-talk determines whether we are our own best friend or our worst enemy. Here is an easy experiment to try right now.

Switch Your Feelings Exercise

Listening to self-talk is a great way to experiment with how thoughts affect feelings. Say to yourself, over and over, "I'm a loser," and notice how you feel. When this is your self-talk, you worry that you might fail. Notice that worrying actually creates feelings of failure: discouragement, defeat, and depression. These feelings inhibit you from wanting to take any risks whatsoever.

192

Now, let that go. Say to yourself several times, "I'm a winner." What feelings come up with that thought? Winning feels like encouragement, motivation, and excitement.

Over the next few days, pay attention to the actions you take when you're thinking and feeling like a winner or a loser. Are you working harder? Giving up? Persevering? Notice how behaviors reinforce your self-concept. This is good information.

Self-Talk

Self-talk comes from our self-concept, self-image, core beliefs, and social influences. Our ceaseless internal commentary creates feelings that we then express through our behavior. In a loop that creates either an upward or downward spiral,[3] our behavior also reinforces our self-concept.

Self-concept is the comprehensive evaluation of ourselves, based on how we see ourselves, value ourselves, think about ourselves, and feel about ourselves. It changes as we change.

Self-image is how we imagine ourselves to be, as if we were describing ourselves while looking in a mirror. It doesn't always align with reality, and it is often distorted by comparison with others. Our self-image affects our performance. A negative self-image automatically sets up a failure mechanism. A positive self-image sets up a success mechanism.

Mindset Magic

How we talk to ourselves about our self-concept and self-image affects our self-esteem. Our mindset can be judgmental or open; it can be fixed or growth-oriented. Someone who says, "I was shy when I was born, I'm shy today, and I'll be shy the day I die," has a fixed mindset about their self-concept. Someone who says, "I get shy around new people," sees their feelings in context, with a growth mindset.

The difference, according to author Carol Dweck,[4] is between being a judger or a learner. With a fixed mindset, we make up our minds, judging ourselves or others as complete, over, done. With a learner mindset, we see a variety of options and enter problems with curiosity.

Mom had a client who cried herself to sleep every night because she thought she was a bad mother. That thought created feelings (guilt, sadness, and anger), which led to her behavior (crying every night), which affected her self-concept (helpless, hopeless parent), which hindered her ability to be with her child (because her focus was on herself instead of her daughter). She decided to change. Now, instead of beating herself up, she tried changing her self-talk when she felt like crying. Instead of discouraging herself, she began substituting encouraging affirmations instead. She said, "I am a loving and effective mother," twenty or thirty times each day. It felt like a lie at first, but it got easier to say, day by day, and more believable. The positive self-talk altered her feelings. Her behavior and self-concept reflected the difference when she started acting like a loving and effective mother.

Say NO to ANTs

When we understand we are not our thoughts and our thoughts come from many different places, it is easier to identify and deal with them one by one. The little paper ants I taped on the back of my kitchen door are named after Daniel Amen's ANTs. When I, or someone else, struggle with a bad feeling, I look closely to find the one that's biting. Here are Amen's nine Automatic Negative Thoughts.

1. All or Nothing (can't see gray area)
2. Always/Never (how dramatic)
3. Negative Focus (can't see the positive in anything)
4. Thinking with Feelings (feeling afraid doesn't mean there's a real threat)
5. Guilt Beating (Mom calls this one "Shoulding on Yourself")
6. Labeling (calling oneself or others names)

Those six are black ants. The last three are red ants: they bite the hardest.

7. Fortune Telling (imagining/expecting the worst possible thing to happen)
8. Mind Reading (pretending you know what somebody else is thinking even though you don't, aka Projecting)
9. Blame (this preserves perceived victimhood)

I've scrawled the following words across the anteater's body: "Talk back to these thoughts. Argue with them; tell them the other point of view. Take a deep breath and stomp, stomp, stomp. They just want to eat your sandwich of happiness."

Draw an anteater with your kids. It doesn't have to be perfect. It just has to have a long snout with a tongue that can lick up ants. Draw ants for it to eat and give them names. Your kids will be able to recognize when they, or you, have ANTs. It's fun to drop them on the floor and stomp on them. (Did you peek at appendix E?)

Stinkin' Thinkin'

When computers first appeared, a popular slogan described the essence of code: "Garbage in; garbage out," or GIGO. It's like a recipe. If you bake gingerbread cake with potato-chip dust, barbecue sauce, and grapefruit peels, it won't come out of the oven smelling delicious and spicy the way gingerbread should. Likewise, when garbage finds its way into your mind, negativity spills into your life.

When your self-esteem drops, listen for garbage; what have you been saying to yourself? Anyone with low self-esteem has a voice inside telling them how awful they are. People who were blamed and criticized a lot as children tend to replay garbage statements over and over again, like a record skipping or a CD track stuck on repeat. Often the volume of negative internal dialogue is so low that people aren't aware of it. Turn up the volume. What do you hear? Write it down. Do you like what you hear? What would you do if someone else said those things to you?

Once you know what you say to yourself, you are free to make changes. *With awareness comes choice.* You can continue to repeat those messages, change the station, or make a new recording.

We all share patterns of "stinkin' thinkin' " — mind games that mire us in a win-lose mindset. We need to learn to catch ourselves practicing faulty mental habits, and even laugh at our assumptions. We all make mistakes sometimes, and there can be serious consequences. Here are common thinking errors and their alternatives.[5]

Polarization

Assumption: There is no gray area, no middle ground. We are either good or bad, perfect or a failure. As a result, emotions swing dramatically from one extreme to the other. One little flaw makes us totally worthless.

Alternative: When you catch yourself making black-and-white judgments, ask yourself how the opposite is also true. If, for example, you hear yourself saying, "The house is a total mess," look for parts of the house that are tidy. Realize that with only 1 or 10 thinking, you block out options 2 through 9.

Personalization

Assumption: When someone doesn't want my help, doesn't like what I made for dinner, or doesn't want to shake hands or hug, I feel like I've offended them somehow. Or I become offended, because I worked hard to please them or I really wanted to connect. A kid might make a real mess of things with this thinking.

Alternative: If it isn't personal, don't take it personally. Check your assumptions. Ask questions. Lots of people have food allergies or aversions. Some people don't like to be touched or have cultural differences. A moment of detachment allows you to step outside of your personal pain. Instead of saying, "How could you do that to me?" to a messy child, realize that the kid had no intention to hurt anyone. It's important for parents not to take kids' behavior personally.

Projection

Assumption: We know what someone else is thinking or feeling. "Everyone is staring at this spot on my shirt." "She must be mad at me since she hasn't called for weeks." Have you been in an argument with a friend or lover and accused him or her of the very thing you discovered yourself feeling — five minutes later?

Alternative: When you catch yourself stating what another person feels, do a reality check. What self-talk are you projecting? Is the person really judging that your house is messy? Do you actually see a look of horror on his or her face? Or are you missing a smile? Negative assumptions (guilt, anger, rejection) come from self-talk. Listen carefully to the words that come out of your mouth after, "You think. . . ." They hold information. When someone projects on you, say, "That's what you think. I actually feel differently."

Catastrophizing

Assumption: Sometimes we imagine and expect the worst. A headache is a sure sign of a brain tumor, a minor financial setback means we'll starve to death, or a missed call means our child is in trouble. The news brings us good reasons to panic every day, but a feeling of doom devastates our sense of well-being.

Alternative: Catastrophes do happen, but rarely in the way we imagine. If your mind creates scenarios, recognize your creative imagination. Let it run wild for a moment. An "and then . . . and then . . ." exercise to play out awful scenarios to the end (we all die, the world ends, the sun burns out) can give you perspective. Consider the odds against your conclusion — brain tumor, starvation, car accident — and think of more likely scenarios. Think of the times you imagined the worst and were wrong. Tell yourself, "Don't make a mountain out of a molehill."

Blaming

Assumption: Self-talk likes to find fault in either ourselves or others. We either assume total responsibility for everything that goes wrong, or we accept no personal responsibility for difficulties and place all blame on others. Often the guilt and shame of the blame game are worse than actual consequences.

Alternative: We're all responsible for our own behavior and its consequences. In relationships, each person is responsible for creating a problem — and a solution. Listen for the words *blame* and *fault* and restate assertions without of them. Instead, think in terms of accepting responsibility and sharing it. When no-fault communication is your family standard, you avoid the flames of blame and solve problems.

Overgeneralization

Assumption: If one thing goes wrong, it becomes a rule of thumb for everything. For example, a child botches one important test in junior high and concludes they are no good at math. An empty toilet paper roll means someone is an awful housekeeper. A child gets the taste of one bad grape and then decides they don't like grapes. A teenage girl who tries sex once gets a reputation. (Yes, people too often make assumptions and then talk about them as if they are true!)

Alternative: Overgeneralizing limits us and hurts others. Test assumptions by evaluating evidence for and against your conclusion, and then weigh information against how much you care for yourself or another person. Pull out math tests your child aced. Have your kid try three more grapes and savor the yummy ones, teaching them how to look for signs of mold. "So what!" is a powerful tool against overgeneralization. Someone is an "awful housekeeper"? So what! They make amazing chocolate cake. A teenager has sex? So what! Everyone has a first time sooner or later. Make sure she's okay, and if she's being bullied, stand up for her.

Being Right

Assumption: Having to be right can make you lonely. It puts you in conflict with everyone whose viewpoint differs. When others differ with you, you ignore them or feel compelled to prove them wrong. You find yourself in frequent power struggles. Minor differences seem major, because self-esteem and personal worth are at stake. When reality differs from the way you think it should be, you deny it.

Alternative: "It is what it is." Reality is rarely what we want it to be. People have their own perceptions, experiences, and lifestyles, and we do a lot of damage trying to force our own understanding on others. We can be firm in our beliefs, but must beware of their being fixed, and we need to teach ourselves to take a breath and listen to someone else's truth. When someone in the family needs to be right at all times, it may take teamwork to change the conversation. Start by affirming things everyone is right about, and then give everyone a chance to state views that differ.

Affirmations

Mom tells this story about going out of her comfort zone skiing. "One winter, I fell every time the trail was steep. But I noticed that just before I would fall, I'd say, 'I'm going to fall!' I decided to flip my self-talk and say, 'I'm doing great!' That affirmation encouraged me and changed my attitude. Soon I was maneuvering down the hills like a pro."

The good news about self-talk is that we can take control of it to support positive change. Instead of letting automatic messages reinforce the negative, we can teach our minds to affirm the positive and bring it about. Affirmations empower us to change our thinking — and our lives.

In workshops, Mom says, "Imagine, for a moment, a blue hippo. Now, *don't* think of a blue hippo!"

Did you do it? How? You probably thought of something else — maybe a red hippo or a blue fox or what you had for lunch. To get rid of the first image, most people replace it with another.

That is exactly how we must work with our unconscious to make important changes in our lives. Replace what you *don't* want with thoughts about what you *do* want.

Affirmations allow us to talk back to negative self-talk. By reprogramming our minds, we transform them. Remember learning to ride a bicycle or swim? When we grow, we move from "I can't" to "Of course I can!" Affirmations release the control of past beliefs and help us create new beliefs and raise our expectations. When we substitute positive messages for negative ones, we not only empty our mental garbage, we also heal damage caused by years of negative thinking.

Affirmations can be used to argue with ANTs, challenge thinking errors and assumptions, and counter put-downs. Remember the self-esteem protection skills in chapter 5? When a bully has told a kid they are stupid, instead of believing it, the kid can counter with positive self-talk. "That's what you think. I'm good at math and making friends."

Close your eyes and imagine someone very special entering the room, walking up behind you, gently touching your shoulders, and whispering something you've wanted to hear. Those whispered words may be your perfect affirmation. Rephrase them in the form "I am _____." Be your own best friend and give this message to yourself, rather than wish and wait for someone else to say it to you. Every morning, when you look in the mirror, say, "I accept and love you just the way you are." You can also say, "I am creating my life exactly as I want it." Repeat affirmations five to fifty times every day (twenty to thirty is the sweet spot), allowing positive feelings to flow, little by little, until you believe yourself — until you *become your real self.*

Another way to use affirmations is to make a list of all the stinkin' thinkin' in your head. Make a chart with two columns. List your doubts, problems, and hang-ups in the first one. Then go down the list, one by one, and write what you want to be true. For example, next to "No one notices the difference I make," write, "People appreciate the difference I make." Jot down examples as

200

proof. How does it make you feel? Remember, what you focus on is what you will find. Go down that list every day and see how fast things start turning around.

This process makes more sense after we understand the nature of the unconscious mind. It really can't tell the difference between fact and fiction, between what's imagined and what's real. *The unconscious will believe anything we tell it and will do everything it can to make that happen.* As with a fertile garden, whatever we plant in our unconscious will grow. If we plant carrots, we won't get petunias; and if we plant nothing, we'll probably get weeds.

What are the seeds for the unconscious? "Imagination is everything," said Albert Einstein. "It is the preview of life's coming attractions." What we see is what we get. Also, the words we repeat over and over in our minds have great power; eventually, they become our reality. Plant words (self-talk) and pictures (visualizations) you want to grow in your life, and take time every day to just feel good about them. *We become what we think about the most.* In the science of visualization, positive feelings allow us to do the things we need to do in order to create our success.

If your children tell you they can't do something, help them turn it around, saying, "Let's pretend that you can!" Read them *The Little Engine that Could* – it's a story about how affirmations help us overcome obstacles and even achieve greatness.[6] Self-talk is especially important to children with learning disabilities or other differences; they get extra negative messages from others and themselves. Encouragement, patience, and skills to compensate for differences are important, but positive self-talk creates ease and flow.

A child with positive self-talk and high self-esteem will choose positive behaviors that reinforce positive self-talk. On the other hand, a child with negative self-talk and low self-esteem will express negative behaviors that reinforce negative self-talk. Teach your children about self-talk and enjoy their positive behavior.

Optimistic Thinking

One last way to look at self-talk is to discover our explanatory styles. When something happens to us, how do we explain it to ourselves? Take a look at the charts below. The first one shows ways we explain events, seeing them as temporary or permanent, coincidental or pervasive, and internal or external (more on this in chapter 22, "Who's Pulling Your Strings?").

Explanatory Style	
It's temporary (transient).	It's permanent (forever).
It's just this once (coincidental/specific).	It always happens (pervasive/universal).
I did this (internal/personal).	Others did this (external/general).

	Good things are	Bad things are
Pessimistic	temporary, specific, and general.	permanent, pervasive, and personal.
Optimistic	permanent, pervasive, and personal.	temporary, specific, and general.

The third chart, on the following page, is a tool we created to help readers flip the switch from using a negative, pessimistic explanatory style, we can change it to a positive, optimistic one. When we listen to our self-talk and hear ourselves make statements, we can tune in to our explanatory style.

Don't feel like you're forcing yourself to change your thoughts. Just say the statements, and see how your thoughts change. Learn more in the groundbreaking book *Learned Optimism* by Martin Seligman.[7]

	Change this	To this
Temporary	"Happiness is fleeting."	"Life is full of joy."
Permanent	"My life has changed for the worse"	"This too shall pass"
Specific	"I got it right this time."	"I got it right again."
Pervasive	"Bad things always happens to me."	"I usually have good luck."
Personal	"I'm always to blame."	"These things happen."
General	"Just lucky, I guess."	"My hard work paid off."

Here's the good news: we know that people are not born optimists or pessimists. Explanatory style is something we learn by example or from decisions we make while growing up. Pessimistic explanatory styles can be unlearned. As parents, we can teach our kids how to choose thoughts of strength that will protect them from feeling helpless and depressed, having low self-esteem, and even having poor immune function.

When you accept responsibility for your self-talk, you take charge of your self-esteem. *By changing your mind, you can change your life.*

22.

Who's Pulling
Your Strings?

*"To be nobody but yourself in a world which is doing its best to
make you just like everybody else means to fight the greatest battle
there is or ever will be."* —e. e. cummings[1]

When I began living on my own, I struggled with housekeeping.
Vacuuming fell somewhere between a necessary evil and
emotional torture, as it always brought up painful memories from
my blended family's screaming matches on chore days.
Unfortunately, I also inherited my dad's tendency to collect piles
of clutter, so I was really in a mess. Literally. Then one day, Mom
heard me say, "I should do a better job keeping my apartment
clean," and she offered a surprising observation. "Haven't I
taught you the Eleventh Commandment? *'Thou shalt not should
upon thyself.'* "[2]

She told me a story about when she was a young mom. One
day, she started hearing her mother's voice in the back of her
mind, ordering her around. "When I tuned in more closely," she
said, "I heard, 'You have to wash the kitchen floor.' I looked over
my shoulder, wondering who had said that. I sat myself down
and had a little talk with myself. 'Self,' I asked, 'do you *choose* to
clean the kitchen floor?' 'Well,' my Self answered, 'I can't walk
barefoot any more. My feet stick to the floor.' After this little
discussion, I decided that I wanted to wash the floor so I could
walk barefoot and enjoy it." Hearing about the beginning of her
long, gradual process of learning to use her internal locus of
control reminded me that, in my own apartment, I could make my

own rules. After that, I found a real pleasure in *choosing* to vacuum!

Growing up is the process of shifting from an external to an internal authority, or locus of control. Young children have an external locus of control. They look to their parents and other important adults for information, values, and direction. Like little sponges, they absorb and accept everything in their environment—believing it—and they internalize it. As kids gradually develop and mature, they learn to trust themselves and stand on their own two feet. Ideally, as parents let go of control and empower their children, kids assume more responsibility and control over their own lives. They gain confidence and competence. They think for themselves, discovering curiosity, critical thinking, reason, independence, and freedom.

For many people, however, this important developmental process has been interrupted or thwarted. Many adults who were not empowered by their parents or their culture still trust others more than they trust themselves. They are overly concerned about what others might say, what others might think, and what might please or displease others. In the extreme, they become unable to tell right from wrong, even confusing the two if someone (in the media or in person) holds their attention, gains their trust, or holds power over them.

Many people trust others more than they trust themselves. They don't know their own values, opinions, beliefs, habits, or identity. They look outside of themselves for direction, approval, a sense of worth, and even happiness. As fully grown adults, they may still look to others to clean up after them or to rescue them from problems.

People with an external locus of control tend to be extremely dependent on persons and things outside of themselves; they give their power away and then feel powerless and out of control. They neglect their own values, desires, dreams, and intuition and as a consequence lack identity, authenticity, and individuality. These people are the ones who, if their physician tells them they have six months to live, die obediently, right on schedule. Seeking solutions outside of themselves, they are vulnerable to manipulation and exploitation by others and can easily become addicted to unhealthy relationships, drugs, food, entertainment, work, and possessions.

Unfortunately, our Western patriarchal consumer culture is concerned with external appearance, performance, achievements, and possessions. Americans have hundreds of times more possessions now than a century ago. The internal world — what we think, what we need, what we value, what gives us meaning in life — is often ignored or considered unimportant. This external focus keeps us emotionally immature. Like children, we become dependent on external displays of identity and sources of self-worth. We yield our power to vague external authorities, fashion, fads, status symbols, and, in the most dangerous cases, political and religious extremism.

When we look around, we notice that the most interesting, impressive, and expressive people we know are those who have decided to take charge of their lives. Truly successful people succeed on their own terms, writing their own rules and becoming their own authority. Bernie Siegel, author of *Love, Medicine, and Miracles*, has this to say about cancer patients who are exceptions to the rule that cancer is incurable.

"Exceptional patients manifest the will to live in its most potent form. They take charge of their lives even if they were never able to before, and they work hard to achieve health and peace of mind. They do not rely on doctors to take the initiative but rather use them as members of a team, demanding the utmost in technique, resourcefulness, concern, and open-mindedness. If they're not satisfied, they change doctors."[3]

Joe Wions, a family friend, did exactly that when he was diagnosed with ALS. Seeking outside opinions and alternative therapies, he lived ten times longer than his doctors said he would and eventually stopped the disease in its tracks.[4] Patients like him tap into their inner locus of control, and their lives change forever.

But we do not have to go to the threshold of death to find it. We can give ourselves permission to do so now.

Where is *your* locus of control? Do you do things more to please others or to please yourself? Do you listen more to external voices — musts, "have-tos," "ought-tos" — or do you trust your intuition?

Dr. Martin Seligman researched learned helplessness. He experimented on dogs, focusing on those that gave up trying to escape shock treatments. Then one day, he had an epiphany: Why not pay more attention to dogs that *didn't* give up? In the following years, he flipped the entire focus of psychology from a disease focus to a strength focus.[5]

Here is a way to bring your locus of control inside of yourself. Make a list of five things you have to, ought to, or are supposed to do today. Start each sentence with "I." Then rewrite your list, beginning each sentence, instead, with "I choose to." Notice how you feel when you are in control. As an adult, you have power over your own life. Perhaps you now see ways in which you have created the life you live now and also how you can choose to make changes.

Turn off the television and put your phone down. Take a deep breath and listen. Close your eyes or take a walk. Reduce the endless bombardment of noise and chatter. Listen to soft inner voices that want to be heard. Really listen! Then do what is good for you. Quiet time can be the most important time in your life. Take time to listen to your body. Learn to trust it. Meditate. Write in a journal.

In Western civilization, we overvalue particular facets of ourselves and undervalue others. Rational and logical aspects are respected and developed, while emotional and intuitive features are too often dismissed, depreciated, and denied. Other civilizations, past and present, approach life with deep respect for and awareness of the intuitive element of existence. Tune in to "inner listening," the divine guidance system that "makes clearer to us what we really want, as distinct from what we have been talked into."[6] When you use your mind and body, feelings and intuition, you become an autonomous adult—your own person. Learn to trust yourself.

When we raise a family, we are given externally oriented babies and small children who learn their value (and everything else) from important people in their lives. In the process of helping them grow up, we can observe their responses to controlling statements, such as "Obey your mother," and empowering statements, like "What do you think is the best choice for you?" With this sensitivity, parents can nudge their children toward becoming internally motivated adults who think for themselves, trust themselves, and have high self-esteem and personal power.

Building Agency

A crucial ingredient of healthy self-esteem is *agency*. When a person feels like they are in the driver's seat and has the tools they need and the right to make things happen in life, they experience the freedom to shape the world. You cannot have agency without an inner locus of control (even if you are working on someone else's agenda or as someone else's agent).

Here are tips to nurture agency in younger children.

- Offer choices: Would you rather have your birthday party at home or in the park this year?
- Give them a box of gold stars so that they can be in charge of rewarding themselves.
- Encourage them to take quiet time in the afternoon, rather than filling their schedule with activities. They may complain of boredom at first. That's okay. Mom says the most creative and best times of my childhood came shortly after I announced that I was bored. I had to look inside myself for entertainment.

Here are tips for older kids.

- Before you give advice, ask what they think. Then ask if they would like your help, suggestions, ideas, or wisdom.
- Encourage them to think for themselves and make decisions and set goals based on what they want and need, what they think is best. If "everybody's doing it," help your kids sort out the situation and its consequences, and help them decide what *they* feel is right.
- When they argue for things they think they must have or do, ask, "Who says?" Help them tune into their own needs, desires, and wants.

Below are tips and ideas for people of all ages.

- Develop and enjoy the bond of love between you and your kids.
- Accept them as they are (though not necessarily all of their behaviors). Give them permission to be individuals. Provide understanding, support, and nurturing.
- Accept and understand their needs and feelings. Your children are unique beings with their own ideas and desires.
- Honor their separateness from you. When possible, let them do things their own way. Give them permission to be individuals. Let them teach you.
- Listen to their experiences, stories, and opinions.
- Support and encourage healthy exploration of their world, while setting reasonable and healthy limits.
- Use assertive communication instead of games, force, and manipulation.
- Use the natural-and-logical-consequences style of discipline. It teaches children to figure things out, think for themselves, and become self-disciplined.

- Use more encouragement and less praise. Praise is a verbal reward that shows children that they are pleasing to others. Encouragement motivates them from within — being pleased with themselves. They gain higher self-esteem directly from the experience.
- Discuss the difference between needs, desires, and wants. Many kids have trouble listening to their own wants and needs. Help them see how simple this can be.
- Encourage your children to go after what they want. Setting goals to achieve little things teaches them important skills they'll need later on in life.
- Give both boys and girls the same empowering messages. Girls have a greater tendency toward learned helplessness, which is detrimental to self-esteem and success later in life.

Foster growth in your children as you cultivate it in yourself. As you get in touch with your own inner wisdom, it will guide you in the fine art of parenting. Your family can become one of centered individuals, each leading interesting and healthy lives.

"Follow your bliss." — Joseph Campbell[7]

23.

Obsession with Perfection

*"A perfectionist is someone who takes great pains . . . and gives
them to others."* — Anonymous[1]

Mom had to be a perfect hostess. She had to cook a perfect meal
and set a perfect table, with no wrinkles in the tablecloth. The
house had to look perfect—no smudges or clutter. She had to look
perfect—hair done and lipstick on. When the doorbell rang, she
had to be calm and smiling, as though she'd done nothing all day
long. She'd be stressed out, worrying about details and neglecting
her own agendas, but she'd never show it. She was living up to
her social conditioning of what she thought a perfect wife should
be. But she doesn't remember ever really enjoying herself or her
guests.

When she realized how deeply she'd lost herself in the pitfalls
of perfectionism, she decided to make major changes. Instead of
chasing unrealistic expectations that inhibited her lifestyle and
cramped her self-expression, she gave herself permission to
attempt things she never thought she could do and enjoy herself
more. In doing so, she took more risks, made more mistakes, and
gained more wisdom. Free from the perils of perfectionism, her
life became much more fun and a lot easier. And she always gave
me permission to just be human.

Women of her white-gloved era were "supposed to" believe
that they had to be perfect to find or hang onto a man. Men
bought into this, and therefore could never experience an
authentic relationship. Today's moms are pressured to feel like
they have to manage career, family, and relationships with the
artfulness of Martha Stewart and make it look *Real Simple.*

But it's the worst for children who feel like their parents will only love them if they are perfect. This happens when parents withhold acceptance and affection, so children feel they have to earn it. They work harder and harder to be accepted, loved, and okay, but the rule is "they don't get love or affection for free." Kids struggle, hoping that in the end their parents will approve of them, love them unconditionally, or see them as okay *just for being themselves*. But when they grow up, they often find themselves in relationships with perfectionists who always look for something wrong and easily find fault. They find partners who, like their parents, have unrealistic or impossible expectations, feeling that *only perfection will do*. A single failing, fault, or flaw proves what they believe deep down: they are total failures.

Perfectionism Kills

Many children feel the pressure to be perfect. If you make a mistake, you'll be late, miss a class, miss a grade. Kids get a lot of messages that if they mess up, there will be trouble.

Although games are great, sports can be a nightmare of pressure for perfectionist kids. Getting up to bat can be terrifying when you believe that you have to hit the ball every time it crosses the plate. The tension is intensified if a perfectionist parent is watching. Competitive parents who shout at and criticize their kids and the team make the game less enjoyable for everyone. A kid who's a talented athlete can be devastated if they get injured or otherwise lose their abilities. Too much pressure can make kids want to quit or not even bother to try. If they don't try, they reason, they can't fail. But if they don't try, they can't enjoy the benefits. Ideally, sports are not about perfection but about play: even the best baseball players in the world only hit one out of three balls!

One problem affecting many teens is intellectual perfectionism. Child perfectionists with straight-A grades have killed themselves after they receive their first B. Their perfectionist perceptions prevent them from feeling content with achievements that are nonetheless absolutely outstanding. High expectations can be energizing, but perfectionism can be deadly, both psychologically and physically.

Believing one has to attend a top college to be okay puts too much pressure on many high-achieving high schoolers who, focusing only on grades, miss out on social and personal growth. Although there are thousands of colleges to choose from, a narrow focus can be harmful. A perfect report card with a 4.0 grade point average is "not good enough" for elite schools that regularly turn away students with a 4.5 average. Heavy intellectual workloads can lead teens into thinking it's okay to use stimulants and alcohol to manage stress. Teens need eight to ten hours of sleep for their growing brains, and those who are deprived can lose the ability to concentrate, compounding the problem, and suffer anxiety and depression.[2] A teen low on sleep is as dangerous as a drunken teen behind the wheel, which can be deadly.[3]

Body perfection messages on social media create serious problems for youngsters, especially girls. Teens who listen more to social media than to parents tend to neglect self-care and be drawn into perfectionism. It's crucial for parents to model self-acceptance when kids are young and reinforce it when children become teens who are growing and developing into adults.

When girls are exposed to entertainment and social media, obsession with body image can begin or intensify. Until very recently, there was a narrow norm for how women should look, talk, and behave. Films, TV commercials and shows, and magazines bombard everyone, women and men alike, with repeated images of particular standards of perfection. Popular kids at school and on TikTok, Snapchat, Instagram, Facebook, and whatever comes next instinctively uphold and repeat these images. Snapping a selfie temporarily boosts self-esteem, but beauty conformity can boomerang on people who compare themselves to each other and try to match unattainable ideals.

Advertising teaches teen girls to be obsessed with perfection. Kids spend more hours learning to use makeup to cover perceived flaws than pursuing sports and good nutrition, which keep the body healthy and attractive. Constant conflict with self-image leads to anxiety and depression, low self-esteem, eating disorders, and self-destructive behavior. Girls who reject gender-role stereotyping tend to have stronger self-esteem. Rather than compare themselves to unattainable standards, they focus on and appreciate their own intrinsic value.[4]

If your teen is on social media, take a peek at their feed and see if they follow any body-positive influencers. If they don't, follow some yourself, share, and start a dialogue.

High Standards for Low Self-Esteem

It's important to have high standards for ourselves, but it's too easy to obsess about being what we think we *should* be — perfect. Striving to be a perfect wife with a Pilates body, a perfect mother with honor-roll children, and a perfect cook serving gourmet dinners nightly sets one up for chronic disappointment, dissatisfaction, and exhaustion. Striving to be a perfect husband or partner with a high-paying job, six-pack abs, and a knack with tools can lead to anxiety and depression. In the perfectionism trap, only when we do things absolutely perfectly do we think we are okay. One widow confessed that she even felt she had to grieve perfectly! Popular cultural pressures are so pervasive it's hard to escape them, but fortunately things are shifting.

Human beings can't be perfect for very long. That's fine. There's nothing wrong with being human. But with perfectionists, one failing, fault, or flaw proves what they believe deep down: they are total failures. Either/or thinking, which we looked at in chapter 20, "Beliefs and Believing," allows no middle ground. *If you are not all good, you are all bad.* Mistakes, therefore, are terrifying. One recovering perfectionist was actually told by her mother, "You are perfect or you are nothing."

Those who have difficulty accepting themselves also have difficulty accepting others. Those who are judgmental and critical of themselves tend to be judgmental and critical of their spouses, children, and friends. And, while good at giving criticism, they fear it from others and easily become defensive. They fight to be right because they can't stand the thought of being wrong, inevitably resulting in conflict. Under pressure to be perfect, they keep up a façade. Playing this role while knowing that it is phony creates a false self, which can tear them up inside.

Decision-making induces intense anxiety for perfectionists, who always want to make perfect decisions. They may procrastinate when faced with a task or avoid finishing it—after all, if they don't start or don't finish, they can avoid being judged. In business settings, they waste immeasurable amounts of time and materials at high cost to the company: for example, a perfectionist can spend hours writing one letter. Those with ADHD or autism, who naturally lean toward black-and-white thinking, can feel pressure very deeply and experience rejection sensitive dysphoria (RSD),[5] a depressive backlash to things not meeting emotional expectations.

The Terror Is Real (or Is It?)

The thought of making a bed or cleaning a bedroom can strike terror in a perfectionist (or someone in a relationship with one) and lead to discouragement and despair. One time my older brother, after spending many hours cleaning his room, called in our dad to inspect it. Dad glanced around the room, stroked the wall, and said, "You didn't oil the paneling." He was kidding of course, but the praise his son deserved—and craved—was masked by a flip response. Everyone connected with a perfectionist suffers from low self-esteem.

Perfectionists may end up doing all the work themselves because no one else can do it "just right," which means perfect. They suffer from chronic fatigue and stress. When they do successfully complete a task, they never give themselves or their team a pat on the back because they are busy looking for flaws. A perfectionist doesn't see the success and savor it; they only see how their efforts weren't good enough.

Perfectionist parents focus on surface qualities. They invest in a façade based on an image/ideal/fantasy of how they think a child is supposed to be. A pimple, spot on a shirt, or unruly hair commands their attention to such a degree that they may not notice what a kid is experiencing. Tattoos, dyed hair, and extreme clothing can freak out parents, and although these things are tough on one who feels it's their job to help a child maintain an image, they may miss their child's feelings, concerns, struggles, growth, and inner beauty. Perfectionists may be developmentally stunted due to confusion and anxiety, stemming from lack of appreciation and support.

No human being is perfect. Anyone who has a body or a kitchen knows that there is no such thing as perfection — at least not for long! A "perfect" child might still have temper tantrums. A "perfect" couple may fight horribly behind closed doors. "Perfect" media models and athletes endure starvation, sickness, substance abuse, and surgery to live up to industry standards. Wrinkles, moles, pimples, fat, and grey hair are eliminated by Photoshop. When comparing ourselves to doctored images, it's easy to think something is wrong with us (see chapter 27, "Guidance in the Digital Age").

Of the thousands of participants in Mom's workshops striving to be perfect, no one ever achieved it. All their lives they worked so that one day they would be *really* okay, which, to a perfectionist, means perfect.

Here's what people like this figure out: it's no fun being a perfectionist. Perfectionism robs us of joy, playful abandon, utter relaxation, and spontaneity. Perfectionism is a compulsion that may predispose people to substance abuse, alcoholism, eating disorders, and obsessive-compulsive behavior. Perfectionism also takes time and energy away from families. When children grow up, their warmest memories will be not of how clean the house was, but of the time the family spent together with their feet up on the furniture.

Recovering from perfectionism, like everything else, requires flipping focus and choosing to change thoughts. Start from the beginning, and take it from there.

Admit that you're only human.

It is our privilege as human beings to be imperfect. Some even say it's our birthright, or even our duty. Persian carpet makers were famously known to weave flaws into their designs, reasoning that only God/Allah was perfect. In Western culture, it takes courage to allow imperfections. Yet, when we accept them and forgive ourselves, we can accept and forgive others.

Who said that parents always have to be right? When we accept ourselves completely — including the fact that we are fallible — the burden lightens. It's a relief not to have to be perfect — not to have to play God.

Admit your mistakes. You can simply state, "Yesterday I said (or did) such-and-such, and I realize today that I was wrong." Kids know how human they are; when you show them how to laugh at your flaws, it gives them hope, it models self-acceptance, self-compassion, and self-love, and it builds a bond between you.

Turn mistakes into teachers.

If "to err is human," children are super-human! They are always losing, forgetting, or spilling things. Feeling bad for being clumsy or confused just makes things worse. When kids cry over spilled milk, just ask them to clean it up and be more careful next time. Self-esteem sags when children make mistakes; when mistakes are fixed, self-esteem is restored. Help kids figure out what went wrong so that they can avoid a repeat performance. A mistake, after all, is just one way that didn't work.

A friend of mine went through many unhealthy relationships before noticing that she kept repeating the same patterns with the same type of man who would never be happy with her the way she was. As soon as she realized this, her "luck" began to change, and for the first time, she met a man with whom she could be herself.

In doing, risking, and trying new things, we develop judgment skills. We learn how to analyze and evaluate old information to determine how it transfers to new situations.

A person who makes mistakes gains wisdom. Thomas Edison made thousands of mistakes; he was also granted more than 1,000 patents. Failure can breed success. There is no successful person, living or dead, who has not failed many, many times. Success is learned and earned. Viewing mistakes as learning opportunities is a life-saving and life-enhancing skill. People who learn from mistakes gain confidence, competence, and judgment skills.

Laugh at your bloopers.

Share mistakes with family and friends — the funny ones, the terrible ones, the ones we learn from. One mom told me that they play "Bloopers" at the dinner table. Mom and Dad begin with stories of their daily blunders, and each kid follows.

Mom once had a doozy of a blooper. After filling her gas tank, she went through the station's car wash. It was only when she turned onto the street and heard a clunk that she realized she had not replaced the gas cap. She and her mechanic spent the rest of the afternoon trying to figure out how to get rid of soapy water in the tank without sacrificing the gas. At home, everyone laughed at her mistake. We kids learned from it and never made the same mistake!

Blooper time is a chance for the whole family to laugh with each other, at each other, and at themselves — and then get on with life. Stories of mistakes can turn pain into pleasure and wisdom. When I told about the time I bonked my head on the sagging hatch of our Prius and ended up walking around Trader Joe's with a bag of frozen peas on my head, the whole family decided to fix the car. Then someone mentioned the scene in the movie *Bridesmaids* when a character opens a bag of peas and pours them onto a bruise. It lightened up everyone's day.

Reorder your priorities.

One mother of three preschool children let slip that she "had to" vacuum the carpet three times each day. Mom suggested that she rethink this. The following week she reported that she had cut back to twice a day. "No one seemed to notice," she announced, "and I had more time for my children." Do you want to be a slave to household perfection? A perfect house is impossible with children. Save the white carpets until they grow up and move out. "When all else fails," the saying goes, "lower your expectations." Or get a dog, I say. Dogs are nature's vacuum cleaners!

Stop trying to be Superwoman or Superman. "Our life is frittered away by detail. Simplify, simplify, simplify," wrote Henry David Thoreau in *Walden*. There are merits in messiness: life can be filled with more fulfilling things than busywork. Design a healthier and more enjoyable family life for everyone. When essential chores are shared, bragged about, and applauded when the cleaning is done, everyone feels the pride and joy.

Life is short; examine your priorities. What's really important in your life? Good parenting? Go for excellence in that area. Be the best that you can be. In other areas, such as planting a garden, "good enough" will do just fine. Seeds will grow fine, even if they are not planted in perfectly straight lines. Missing a day of school will not go on a child's permanent record. Make yourself a sign and hang it on your refrigerator where your kids can see: "Nothing is perfect, and it's all OKAY!"

Relax. Breathe deeply. Be flexible. Be gentle with yourself. Focus on and enjoy the *experience* of life rather than the *accomplishment* of it. Your emotional and mental health are more important than perfection, and that's true for your kids, too.

Compara-sins

"If you want to be unhappy, try to choose someone who is doing better than you and keep comparing. It's the best way. It really works." — Ilona Boniwell

"There were four girls in our family," a workshop participant told me. "We were always compared to each other in looks, intelligence, athletic ability, and so on. For the most part, I tried to hold my own by competing with my sisters. My youngest sister felt defeated and reacted by not participating at all. Most of my self-esteem problems stem from the fact that I was never as 'wonderful' as my oldest sister." Comparison is a setup for low self-esteem. Did your parents compare you with your siblings? Did they play favorites? How did you feel when they did that? What were they trying to do? How well did it work? What is your present relationship with your siblings?

Social comparison is a basic drive, a normal human function. Observing how others do things helps us know where we stand and figure out how to get the best for ourselves. Since we cannot see ourselves, we anchor on others and mimic what appeals to us. But when we don't feel like we measure up, constant comparison can make us feel constantly insecure. In fact, in studies about happiness and unhappiness, unhappy people have something in common: they compare a lot and care a lot about the results.[6]

People motivate themselves by comparing themselves to others, but comparison can be tremendously damaging to self-esteem. Theodore Roosevelt called comparison "the thief of joy," because it can make us judgmental, biased, overly competitive, unkind, and sad. When we base our judgment and behavior on someone else's values, we separate ourselves from our own truths (see chapter 22, "Who's Pulling Your Strings?").

Sin means "missing the mark." In comparing ourselves to others, either we miss the mark or someone else does. We miss the mark of joy when we do it, so we coined the word *compara-sin*. We miss the mark when we give away so much of our power. It keeps us from feeling whole, happy, and loved. Compara-sin is a sin against our joy.

When we're not in our right mind, we greatly fear being judged by others. When we care so much about what others think of us, we not only judge ourselves, we judge others as being judgmental. The tyranny of social comparison is a toxic thought circle that keeps us from knowing what we value and need and keeps us trapped in a perfectionist mindset. Both feeling smug and feeling guilty lower our energy. Start noticing when you compare yourself to others and wonder what other people think of you. Remember (from chapter 21, "Monkey Talk") that mindreading is an ANT (Automatic Negative Thought). When we stop comparing and judging, we feel less judged and more appreciated. We feel less intimidated and more at ease. We can help and support each other.

Comparison Is Competition

Competition is a wonderful thing when goals are well defined, rules are clear, the playing field is equal, and fairness is the bottom line. But in order to let go of the win-lose struggle that pervades mind chatter, we can choose to be sincerely happy for others' achievements and successes. As one woman stated, "Edna's a good cook, so let her cook. I'm a good eater!" A win-win attitude fosters cooperation essential for having a winning family team.

Cooperation is necessary for healthy families and also for business success. Working and pulling together is the solid foundation on which both successful businesses and winning families are built.

Comparison both encourages and enforces conformity. But no one has to be like everyone else. As a matter of fact, you *can't* be like everyone else, because you are one of a kind. It's okay to be who you really are. If you aren't you, who will be? Judy Garland used to tell her daughter Liza Minnelli, "Always be a first-rate version of yourself instead of being a second-rate version of someone else."

Since the beginning of time, billions of people have inhabited our planet. Yet there has never been anyone like you. You are unique. You are special. Your personality plus your experiences make you a divine original. The only person with whom you can compare yourself is you.

How are you today, compared with three months ago or three years ago? Are you more loving, more accepting? Are you a better person or are you backsliding? Compare yourself only with yourself and your own personal growth. Challenge yourself to become your own personal best.

If you notice that you are comparing yourself to (and competing with) another person, change your self-talk. Instead of putting yourself down, consider the other person a model and lift yourself up. Even our children can be models. My son blows me away with his capabilities. Mom used to tell me (and still does, which is adorable coming from an eighty-year-old), "I want to be just like you when I grow up!" I say the same thing to my kid. We are hungry for models. Seeing with new eyes, we find people everywhere who inspire us to excellence. When we change our thinking from "you or me" to "you and me," we enjoy ourselves and each other far more. We feel a connection rather than a separation from others.

No More Stinkin' Thinkin'

Stop the stinkin' thinkin' that says, "I'm not good enough." Listen to whose voice is stuck in your head. Then pause and realize that it is *only an opinion* at *a moment in time* based on *someone's perfectionist expectations*. The fact is, you *are* good enough and *always have been*. Stop giving nagging, damaging messages power. When you hear them, repeat the following affirmations:

"I am good enough."

"I am not perfect, but I am okay."

"I don't have to be perfect; I like myself just the way I am."

"I make my best effort."

Repeat these affirmations a few times. They may feel strange at first, but that will change. Over time, these sayings will heal you and help you transcend perfectionism. Meanwhile, celebrate your achievements. List your successes! Acknowledge your efforts! Appreciate yourself!

Be an Imperfectionist!

Wabi-sabi is the Japanese idea of finding beauty in the

imperfection of nature. It honors things that are "imperfect, impermanent, and incomplete." When we start to see life through this gentle lens, we can relax and get into the flow. Any time you walk away from judging and toward acceptance, you become a better parent and a better person. In spite of images that tell us otherwise, there is no authority greater than your own beating heart.

I feel very fortunate to have witnessed my mother, over the years, releasing herself from the trap of perfectionism. Because of her journey, I was able to discover the happiness that hospitality is really about, rather than feel enslaved by perfection. I'm not very good at folding napkins, ironing tablecloths, or polishing silver, but as a hostess, I have come to own my personal style, mixing formal with fun and beauty with messiness, and relishing realness, not perfection. When the doorbell rings, I do my best. No one expects perfection from me, nor I from them. A house full of people who feel comfortable brings me great joy. Any guest who looks for it can always find a pile of papers or dust on a windowsill. They never say anything, but if they did, I'm prepared to smile and say, "Better sane than sanitized."

24.

Internal Barriers to Self-Esteem

"The first problem for all of us, men and women, is not to learn, but to unlearn." —Gloria Steinem[1]

Self-esteem is as important to our well-being as legs are to a table. It is essential for physical and mental health and for happiness. The bad news is that there's a pandemic of disrespect in society, magnified and spread by media and a culture of falsehoods. Hurt feelings cause reactivity and low self-esteem. Rudeness, bullying, and verbal abuse have increased exponentially, armed with self-righteous justification of violence, which escalates hatred of individuals and groups.

Since self-esteem is formed not just by our family but also by society, it is a cultural issue as much as a personal one. We live in groups—families, communities, and countries—and our mental and emotional health are interconnected. Contagion science shows how viruses spread, but it also demonstrates how one person with a high level of well-being can affect everyone around them.[2] When we care for ourselves, we care for others. The next three chapters look at how internal, external, and cultural blocks to self-esteem, well-being, and wholeness, challenge us and keep us stuck.

Some of the biggest internal blocks to self-esteem are common to many cultures.

Othering/Objectification

The philosopher Martin Buber observed two ways humans see each other: *I-Thou* and *I-It*.

- I-Thou indicates a relation of reciprocity and mutuality, subject to subject.
- I-It refers to a relation of superiority, in which one uses or controls another, subject to object.

In I-Thou relationships, we accept people as themselves, viewing them as sovereign beings; but in I-It relationships, we objectify people, seeing them as less than we are — as problems or servants. Objectification — real or perceived — creates alienation. Here are ways it affects our lives.

1. **Comparison.** Closely linked to competition, this way of seeing each other is fundamentally about winning and losing. If you fail, I succeed. Competition in everyday family life leads to anxiety, loss of self-confidence, and damaged trust. Comparison interferes with cooperation and teamwork. No one really wins. Comparing ourselves with others is not an accurate measure of our inherent self-worth.

2. **Labeling.** For kids and adults alike, labels can be more powerful than they are meant to be. Value judgments applied to a person can affect self-esteem for years to come, whether the label is "selfish and stupid" or "gifted and smart." Adults who apply negative labels to a child instead of addressing unacceptable behavior reject the whole child, who feels wounded, shamed, worthless, and devastated. Naming a *problem* is a powerful tool that helps us solve it, but when we label *people*, we objectify them and judge their identities. All stereotypes are labels.

    What labels have defined and hurt you? Selfish? Stubborn? Untrustworthy? Wouldn't you rather have heard, "That was a selfish thing to do," or, "Did you forget something?" A "bad" child is inherently a good person who feels confused or has exercised poor judgment. Instead of getting a heavy dose of rejection, punishment, or shame, he or she needs understanding.

3. **Prejudice.** Our minds make assumptions all the time based on previous experience, but prejudging a person objectifies them. Stereotypes help us temporarily make sense of the world, but when we take shortcuts, we run the risk of bigotry, which is true intolerance (see chapter 25, "External Barriers to Self-Esteem.")

4. **Body shaming.** All of us on the spectrum of male to female feel self-conscious of the way our bodies are shaped, colored, and smell at one time or another. The world is full of products and advertising that create norms to which we are "supposed to" conform. When we look in the mirror or at photographs of ourselves, which are everywhere, we see ourselves from the outside and often focus on our flaws. Many adults and children suffer from a warped self-image that keeps them from fully loving every part of themselves.

5. **Impostor Syndrome.** "Smile for the camera!" People who are accomplished and held in high regard by others can experience an undercurrent of negative self-talk that undermines confidence. When we focus on performance, second-guessing, and pretense, we can't reveal our insecurities without betraying our self-image. Maybe we are getting away with something we don't deserve. We wear so many different hats/masks in order to perform different tasks—at work, on social media, and in social settings—that we can lose track of our authentic selves when self-esteem takes a back seat to externals.

There are many ways we adopt a false self that does not align with our core being. We can share only certain parts of ourselves with others — and with ourselves. We can cope with fears around this disconnect by learning to tolerate discomfort and accept imperfection.

6. **Pornography.** The porn industry sets up humans as objects to be used for pleasure and then thrown away. Pornography consumers learn to objectify humans. Women and girls really do get hurt. Alarmingly, the largest consumers of pornography are children from twelve to seventeen years of age who seek to understand emerging sexuality, but fall, instead, into addiction and unhealthy relationships. Even more alarmingly, there is more human slavery in the world now than ever before, and most of it is to service sex.[3] Secrecy surrounds pornography, which is mentally stressful and emotionally unhealthy.

People naturally sort each other into categories, just to make sense of the world. But when categories become stereotypes, filled with hand-me-down beliefs, fears, and other emotional baggage, we remain trapped in destructive patterns of disconnection, distrust, disrespect, and control. And when people *look* for differences, that's what they see.

Members of a winning family work to see themselves and others as dynamic, worthwhile, capable persons, not trapping others as objects of the roles they play.

I-It objectification causes pain and problems. I-Thou relationships move through pain and problems to the other side.

Alcohol and Substance Abuse; Addiction and Codependency

Alcoholism and drug addictions devastate families. In about 90 percent of child-abuse cases, alcohol is a significant factor.

Children of alcoholics are at the highest risk for physical, sexual, and emotional abuse; neglect; and other forms of violence and exploitation. When parents are drunk and/or high, they may do things they later regret. A sober adult should always be around when children are present. In addition to physical damage, children of alcoholics experience a wide range of psychological issues, including learning disabilities, eating disorders, compulsive achievement, depression, shame, and guilt.

Adult children of alcoholics often struggle with guilt, shame, control, trust, denial of feelings, and intimacy. They're far more likely to become alcoholics or marry one and to suffer from relationship problems. Everyone's self-esteem and mental health is damaged.

An estimated 28 million Americans are children of alcoholics. They learn certain attitudes and behavior to survive. The first rule of alcoholism is to deny there is a problem. *Don't talk. Don't trust. Don't feel.* These habits may help kids survive at home, but they prevent them from having healthy adult relationships. Addiction is a disease that infects everyone in the family.

Alcoholics Anonymous is a global support group that has expanded into others, such as Adult Children of Alcoholics (ACA), Al-Anon, and Alateen, as well as Narcotics Anonymous, Debtors Anonymous, Marijuana Anonymous, Crystal Meth Anonymous, and more. Their model has inspired thousands of recovery support groups for all kinds of addiction. Understanding the dynamics of addictive family systems helps adults learn to become loving parents to their own wounded inner child and prevents the disease from occurring in the next generation.

One ACA member in my workshop said, "Joining these meetings has been the single most helpful and supportive thing I've done in my adult life. For the first time I understand why, for the past thirty-six years, I haven't felt good about myself, why I'm a caretaker and a perfectionist. It's such a relief to be in a room full of people who accept me as I am, who understand from the inside out what it's like, and to realize that I'm not bad, crazy, or sick, that I'm not hopeless. I've learned that it's okay to take care of myself and to like myself."

AA members learn these three hard truths about alcoholism.

1. Alcoholism is the only disease that tries to convince you it is not a disease.
2. Alcoholism is a self-diagnosed and self-treated disease — only the alcoholic can identify it and choose a path of recovery.
3. Alcoholism cannot be cured or healed. It is called Alcohol*is*m not Alcohol*was*m. A drinking problem can always come back.[4]

So if your parents were alcoholic, you need to let go of blame and shame to begin your own recovery. In spite of messages they may have given you, you are not responsible for their problems. You are responsible for healing yourself and not passing damage on to your children.

Alcohol and recreational drugs, which are pervasive now, go hand in hand. Marijuana is cultivated to be stronger than ever, and kids try it younger than ever. With these factors and greater accessibility, we find more adverse reactions, including acute psychosis, most notably in first-time users.[5]

When used correctly, medicines help and heal, but prescription drugs can be deadly. While police warred against crack, pharmaceutical companies and doctors created national dependencies on stimulants, sleep medicines, and painkillers. The meth and opium epidemics have taken the lives of millions of parents and children. When I was a child, it was illegal to show alcohol consumed on TV, but the government deregulated control, and kids are bombarded with images of consumption. Alcohol became more, not less, accessible during the Covid-19 lockdown.

When there's addiction, there's codependency, a common, widespread, and painful dysfunctional psychological pattern. Barry and Janae Weinhold see codependency as responsible for most human misery. "Codependency is learned dysfunctional behavior and is the result of the failure to complete one or more of the important developmental tasks during early childhood," they say, and it occurs in most adult relationships.[6]

Major symptoms of codependency are

- low self-esteem,
- being a people pleaser and approval seeker,
- feeling like a martyr,
- having poorly defined psychological boundaries,
- seeking outside stimulation, such as alcohol, food, work, shopping, or sex, as a distraction from feelings,
- feeling addicted to and trapped in damaging relationships and powerless to change them, and
- being unable to express love and true intimacy.

Recovery from codependency means sifting through and unraveling what doesn't work and replacing it with what does. This can be done in therapy, in twelve-step meetings,[7] or with personal research and dedication to unlearning the "bad stuff" and relearning the "good stuff." We've discussed beliefs, self-talk, perfectionism, and boundaries in previous chapters. Revisit them if you need support, and reach out to find a group in which you can grow. You are not alone.[8]

Loneliness

"The truth is, you cannot love yourself unless you have been loved and are loved. The capacity to love cannot be built in isolation."
—Bruce Perry and Oprah Winfrey[9]

Human beings are hardwired for connection. Life's hard when we are, or feel, disconnected. We can be alone and not be lonely, or we can feel alone in a crowd. Loneliness is usually temporary, but it can become chronic. Loneliness is at the root of much diagnosed depression. Social distancing during the Covid-19 pandemic has painfully intensified collective loneliness, sometimes in ways that are hard to heal. Children and older people are especially affected.

Loneliness can cause many stress-related symptoms, such as

- getting sick a lot,
- gaining or losing weight,
- constant negative focus,
- social media or gaming addiction, and
- substance addiction.

Loneliness has many causes, such as

- depression,
- anxiety,
- mood disorders,
- neurodiversity,
- chronic illness,
- bereavement, and
- fear.

When something causes a child or adult to feel separate or different, be it a personal trauma or a pervasive negative thought, a lonely mood can interrupt close connections with friends and even attract bullies. Loneliness can cause low self-esteem and be caused by it.

When we don't have people in our lives who reflect our goodness and value, we feel isolated and alone. When we feel bad about ourselves, we have a harder time making and keeping friends. Western culture focuses on individual accomplishment and self-interest, encouraging us to get what we want and stand out from the crowd. Social media gives us new ways to be connected, but it can magnify differences and loneliness. It's hard to admit being lonely when everyone else seems connected — and we can also feel ashamed about it.

Healthy connections with people increase oxytocin (love hormone) and decrease cortisol (stress hormone). Just recognizing loneliness can give relief. Talk with children about it and brainstorm things that make us all feel connected. That can lead to action that fills each other's cups . . . and buckets!

Internal barriers may be worsened by external circumstances, and there are many external barriers that contribute to low self-esteem and dis-ease, as we shall see in the next chapter.

25.

External Barriers to Well-Being

"Owning our story and loving ourselves through that process is the bravest thing that we'll ever do."
— Brené Brown[1]

A famous study by Kaiser[2] found that Adverse Childhood Experiences (ACEs) such as being a victim of violence, witnessing violence, and having a family member in jail cause health problems later in life. Many external, societal experiences negatively affect self-esteem and are beyond our control, particularly when we are children. Below are several of these major barriers.

Poverty

In 1776, social philosopher Adam Smith suggested that poverty was "the ability to go about without shame," yet people who experience poverty struggle with shame and humiliation in ways those with means cannot know.[3] There is a double injury when your basic needs are not met and you feel humiliated because of it.

Any political party that passes laws that make the rich richer and the poor poorer adds injury to the economically challenged. Belittling speech and labels perpetuate the myth that poverty is the result of personal failure. When money is always tight, it's easier to buy into negative self-perceptions. It's difficult to better yourself when you are struggling to find self-confidence. A recent study shows that living in poverty can trigger serious mental health issues, including schizophrenia, depression, and substance abuse.[4] Impoverishment can also create a scarcity mindset that lasts a lifetime, perpetuating poverty issues and making it impossible to plan for the future.

To help fight the pain of poverty, there are things we can do other than vote for government policies that protect and help the poor. Contact between communities of different socioeconomic backgrounds helps humanize the experience of financial stress and build relationships, so churches and other organizations that provide food and material items are crucial. It's also important to engage in conversation. People on the street who ask for money need smiles and a chance to tell their stories. It's also good for them to hear stories that uplift their spirits.

Living without enough money is incredibly stressful. Under financial stress, it's especially important to guard against a pessimistic mindset (see chapter 21, "Monkey Talk"). Remember, thoughts are something you can change. Remind yourself that your hardship is temporary and it's not personal.

When talking to children, use protective statements.

- "Kids are just noticing, not teasing. They don't know better."
- "A lot of people are poor these days. It's normal, it's not their fault, and we hope it will change."
- "Let's count our blessings. What makes us happy that doesn't cost money?"
- "Let's savor the good things. That will help us get through each day."[5]

Savoring and gratitude are powerful. My paternal grandparents were poor, and yet between Grandma's chocolate cake and her laugh, we always felt rich when we were with them. They grew raspberries in the yard of their mobile home and took us fishing for bluegills in their beat-up old truck. At Christmas, Grandma put oranges and apples in our stockings and splurged on a jar of pickled herring, praising it as if it were the finest caviar. Grandpa wrote poetry and read it to us. But we didn't talk much about them at school.

In school, kids can be mean without meaning to be — for example, by pointing out when their peers wear the same clothes all the time. Teach your kids kind responses that feel supportive, positive, and empowering to friends in hardship.

One interesting thing about money is that it does not make us happy. Not having enough can surely make us suffer. And there's a measurable happiness boost when people go from having not enough to having about $10,000 extra per year to "play" with. But having much, much more than that does not measurably improve happiness.[6] There really is enough to go around.

Another interesting thing about poverty is that giving to others, even if you don't have enough for yourself, powerfully boosts happiness. My husband, who teaches at a school where most of the children need assistance, runs an after-school program that gives kids a chance to give back. Each semester, they pick a problem and work together toward a solution and then take action. Their small teams have collected toothbrushes and soap to give to people in halfway houses, helped animals, and cleaned neighborhood streets by picking up trash. Those kids get a self-esteem boost that lifts them into an empowerment mindset, and they do better in school.

Structural Inequality

Poverty has become worse in the past two decades. Laws protecting the middle class are weaker, and the economy has changed. It has long been the case that the wealthiest 10 percent of households have controlled over 50 percent of all wealth, but over the past twenty years, that's changed dramatically. According to recent research,[7] the top 10 percent now own 70 percent of all wealth, and now nearly a third of all wealth in the United States is owned by 1 percent of the people. Meanwhile, the bottom 50 percent of Americans control less than 2 percent of the nation's wealth, and over 70 percent of children in poverty are children of color.[8]

Money is not the only inequality hardwired into our country's laws. In spite of America's inspiring commitment in 1776 to create a country where "all men are created equal," it has yet to live up to this ideal. Native Americans were not seen as citizens or, in some cases, even as people. They still suffer inequalities.

It took nearly 150 years for women to win the vote in 1920, and the Equal Rights Amendment, introduced three years later, has never passed. Gender bias continues to create huge barriers for women, who still face violence, discrimination, and institutional blocks to equal participation in society. Although change is afoot, family leave in America is embarrassingly inadequate compared to that in all other countries. Women's basic needs are marketed as luxuries[9] and, in some cases, are considered "evil." Under structural sexism, divergence from the idea that women are on Earth to serve and please men is seen by patriarchal culture as deviant, if not criminal. Misogyny also makes life unsafe for gay and transgender people, who are made, worldwide, to feel as if they don't exist, or have a right to exist.

During World War II, Mom's German immigrant family was the target of suspicion and prejudice. Her uncle, a barber who spoke imperfect English, was assumed to be a Nazi by association. The misperception was typical in a time of war and fear, and being treated with prejudice was a threat to the entire family, frightening Mom and her siblings into silencing their accents, and even their voices, in public. At the same time, tens of thousands of Japanese Americans were rounded up and taken to concentration camps. Almost all ethnic groups, including many Europeans, have at one time or another been objectified and have suffered for it. Today's Muslim, Asian, and Latinx immigrants and longtime US citizens experience the same suspicion. During the first few years of the Covid-19 pandemic, Asians experienced a fresh wave of hatred.

White supremacy enforces inferior stereotypes on people who are red, black, brown, yellow, Jewish, disabled, female, gay, and trans. This is a thought problem that has shaped politics and culture worldwide, for many centuries. Stories from "minorities" are not taken seriously, and their needs are ignored or neglected, because they are seen as objects, not as worthy humans. Negative judgments are based on comparison to an "ideal" image of how an objectified group is supposed to behave according to stereotyped roles. Meanwhile, most white people suffer from a perfectionism they don't even realize. These assumptions lie outside of our awareness until they are challenged in some way and our blinders are removed.

In recent years, the general public has been coming out of denial around what black Americans have been protesting for centuries—that structural racism in our country is a continuing reality. After slavery ended, punitive Jim Crow laws kept white people separate and feeling superior until the Civil Rights amendment in 1964. Since then, discrimination has continued in subversive ways, criminalizing black people unequally. People of color are still kept separate from whites by real estate practices and banking laws. A practice known as "redlining" keeps them living literally on "the wrong side of the tracks" in all major cities.

Historically, all European immigrants have been lumped into the color (or absence of color) white. Even though life may have been a struggle for them, and even though they may have been discriminated against, society still gave them preference over nonwhites. No matter what their personal beliefs were, all white people of my grandparents' generation were encouraged by common speech and culture to hate and fear blacks. Even now, many immigrants of color are dismayed to be treated with an unexpected prejudice counter to America's legendary openness. Racism thrives in secret when lawmakers are appointed who uphold standards of white supremacy, when voting laws are manipulated to keep poor people of color from having a voice, and when political hate groups are supported by those in power.

What does it do to a person's self-esteem to be told they're not worthy of human rights—that they're not welcome in public spaces or protected by law because their skin color or the contents of their pants are incorrect? When racism and sexism are internalized, self-esteem plummets and negative self-talk creates a sense of inferiority.

Representation in media, in sports, and on the political stage is crucial for all minorities. Self-esteem can rise when racial or gender esteem rise. How can you do this in your family? Think of what your family and ancestors did to create good luck, good feelings, and connection. What have your people done, throughout time, to define themselves? What are the dreams that keep you going? Everyone who suffers from structural inequality can find strength in their stories and imagination and by using their voices to declare themselves worthy. Social structures change over time, and our generation is doing it. Those of us who are alive in this moment have many successful ancestors. Teach children their messages of strength: *You're important. You're loved. You're blessed.*

We need self-acceptance and self-respect to have healthy self-esteem. It's crucial that we give it to ourselves and to others. No matter what your race, ethnic origin, gender, or sexual preference, you are OKAY. You are the subject of your own story. To counter and heal destructive prejudice, affirm your own worth and that of others. Remember the Golden Rule: "Do unto others as you would have done unto you." This concept, shared by all world religions, teaches empathy and respect, which is I-Thou thinking.

Win-Lose and Dominance Thinking

In our book *The Bullying Antidote,* we teach parents to watch for and defuse what we call the bullying, or punishment, dynamic. This tired historical mindset can also be called the dominance model, or win-lose thinking. Riane Eisler, founder of the Center for Partnership Systems and the author of *The Chalice and the Blade,* observes, "The struggle for our future is . . . the struggle between those who cling to patterns of domination and those working for a more equitable partnership world."[10] In this model, we see things as opposites—black and white, rich and poor, crazy and sane, and heaven and hell, valuing one more than the other. This dualistic language affects our children. One woman related, "I did a dumb little thing, and my mother wiped me out with her words. Yelling that I 'blew it' and was 'so stupid' devastated me. I felt rejected, worthless, awful, and unlovable. Looking back, I realize that I wasn't a bad girl; I was a good girl who had made a dumb mistake."

The punishment model rejects the whole person, using punishment and shame as tools to keep power dynamics unbalanced. Comparison and competition are part of this system. Spirited competitiveness is considered a virtue that brings out the best in us, and we are hardwired to compete with others to better ourselves. But a winning-is-everything attitude in life and sports can devastate the self-esteem of everyone around you. In personal arenas, where rules are not clear or obvious, competition can make people suspicious and hostile toward others. Comparison creates separation. Competition creates a desire for dominance.

Structured competition, like sports, provides connection, teamwork, and life lessons in the context of fairness. If children are treated with dignity, encouragement, and support, being on the team can foster a sense of belonging, self-confidence, and fun. But coaches, teachers, and parents — with good intentions — may cause humiliation and frustration, anger and anxiety, and failure when they focus on domination. A sense of rejection can have lingering effects far beyond game season. How the game is played and coached should be more important than winning.

We need to expand our definition of winning. Best-selling author and success expert Stephen Covey observes, "As people really learn to think Win/Win, they can . . . transform unnecessarily competitive situations to cooperative ones." Like Eisler, he demonstrates again and again that partnership and interdependence are better systemic models. We can take the idea of winning even further, seeing each success build on the last and each win take a step toward greater happiness. Consider every success, accomplishment, achievement, and task crossed off a to-do list a win. When we notice our wins, our self-esteem soars and we do better, even without the concept of "personal best," competing against ourselves.

In your daily life, notice and be cautious about dominance culture. Seek out partnership culture. One of them cares about everyone's well-being.

There are many more external barriers to self-esteem: too many to list. But once you start to recognize them, they begin to lose their grip.

"Don't you ever let a soul in the world tell you that you can't be exactly who you are." – Lady Gaga

26.

Cultural Barriers to Wholeness

"One of the best decisions we can make is to reject the cultural expectations that shift and change with the wind. And to accept the fact that we don't need to run with the cool kids to be happy."
—Joshua Becker[1]

We've talked about internal barriers and external barriers to feeling your full self-worth. This chapter discusses barriers that come from both inside and outside — and are culturally considered "normal" behavior.

Avoidance

Everyone has pain and discomfort at times. Here are three common strategies for dealing with them.[2]

- **Denial.** On their honeymoon, my mom and dad agreed that, unlike other couples, they wouldn't have problems. Hahahahahaha. Their relationship — sweet at first, dysfunctional at the end — was based on denial and gunnysacking (withholding).

- **Distraction.** A movie, a phone call, or a change of scenery can provide a needed break from the intensity of life. But distraction can go from being a crutch to being an escape to being an addiction.

- **Drugs.** A glass of wine. A puff of smoke or steam. A pill. Drugs help us relax, cope with fatigue, socialize, and sleep. But often these rituals keep us from confronting and dealing with our problems.

Avoidance is a coping mechanism in which a person changes their behavior to avoid thinking about, feeling, or doing difficult things. Other forms of avoidance coping are procrastination, running away, changing the subject, and driving out of your way so that you don't have to think about a place or situation where you got hurt. Avoidance strategies can provide a brief vacation — time for regrouping or changing perspective — but ultimately cause more anxiety and stress than they relieve.

It takes more energy to avoid pain than to face it. When we avoid pain, we hold on to it. It becomes chronic. As long as we keep avoiding, we remain stuck in feelings of helplessness and numbness. Avoidance interrupts the process of healing. Sharing pain with others, as we do at funerals with close friends and family members and in therapy, creates opportunities to shift out of pain, give and receive support, and bond.

Unhappy people and families don't become happy by denying or avoiding reality and pretending. They become happy by talking, listening, negotiating, and making positive changes. They let go of self-defeating behavior that does not work.

Avoidance is also a cultural problem in families, communities, and even politics. We resist upsetting people, not wanting to create drama, so we don't address unacceptable behavior. Fear of rejection, dislike of confrontation, domination, alienation, and unresolved pain can contribute to a culture of avoidance. When we don't have assertiveness or listening skills and don't know how to use Non-Violent Communication (see chapter 18, "Problem Solving"), our relationships decay. Bad habits, like weeds, can take over the garden. As happens when we defer maintenance, our relationships can crumble.

Notice when you are part of an avoidant culture. Politicians use avoidance to control special interests. For example, directors at the Center for Disease Control avoided all research on gun violence for decades, fearing the center would be financially penalized by the NRA. In 2016, it was restricted from using words such as *vulnerable, evidence-based,* and *science-based* when discussing a global pandemic.

Malcolm Gladwell writes about how a culture of respect in an airplane cockpit prevented flight attendants and co-pilots from confronting a pilot who was making a bad decision: everyone died.[3] In hospitals, patients, families, nurses, and physicians tend to delay or defer conversations about end-of-life concerns until there's a crisis. Avoidance culture appears at individual, relational, and systemic levels. Addressing problems, differences, and power issues can be exhausting, but we need to lean into our strengths and strengthen our ability to communicate if we want to do better.

If you have a flat tire, you think about what you can do — it does not fix itself. In figuring out how to solve a problem, we *do* something, we *change* something, and we *learn* something. When the problem is resolved, the pain is gone, and we move along. When we grow through our struggles, we feel joy.

Toxic Speech

When I was young, foul language was rare and shocking. Now it's in music, movies, video games, and everyday speech. We are constantly exposed to offensive language, racial slurs, gender slurs, and aggressive speech. It leaks into our workplaces, friendships, and families. Toxic language is rarely studied in psychology or sociology, but anyone who has a negative work or family environment will agree it's a problem. When swearing feels normal, people more easily abuse each other and are defensive and contemptuous.

Few psychologists look at the connection between common language habits and mental and emotional health, but the ones who do notice a real problem in men's culture, where insults like "man up," "grow a pair," and "don't be such a girl" reinforce damaging toxic stereotypes. "Do yourself a favor," "get over yourself," and "f— that" may feel very natural to say, but they are examples of violent speech. Hard language often goes along with The Four Horsemen identified by the Gottman Institute for relationships: Criticism, Contempt, Defensiveness, and Stonewalling.[4]

In 1996, the speaker of the house, Newt Gingrich, released a memo with a list of words his party should start using to attack political opponents.[5] Trolling came next, when anonymous sources (many of whom were later discovered to be paid trolls and even bots) said and wrote the ugliest things to and about politicians. Ugly, aggressive language became common on all social media. Name-calling, lying, and expressing hurt through aggression have been normalized. Divisive language demonizes sections of the population. Some politicians and media still use toxic rhetoric that shows they believe certain people are more entitled to human rights than others and it's okay to do harm. In arenas that are supposed to uphold our highest values, this has become a serious problem that hurts kids. After the 2016 election, for example, bullying incidents on schoolyards rose sharply.

In *The Bullying Antidote*, we call this trend "casual cruelty." The problem with toxic language is that it's disorienting. It's easy to forget there are real people involved and that real people get hurt. Some industries have a culture of toxic speech that only allows the "toughest types" to participate. This creates barriers to minorities who get the brunt of the jokes.

Negativity lowers self-esteem. Negative talk comes from negative thoughts, which lead to negative feelings and negative behavior. It's no wonder so many people are struggling with poor mental health. When we see that toxic speech is a cultural problem, we can better protect ourselves and our families. Here are some tips.

- Often there are good intentions behind toxic speech. Look for them and restate them without slurs. For example, "I can see how much you care about children." Leave it at that.
- Listen to how your children talk about themselves.

243

Negative statements, such as "I'm so dumb" or "I never do anything right" let you know what they repeat over and over again to themselves. Point it out. "It sounds like you are really picking on yourself. Where did that come from?"

- Some parents start a swear jar and add a nickel anytime they get caught using bad words. Let your kids help clean up language in your family by holding each other accountable for negativity.
- Look for good qualities in yourself and in your kids. Ask them to tell you what they like about themselves, starting with an example. Help them see their special qualities and start thinking positively about themselves. Parents and teachers alike report that kids love doing this, and their self-esteem increases instantly.
- Establish a rule that every negative statement is to be countered with two positive statements. This will help you become aware of how you talk to yourself — and about others — and will flip focus to the positive.

When I realized my kids had a difficult time with toxic speech outside and inside their heads, I introduced the Twelfth Commandment: "Thou shalt not speak negatively of thyself or others."

Our Bodies Are Never Okay

Most women think that something is wrong with their bodies. They compare themselves to the current "perfect" body type, put themselves down, and feel bad. Like fashions, the ideal figure keeps shifting. Perfect body types go in and out of style — but our bodies are our bodies.

The cultural stereotype for women's bodies is not only damaging, it is also absurd. Jane Fonda discussed becoming bulimic in high school. "For several of us at my school," she writes, "it was the beginning of a nightmarish addiction that would undermine our lives for decades to come."[6] She and her

244

friends became obsessed with an external ideal, rather than concentrating on the person inside.

Especially after the stress of the pandemic, bulimia, anorexia, and other eating disorders have reached epidemic proportions. Obesity is also considered a global epidemic. All of these issues intersect with the cultural value that it is okay, and even desirable, to be obsessed with physical perfection. Men, women, and children have learned to hate their bodies and reject themselves.

Those who can afford it, spend billions worldwide on cosmetic surgery and procedures in an industry whose profits have increased tenfold since the emergence of social media.[7] These numbers suggest that the pursuit of perfection is not a personal problem, but rather a social issue. Physicians are alarmed by a new phenomenon called "Snapchat dysmorphia," in which patients bring heavily edited or filtered selfies as models. We need to ask ourselves if there aren't more important things to spend money on than the illusion of perfection.

People come in all sizes, all shapes, all colors, and we are all okay. Any cultural model is bound to be damaging and unhealthy if it becomes a requirement. Your body is not an object—it's *you*. Accept your body. Take good care of it. Love yourself just the way you are. If you do want to make changes, remember, *it's more important to be healthy than to be perfect*. Your body has much to teach you about self-compassion. You can't have high self-esteem unless you love all of yourself.

Materialism: Comfort Addiction

Just ten generations ago, on this land where I live, people like me were foraging for food every day, cooking outside. Even my grandparents could never have imagined doing what we can do now when we are sick: order soup on the Internet. We have created a world in which we can create, purchase, and realize nearly anything we can think of if we have a credit card. There's a new term today: *comfort addiction*.

"When we were kids," my aunts and uncles tell us, "we would

play outside all day." Now more and more children spend their days indoors using technology. "We would take the bus up to the lake in the winter to ice skate." That lake doesn't even freeze in the winter anymore. The world is literally changing beyond recognition, and we are all part of the problem. People know we have to stop ALL carbon emissions if our grandchildren are to survive, much less thrive; yet, we idle our cars while waiting at the curb to pick kids up from school.

For a century, we've become consumers of everything we can borrow money to buy. Our world is defined and shaped by materialism, and our lives are impacted by its challenges. In the last fifty years, houses and cars have tripled in size, but we still need storage facilities. We have holidays designed around increasing the number of our possessions.

Here are facts gathered by the website Becoming Minimalist.[8]
- 3.1 percent of the world's children live in the United States, but they own 40 percent of the toys consumed globally.
- The average American woman owns thirty outfits — one for every day of the month. In 1930, that figure was nine.
- The average American throws away sixty-five pounds of clothing per year.
- Nearly half of American households don't save any money.
- Our homes have more television sets than people. And those television sets are turned on for more than a third of the day — eight hours and fourteen minutes.

"Discomfort is internal, but its antidote is external," says Robert Biswas-Diener in his "Comfort Addiction" TEDx talk. We confuse comfort with happiness, and our economy is driven by our desire for comfort. Parents who try to give their children everything they want deprive them of the ability to discern wants from needs. A spoiled child cannot bear disappointment or discomfort; parents need to help them learn to cope with these very real feelings. In fact, their future depends on it. Efforts to slow down climate change have met resistance in the form of bigger cars, bigger houses, and more consumption. Whether it's because of human nature or the way our thoughts are programmed is unclear. Now our kids have to cope with the discomforts and real dangers of climate catastrophe.

In the big picture, how we treat the poor, how we treat minorities, and how we view all of our barriers to self-esteem have to do with maintaining our own personal comfort level. We need to challenge our beliefs around all of these things if we are to survive.

Cultural barriers affect our self-esteem and sense of wholeness, but we can work together over time to change them. With awareness comes choice. With awareness, you empower yourself to improve your own family culture. In my mom's childhood, it was common for parents to tell a kid to wash their mouth out with soap when they spoke profanity. Taken literally, that's abusive, but so is toxic language. There are better ways to create acceptable behavior and improve the family atmosphere.

Since this book was last published, researchers have developed psychological tests that measure self-esteem. Mental health is now seen on par with physical health. We have discovered that trauma is a US national health issue, and help is widely available (for example, right here in this book), which will stem its affect on further generations. Global and historical cultures offer inspiring and more-loving models than ones we know now. Measures of global well-being have been established, such as the United Nations annual report card on how kids are cared for in rich countries. Information is power. Paradoxically, our information-rich world creates many stumbling blocks to wholeness.

27.

Guidance in the Digital Age

"If parents don't shape kids, they will be shaped by outside forces that don't care what shape they are in." —Louise Hart[1]

In the previous edition of this book, this chapter was titled "Guidance in the Age of TV." When Mom and I planned a revision in the mid-2000s (which never happened), we were going to call it "Guidance in the Media Age." Even then, who could have predicted today's digital age, where smartphones, smartwatches, and even smart refrigerators are part of our everyday lives? When our kids are making content almost as much as consuming it? How could parents have known new forms of addiction would appear after they went out and bought toys, or that sharing photos could cause trouble and harm?

On a trip to Nepal, Mom visited a village at the edge of a jungle inhabited by rhinos, tigers, and wild boars. In the river were even crocodiles! Children growing up in an environment surrounded by imminent dangers learn very early how to avoid them. Everyone in the village knows that rhinos travel after dark, so young children (and tourists) are taught to stay off the path if they value their lives. Mom learned from the youngest children not only how to avoid rhinos, but also how to climb a tree—fast— when she heard one coming!

Every culture, whether rural or urban, has teachings transmitted from parent to child. Rhinos are a fantasy in developed countries, where kids all learn how to safely cross a street. But as rhinos, and many other species, are disappearing, new dangers take their place. In some ways, a parent's job is harder now, when everything in modern life seems so much safer. Kids don't expect danger. And there are no clear ways to label all the poisons that can damage kids emotionally, physically, and mentally.

Today's kids have never lived in an Internet-free world, yet much of what's available to them is brand new to their parents. This disconnect makes it hard for parents to guide and protect their children.

Parents assume that items sold in stores are safe, and they trust objects other parents purchase or allow in their home. Aside from game and movie ratings, the virtual world doesn't come with warning labels. In late 2021, the Office of the Surgeon General reported that young people have shown alarming increases in mental health challenges: one in three high school students and half of all female students reported persistent feelings of sadness or hopelessness. This is nearly twice what was reported a decade before, when mobile phones were not yet ubiquitous. The Covid-19 pandemic just made things worse.

"Young people are bombarded with messages through the media and popular culture that erode their sense of self-worth—telling them they are not good looking enough, popular enough, smart enough, or rich enough. . . . Progress on legitimate, and distressing, issues like climate change, income inequality, racial injustice, the opioid epidemic, and gun violence feels too slow."[2]

The digital world is affecting our kids. Here's how.

Devices and Diversions

Each form of media wants something different from us. TV wants us to sit still and watch. Social media wants us to check in constantly and interact. Email wants us to stay connected. Radio programs and podcasts want to be with us while we're doing things. Smart devices want to respond to our every desire. Books want us to be quiet and lose ourselves for a while. We need to be more aware of what else they ask of us, the users.

What's on TV

Because images are accepted as truth by children trying to understand how the world works, TV has a psychological impact. TV programs that show people managing emotions and life struggles in positive ways—talking about them with their friends, taking appropriate action, expressing love, and doing good for others—add to our sense of well-being and model good mental health. But TV holds dangers, as we have known since 1985.

- Watching TV promotes obesity.
- TV encourages the use of drugs, alcohol, and tobacco by glamorizing them.
- Unrealistic sexual relationships portrayed on TV contribute to the risk of teen pregnancy.
- Repeated exposure to TV violence can make children violent and make them accept real-life violence.[3]

The typical American watches four hours of television a day, or nine full years by the time they're sixty-five.[4] Do you watch more TV or less? Think of the role TV plays in your family. Is it a hearth? Is it a family activity or a family "passivity"? Is it a companion? Is it a lifeline? Is it a babysitter? What was your relationship to TV in your childhood? Has it changed for your kids? Parents need to be conscious and careful of the mesmerizing nature of TV and the messages it sends us. We need to be aware of how TV can be addictive, isolating, and influencing.

There's an App for That

Social media emerged the year I became a mom. Now I can hardly remember a world without my smartphone, aka everything device. There's a lot more for parents to keep track of, and devices seem to have more influence than we do.

Below are healthy device management tips.

- Make face-to-face people time the highest priority.
- Make gadget-free times and spaces.

- Create in-person "programming" centered on family connection (conversations, off-line games, touching, cooking, building, etc.).
- No screens in bedrooms.

Parents had enough challenges when TV was the only medium. Media is now ubiquitous and decentralized, and our generations have been guinea pigs for innovators and developers. We have to understand what we're part of.

Who Pays for the Media?

"Whoever controls the media, controls the mind."
—Jim Morrison

It's wonderful how free the world is now, with so many opportunities to learn, search for, and share information. But media isn't free of finance. Whenever we view programming, it's because someone has created a host platform: an outlet, a channel, an app, a website. Someone paid for it and needs to make money to stay in business. Selling media is kind of a free-for-all. The way business is done affects us.

- **Commercial Media** is owned by private companies that make money by selling advertising during the programming they pay for. Most media is commercial, and our kids are exposed to ads. This goes for TV, radio, and nearly all social media.
- **Public Media** is supported by local or national governments and protects kids from harmful advertising: or at least it used to. Those who believe in limited government have stripped public programming budgets, so we often see "sponsors," which are ads. Also, public media now relies on listener or viewer support.

- **Subscription Media** is supported by users, which makes for a more community-driven experience, or at least one with fewer ads.
- **Data Harvesting** is how many platforms make money. Whenever you engage in something that seems free, you are giving up your privacy. This happens in small and large ways. Small: If you like a post about fashion on social media, you will suddenly start seeing a lot of ads for fashion. Large: Data leaks and thefts can expose you to identity theft.

Commercials confuse us and prey on our self-esteem, blurring the distinction between real and artificially manufactured needs. Traveling to other countries points out the absurdity of our consumer mentality. We do not need high-definition screens; kids do not need designer tennis shoes. Our real needs are simple: food and shelter, safety, belonging, love, pleasure, respect, and self-esteem. All other needs are really only wants, desires, and wishes — or things we've been talked into thinking we must have. Historically, self-esteem started becoming a problem for people after lifestyle advertising was invented. Instead of just selling products, commercials sell images of *who* you can be.

Your kids are in the middle of a real fight out there. Media sees all viewers as consumers, even kids.

Consumer Values

When children look to television and social media to learn about life, what do they learn? They learn about nature, drama, pop culture, and social norms. Depending on the media they consume, kids also learn to be entertained, to use their thumbs, to get instant results, and to be in control at all times. They are also constantly guided to be consumers, to always be on the lookout for something to buy. Granted there are exceptions to every rule, but, overall, we are all conditioned by commercial media to believe that

- happiness comes from material possessions and external conditions,
- drugs will cure everything and are the only cure for physical problems,
- violence is a justifiable problem-solving behavior,
- neuroses are normal,
- dirt, smells, and calories are problems,
- sugar, salty foods, and alcohol are awesome, and
- nature is for driving on.

Watch prime-time TV some night with your kids and pay attention to the underlying messages about sex, alcohol, and violence. Write them down. Count the times a gun is fired, a glass of alcohol is poured, and a woman is hurt. Notice statements about and attacks on self-esteem and talk about them. Watch out for alcohol commercials during football season.

Media Violence

A 1986 report by the University of Pennsylvania's Annenberg School of Communication stated that the "family hour" on TV (which has the most child viewers) is, in fact, the "violence hour." Nearly nine out of every ten minutes of programming in the first hour of prime-time viewing contained violence, and there were eight violent incidents every hour.[5] By the mid 2010s, family hour was a thing of the past. Shows that weren't violent were full of vulgarity disguised as appropriate behavior. Inappropriate subjects and language create a sense of disgust and unease in people of different ages and cultures. There are still very few shows that a family can watch together. Almost all popular cartoon shows that appeal to adults contain vulgarity and adult themes.

Here are tips for coping with violent programming and ads.
- Create boundaries around violent media.
- Turn off violence when children are present.
- Make a rule to follow movie and game ratings.
- Research shows and games on Common Sense Media

before watching or playing them.

- Talk about how it feels to witness violence on a screen when you walk into a room. Find compromises.

Brand Loyalty

One aspect of advertising that really affects kids is religious loyalty to brand names. As soon as a child is exposed to commercial TV, they begin seeking brand connections. They will connect favorite characters to toys, and toys to food. They soon measure their own "coolness" by the brands they choose and link that to their self-worth.

Creative and imaginative play is crucial for healthy development. Research shows that commercialized play — playing out storylines from movies or video games, playing with licensed characters, and playing on ad-supported screens — can limit kids' imagination, creativity, and physical development.[6] Younger and younger kids are playing roles shown to them by media programming instead of imagining original ideas. Today's three- to five-year-olds behave like kids five years old and up when playing with action figures and dolls.[7]

Who's Watching You?

Before allowing children to open any sort of social media account, parents should watch the documentary *The Social Dilemma*. This film addresses much of what we discuss in this chapter and also gives a chilling behind-the-scenes look at how every user's information is tracked. What we like, how much time we spend, and who we connect with all add up to data designed for businesses to take advantage of us.

Blurry Boundaries

What's in one generation leaks into another, and what's in one home leaks into another. Kids get exposed to movies, games, and Internet programming when they play with each other. Anywhere there's a screen, there's a chance kids are being lured out of bounds by advertisers or are making their way into danger without knowing it. Pornography pushes into email accounts and innocent web searches. Exposure forces kids to grow up faster than they are ready to. When our young son started asking about how to erase browsing history, we wondered why and discovered that kids were accessing porn in a computer club at school without the teacher's knowledge. A sudden loss of innocence causes kids to feel divided, hide, and lie. When — or before — this happens, we have to be honest and teach kids about an industry that preys on young boys to make them consumers, as does all advertising. However, porn is much worse than cookies with trans fats. It disturbs normal sexual and relational development,[8] and what's worse, this product is made of human beings, many of whom are young boys and girls forced into slavery.

Slippery Slopes

Innovation precedes regulation. When someone invents something new, no one knows what to expect, and the outcome is an experiment on an unknowing society — often on our children. Entertainment is generally designed to provide pleasure, happiness, and moral guidance, but there are holes kids can fall into, sometimes with dire consequences.

There are many slippery slopes in the media and digital world, where seemingly innocent activities lead to trouble. For example:

- **More, more, more** is the most common slippery slope: it's not just needing more things, but needing more time.
- **The fuse leads to the bomb**, sometimes literally. Squirt guns and foam-dart guns were a big part of play in our house. But as my son grew from a child to a tween to a teen, he and his friends became exposed to more realistic toy weapons and first-person shooter games that actually sold weapons. During my son's childhood, military

spending doubled and mass shootings increased twelve-fold.

- **Radicalization** by watching videos online. A generation of young men, frustrated by the world's problems, has turned to videos that explain things, and they click links suggesting other videos. Soon their worldviews become less empathetic and more extremist.

Making Friends

Facebook has changed the definition of the word *friend*. A friend used to be a very meaningful person you felt particularly close to. You were lucky to have one, and a small group of friends could open the world.

Socializing online allows us to find people we relate to and can be a salvation for the lonely. By writing, we can become close to people we never meet and have friends around the globe. At twenty-four years old, my son is closely bonded with friends online that he met long ago playing Minecraft. The online world works for him because he has a capacity for closeness. He knows what friendship really means. When he was a kid, he always had someone to talk to in real life (IRL) about what was happening with his online relationships—me.

Without parental supervision, there is real danger to kids in the social media space. Kids are easily exposed to online predators and can fall prey to grooming and psychological abuse, addiction, withdrawal, anxiety, depression, online abuse, bullying, pervasive pornography, sexting, online pedophilia, and sexual predators.

A Facebook whistleblower testified that the company knows its products harm kids and does not focus enough on safety.

Parents need to observe, listen to, and monitor kids and help them discern what they are experiencing online. Show them how to check out a person, block profiles, and curate their social circle carefully. Teach them to ask themselves these guiding questions.

- Is this an appropriate friend for me?

- Is this a friend, an acquaintance, or a stranger?
- Does this person make me feel uncomfortable?
- Can I be myself with this person?
- Have I ever met this person in real life? Would I want to?

Emphasize the influence kids have in setting a tone in all social media. What kind of person do they want to be? What kinds of people do they want to have around them?

Making sure your kids are playing age-appropriate games and giving them a chance to talk about how their interactions make them feel will make them less vulnerable to bad actors and more aware of who they are and what they value.

Crushing Regrets

Even the most upstanding kids who want to do the right thing can be lured into immoral behavior by the gaming industry. Gaming microtransactions account for billions of dollars in legalized gambling, targeting children and low-income communities who become emotionally addicted. "I couldn't believe it, afterwards," my son confessed later about his sixteenth birthday. "I'd spent all of my birthday checks and savings on fake cars in a game that doesn't exist." Be ultra-vigilant if your children play Candy Crush, Roblox, Fifa Ultimate Team, or anything by EA. And be cautious about websites such as Internet Matters, which provides safety information, but also partners with game providers. Loot box monetization is so damaging to boundaries that it has been banned in several countries.

When Play Leads to Pain

*I think there should be regulations on social media to the degree
that it negatively affects the public good.* — Elon Musk

The digital world is designed with our pleasure in mind. The pleasure of having whatever we want, whenever we want it. The pleasure of being able to talk to anyone at any time. The pleasure of seeing things far beyond our immediate surroundings. The pleasures of learning, of connecting, of play. Because these things are seductive and kids crave them (as do adults), we need to carefully maintain a balance. A parent's voice is important in guiding kids away from pain.

Pain in Our Bodies

Constant use of devices causes repetitive strain injury, from painful thumbs to carpal tunnel syndrome. Adults spend over eleven hours a day interacting with media,[9] and kids are not far behind. We are increasingly affected by forward head posture (text neck, tech neck, nerd neck, iPosture, iHunch), a physical problem caused by bending over laptops, tablets, and smartphones. Every inch the head tips past the balance point over the neck adds ten pounds of strain to the neck and shoulders. Think protectively if you or your child needs to carry a heavy backpack. Many American children under the age of eight have their own tablets or similar products, and parents don't know if they are even safe. Our bodies are powered by electrochemical interactions, and electronic appliances create electromagnetic fields. Fetuses, babies, and children are more sensitive than adults to microwave radiation (MWR) given off by wireless devices, and safety information is outdated. Keep devices at least six inches from a child's face, and be sure all devices are in airplane mode when they (and you) sleep.[10]

Planetary Pain

The virtual world, even though it allows escape from discomforts, also creates problems.

- There are no media restrictions on advertising environmentally harmful products; in fact, car culture, meat products, fashion, appliances, plastic toys, and air travel all contribute to global warming.

258

- Corporations that advertise to children do not always have the best environmental or social practices.
- Nearly all tech uses electricity.
- All new products create waste.
- Kids own more toys than ever and are burdened by their own possessions, living in clutter and/or creating waste.
- Plastic toys and packaging clog our oceans and break down into microplastics that harm our bodily functions.
- With less time spent outside, children lose their connection with nature. Several clubs that used to promote outdoor activities for sport, like the National Rifle Association, have been warped by politics, and now focus on fear and violence rather than the need for food, responsibility, sportsmanship and companionship.

Mental and Emotional Pain

The problems we mention in regard to TV (addiction, isolation, influence) can be magnified by all technology. In fact, mental illness and suicide have become the greatest threats to school-aged children, more so than accidents and physical illness. Tech companies know this. In 2021, a Facebook executive leaked information proving that the tech giant (which now owns Instagram) knows it places kids in danger. In fact, the majority of tech leaders severely limit their own children's screen time to protect them. Meanwhile, the average child spends much more time on screens than on the playground.

Kids are exposed to media before they have a sense of self or discernment, which develops as the brain grows. Being asked to create a personal image causes kids to become people pleasers, easily manipulated and persuaded, living from the outside in with an external locus of control (see chapter 22, "Who's Pulling Your

Strings").

Governmental policies have forced educators to teach to test, making kids anxious to give the right answers rather than focus on internal, subjective learning, all at expense of mental and physical health and well-being.

The distorted self-image children get from their exposure to screens and, especially during the pandemic, fewer positive real-life activities has created a mental health crisis. The loss of playtime, imagination, and autonomy combined with the access teens and younger children have to shows, websites, and forums that show users how to commit suicide put kids in grave danger. One has to ask: why would kids want to die? Because they are trapped in their pain.

How can parents lessen the pain and guard the pleasures of play?

- Know what your kids play. Play games with them.
- Choose or encourage games that permit prosocial behaviors and creativity, such as free play and problem-solving, rather than competition, materialism, and violence.
- Talk to kids about who they attract and meet online. They are real people.
- When kids are exposed beyond their innocence (or caught using social media for bullying), talk to them about how it makes them feel. Then talk about how you feel and how other people involved might feel. Then ask how they feel again. Discuss the moral responsibility that comes with knowledge so that they can become protectors of younger, more vulnerable people.
- Turn off notifications for all but crucial apps. YOU are in charge of your attention. Turn off all notifications on children's devices. "Pings" make the device the boss of you.

- Talk to kids about cyberbullying, data harvesting, game subscriptions on credit cards, information sharing, good taste, and good online behavior.

An IRL Childhood

In the history of humankind, people have never been so connected and so disconnected!

Our lives are greatly enriched by digital technology. Learning, engaging, accounting, exercising, cooking, shopping, communicating, and playing will never be the same. But our relationship with computers takes up a lot of time and attention, and in many ways makes us more vulnerable. When our Internet goes down, when our computer gets a virus, when we experience a crash or failure, or when our identity is stolen, our lives are thrown out of balance for days, weeks, and sometimes even years. Often we don't know how to fix what is broken. Feeling stupid, dependent, and out of control, we lose track of our self-esteem.

When technology works, it brings us closer than ever to each other and the experiences we want. But kids and families, as well as close friends and relatives, need in-person, regular connections to build and keep strong bonds.

Human Values, Not Media Values

Children need guidance to help them handle their physical, emotional, spiritual, social, and sexual development. They need guidance to understand themselves and the world they live in. They need guidance to find media that support their tasks, not those that distract them.

Away from screens, kids spend more time using their hands, muscles, and imaginations to interact with people and participate in life.

Ask them questions about the content they watch. Challenge them to understand what they are watching. Ask them their opinions on the content of shows and commercials. "Do the girls you know really like toys like that?" "Is that the right thing to do?" "What do you think this is teaching you?" "Which shows make you feel smart?" Be especially protective around images of sexualization and racial stereotypes, since kids are taught sexism and racism from toddlerhood. Be critical of tropes like the one cute and giggly female in an otherwise all-male cast, the girl who is not happy until she's pretty, or dumb or passive female characters.[11] Knowing one's opinions and trusting one's judgments is a key part of high self-esteem.

Use your influence to shape good programming. Turn off radio stations that spoil your pop radio experience with vulgarity or violence while driving kids to school—and tweet about them to warn other parents. Call TV stations to express your opinions about their programming. Protest violence and praise good storytelling and ethical messaging. Use your consumer influence to communicate with advertisers and sponsors about programs that glorify guns. Request that your school principal establish strict guidelines about ratings on movies shown at school events. Join organizations such as Common Sense Media, Child-Friendly Initiative, and Fairplay and work with other parents.

Protect Your Data

How can parents monitor what's on all screens? If you are not able to adequately supervise your children's media consumption 100 percent of the time, which no parent can or wants to do, be sure you keep lines of communication open. You have a right to review kids' text threads, but be respectful of their growing need for privacy and increasing ability to exercise caution and good judgment.

Use spam filters to keep pornographic emails away from your screen. Learn to spot phishing and fraud. Change your passwords often, and keep a list of your children's passwords until they are paying for their own media. Err on the side of protection, and keep age-appropriate boundaries in mind—not just between yourself and your child, but also between them and all of the people they connect with. Be a good example to kids and talk about what you do to protect yourself, manage settings, and block intrusive content.

LIKE Yourself

Understand what it means to be a content creator. Get kids to think about what they want to put out there, what messages and feelings their content gives to other people, and what "Likes" mean to them. Sadly, social media can make money on a child's pain. Kids have committed suicide when their peers Like posts in which others are teased and bullied. Be very, very aware of how social media makes you and your kids feel. Likes can be addictive. But the pleasure rush we get from seeing outward approval is NOT self-esteem.

Having an open family dialogue about creating content can protect kids. One of the best things we can do as parents is teach kids to never, ever say anything on social media that is hurtful or that they wouldn't say in front of a person's face. We also need to guide them in what Liking really means. Check out Pat Palmer's classic book *Liking Myself*, a great resource for teaching kids how to understand and manage their feelings.[12]

Part of the Family

Our book *The Bullying Antidote* provides additional resources and guidelines for coping with the tsunami of technology that has crashed upon this generation of parents.[13] We discuss appropriate media for every age, from the time of early brain development (NO screens for the first two years) to legal age (kids must be thirteen years old to start a social media account). We also describe "netiquette" and provide more information about media addiction and protective tactics.

Seek professional help if you spot any of the following signs of media addiction:

- Preoccupation with online activities — always at the back of your mind.
- Needing increasing amounts of time online.

- Can't seem to control, cut back, or stop Internet use (feeling restless, moody, depressed, or irritable when attempting to do so).
- Staying online longer than intended.
- Significant relationships, jobs, and educational or career opportunities are compromised because of online activity.
- Lying to family members, therapists, or others to conceal the extent of involvement with the Internet.
- Going online to escape from problems or relieve a dysphoric mood (e.g., feelings of helplessness, guilt, anxiety, depression).[14]

Parents have the responsibility — and the power — to declare a digital detox whenever it's needed.

For the most part, our children's lives will be integrated with technology in ways we cannot even imagine. It's our job as parents to help them build a good relationship with it, one that allows them to be fully human and healthy and bring their best selves into the digital world. As for my mom, she loves telling stories of the Nepali forest, but she prefers to encounter her rhinos on the small screen!

28.

The Power (and Pleasure!) of Play

"Human beings need pleasure the way they need vitamins."
—Lionel Tiger

Mom and I once attended a kazoo concert—a "Kazoophony." The musicians played the "1813" Overture and *The Plight of the Kazoomblebee*.[1] "The kazoo," they said, "is to classical music what a total body cast is to ballet." We laughed for days afterward, appreciating the gift of silliness we'd been given. Mom bought kazoos for the whole family, and we reached for them whenever we needed a boost.

Play is a universal language and serious business for creating a healthy family culture. When we play, we give to one another a gift of joy and spontaneity. The thrill of being alive pervades the entire body when we play. Life is supposed to be fun!

When my brother and I were in grade school, Mom said, "Take me into your world, and show me what you see." Leaving her parent-self at home, she followed us along an irrigation ditch to the bridge where the troll lived. We stopped along a narrow path in front of a crooked tree, and told her where to plant her feet and squint her eyes. When she saw the Cat in the Hat in the trunk, she squealed with delight. She'd passed that way many times before, but she had never seen this very obvious, to our young eyes, figure. She never stopped talking about her initiation into our magical, mystical, and wonder-full world. That experience bridged our separate worlds of parent and child, and that memory delights her still.

Children are natural teachers, and we best learn from them when we meet them at their own level, when we enter their world. Kids help us remember how to play — how to break all the rules and write our own. A chair can be a fort or a fire engine; an adult can be the baby when kids play "house." We encouraged Mom to try new ways to play — like kicking a Hacky Sack and riding a skateboard — and she taught us hers, like playing hide-and-seek and jacks. We had epic squirt-gun fights and Nerf-gun wars. Through our children, we can see the world with fresh eyes, cut loose from stuffy adultness, be totally foolish — and get away with being unforgivably silly! We can reclaim forgotten parts of ourselves and rediscover the finer points of childhood.

Play is so important that there is even a museum dedicated to it, the Strong National Museum of Play. Recognizing how important play is to a child's development, Margaret Woodbury Strong, a collector of dolls and toys, founded a place where we can celebrate everything about it.[2] Play makes our bodies stronger, trains us for the unexpected, and is a universal common denominator that brings people together, even with animals. When kids are in play, they feel stronger, smarter, and bigger than they are in real life, and reflecting on it later brings deep growth and learning. To be human is to play.

Why do we love watching sports so much? Because sports are games. Basketball star Steph Curry is grateful for the fact that he doesn't work for a living: he plays for a living. There is magic in his movement because he lives on that genius edge of discovering new possibilities with confidence. This childlike quality allows a flow of energy and intelligence that creates an absolute sense of awe.

Kids are born with inner joy. Play is as natural to them as breathing. Mister Rogers liked to remind grown-ups that play is the work of childhood. Work is play until parents teach children that it's work — and only then do kids learn to resist it. They quickly pick up adult dualistic thinking: work is what you have to do and don't like, and play is what you love to do but don't have time for. Yet work can become play when adults change their attitude. Having a vegetable garden, for example, can be drudgery or pure joy. If we put fun back into our work, we will want to do it, and our kids will be more eager to join in.

Childhood is a time of phenomenal growth, aliveness, and discovery. Sadly, growing up can feel like the end of this amazing process. One young man observed, "Growing up in America is the process of growing numb." Many have come to associate growing up with a loss of excitement and their eagerness to learn. Playfulness has slowly disappeared from their lives. Yet this need not be a terminal condition. Ask a kid how to play, and you can recapture dormant parts of yourself, rekindling aliveness, spontaneity, and joy.

When we were young, Mom collected rhythm instruments — tambourines, claves, a guiro, a triangle, and hand drums. Periodically, we turned on lively music and we all became percussionists. Sometimes we put on hats (sometimes, making our own) to add to the fun and marched and paraded around the house. (Rhythm toys are great for adult parties, too. Mom made sure to give cymbals to the most reserved person in the room!) Mom put on a record of *Peter and the Wolf*, and we'd act it out. The living room was transformed into a meadow, and each of us played a character identified with instruments and themes. We argued over who got which parts, but there was always a "next time." It also built our appreciation for classical music.

If you aren't already playing with your kids, here are a few tips.

- Play needs to be fun for everyone. When you tease or tickle your kids, watch them; if it's not fun for them, stop doing it. Some parents toss a toddler into the air, saying, "What fun!" and continue even when the child starts to cry. If you're both not having fun, change the game. Kids may feel violated by well-meaning parents and older siblings who tease them too far.

- Play is best when everyone comes out winning. Playworks is a great source of noncompetitive games that involve everyone.[3] Tail of the Dragon, for example, involves a line of people, each holding onto the waist of the person in front of them. A kerchief (the tail) hangs from the back pocket of the last person, and the first person (the head) tries to catch it.

- When parents feel they have to beat their kids at a game, the kids are set up to lose. This isn't play: it's a power ploy and losers are victimized. It's okay for kids to lose a few rounds, but parents are bigger, older, and smarter than kids. They can win all the time if they want to. Kids who lose all the time become discouraged and don't want to play anymore because they know they will lose. Nobody likes to lose. The parent may win the game, but the relationship suffers, as does the child's attitude toward play. If your parents played with you in this way, remember how it felt. Did you ever shrug and say, "It doesn't matter," when, in fact, it did? That kind of play wasn't fair — and it wasn't fun. Try a new kind of game with your kids, or at least let them win sometimes.

- According to folk wisdom, a dirty kid is a happy kid. Telling your kid to "go out and play, but don't get dirty" sets a double standard and can lead to disappointment. Kids often get dirty when they're having a good time. Science tells us that touching sand and soil helps build a healthy immune system.

- Keep it simple. Use resources you have on hand. My son's favorite play on rainy days was with a flour-filled baking pan and a handful of toy cars.

He called it his "Snow Project" and spent hours engaged in imaginative activity.

Let Kids Show You How

Make play time a high priority in your family. Set aside a half-day to have fun together. Go for a walk or bike ride. Go to the museum or zoo. Play cards and games. Be silly with your kids *at least* once a day, and set time aside on weekends for pleasure. Put more spontaneity, silliness, and joy into your life.

Kids can teach you how to play. If you don't have any, borrow some! When you pick up your child from daycare, stop at a park to unwind and reconnect. Roll down a grassy hill, go down a slide, skip rope. Pretend. Children can help you make a fool of yourself, and it might be the best thing for you. When you laugh and play together, stress goes down and self-esteem goes up. Here's a secret: play is the antidote to perfectionism.

Kids are a great excuse to be silly. Alone, you might not spontaneously roll down a grassy hill, lest someone think you berserk, but if you take a kid along, no one will think twice. If they do, it will probably be, "How wonderful to see parents playing with their children."

Playing will develop your sense of humor, along with those of your kids. A regular dose of giggles and snorts does wonderful, even astonishing, things for your emotional and physical health and well-being. A sense of humor can be a saving grace in times of stress and a survival tool throughout life. When play is present, people feel safe and happy. When play is absent, they feel tense and insecure.

Laughter stimulates your immune system, relaxes you, and raises your guard against depression and pain. Exercise — running, dancing, hiking, swimming, and biking — is play, if you find the kind you like. People you play and laugh with easily become your friends. Play in a family increases health, happiness, and harmony. It creates bonds between people and enhances personal growth and self-esteem. Play is a gift that keeps giving, building a store of rich memories from which to draw and bonds that provide support in hard times.

Kids can fill up their time with lessons and activities. Make sure your child has time for Freewheeling, Imaginative Play. Old-fashioned play, where kids get together and make up their own rules, is crucial for development. Kids learn self-regulation and work out social interactions. In some schools, recess time was reduced to 15 minutes because kids started getting into conflict after that amount, but entering and resolving conflict so play can continue is a building block for social success. Free play allows for creativity and invention. I was in awe of the games my son and his friends invented, using tiles on the kitchen floor as a giant board game and all of his cars and action figures as players. They directed me to step on "safe" squares when I walked through the room. It was silly, but the word *silly* comes from ancient roots and means "happy," "prosperous," or "blessed." The ability to be silly (*sillability*?) and to allow silliness in your kids is a sign of aliveness: depressed children are not silly.

Playing outdoors in nature is most important. Sharing time in nature builds respect of and love for the Earth and easy bonding with friends and family. A walk in the woods reduces tension and stress and heals strained relationships, especially if you hold hands or play little games as you walk. It can also give children a deep sense of security — feeling connected as part of a grand plan. Mom loves telling the story of the time we were playing at the edge of a small lake, catching tadpoles. My younger brother came to her with a closed fist and wide-open eyes. His face lit up, and he said, "I can feel its heart!" The magic and mystery of that memory still thrills her.

Watching sunsets and rainbows creates a shared sense of amazement. Awe builds our capacity for positivity. Natural highs are an important key to substance abuse prevention and recovery. In the 1960s, people said, "When people are high on life, they don't need alcohol and drugs." Now they say, "When we stimulate and increase the brain's natural reserves of feel-good neurotransmitters like dopamine, we can avoid addiction."

The Family that Plays Together . . .

Family playtime increases closeness and positive feelings. Everyone relaxes and feels more alive. Love just happens when you're having fun together. Tape this cliché to your refrigerator: *The family that plays together stays together*. It's a cliché because it's true. Hikes, board games, jokes, tag, and music — win-win creative play has always been essential to our family's continued bonding. It didn't matter that we didn't have money when it came to creating a great experience. When my younger brother, Felix, was in high school, he couldn't afford a typical prom experience, but he saw this as an opportunity to be creative and make the day fun and memorable. He and his friend Jeff decided to cook dinner at Mom's apartment. Mom ironed her best tablecloth and borrowed a silver candelabra and serving pieces from a neighbor. My older brother, Damian, borrowed a Mercedes Benz from a college professor, decorated the interior with silk roses from Mom's bathroom, and dressed the part of chauffeur to pick up their dates. Exchanging cap for apron when everyone returned home, Damian became the waiter. When Felix snapped his fingers nonchalantly and called for wine, Damian, with a flourish, removed the wire champagne cap from a bottle of sparkling cider and unscrewed its metal cap, which everyone sniffed without cracking a smile. The boys had found frozen lobster tails on sale, and when Damian brought them to the table, he announced that the main dish was Giant Roly-Polies.[4]

Play is just absolutely crucial for family connection. Patty Wipfler, founder of Hand in Hand Parenting, suggests thumb-wrestling, arm-wrestling, hide-and-seek, and sock battles. She writes about indoor games, and games you can play when you're too tired to play, like "squish games" and comedy snoring.[5]

Using play is a great way to motivate kids. Here are a few examples.

- A TV show gave us the idea to do a "ten-second tidy"

271

before naptime. The kids picked up as many things as they could while I counted slowly to ten; it didn't matter who won!

- One mom told this story as an example of a tiny parenting victory: "I got my kids to pick up their own clothes by yelling, 'I'm cleaning up this mess because I love you!' Eventually kids began doing the same thing to each other. Less mess, more love!"[6]

- Wanting to teach my young son how to help me fold the laundry, I piled all the socks in front of him to pair and fold. He matched a couple, and when he figured out how to fold them, he proudly announced his "sock burrito"!

Play Fighting

Arguing in a playful way diffuses tension and builds verbal self-defense skills. Here's a famous dialogue held by my brothers in the back seat of the car.

Felix: "We really don't have any sibling rivalry; I just know I'm better."

Damian: "No. I'm better loved."

Felix: "Mom loves me best, though."

Damian: "Mom loves me best! She had me first."

Felix: "She didn't know what she was doing."

But beware — insults and teasing can be play if everyone is in on the game.

Play can even be used to address troubling behavior & conflict in a lighthearted way. I got this idea from a friend who's a big sports fan: Buy or make your own sports "penalty flags" (I use tissues, tape, and lollipops with the stick broken off, like little ghosts), and keep them handy. When things start getting out of control, toss one on the ground and call out sports-related misbehaviors such as, "excessive force," "delay of game," "false start," etc. It's a fun way to point out when someone in the family is being rough, dawdling, or needs a do-over — without shaming or blaming—and then "returning to play."[6]

One more reason play is magic sauce: games have clear rules that create fair competition and engagement. When someone goes out of bounds, action stops until things are sorted out. And consequences aren't terrible; there aren't spankings or screaming. You give up some ground to make things even.

Life is a burden to those who don't enjoy themselves. Other people are a burden to them, and they are even a burden to themselves. Enjoying ourselves is one of the greatest things we can do. Joy is contagious, so others will benefit, too.

Start to play today. Look for things that tickle your funny bone. Record or remember the really funny words and events of childhood (your own and your children's), so you can recycle the joy when you are all older. If you don't have that resource, watch comedy and jot down ideas. You deserve joy in your life. Claudia Black, a founder of the Adult Children of Alcoholics (ACA) movement, teaches *it's never too late to have a happy childhood!*

29.

Bodies and Brains

"If a seed is given good soil and plenty of water and sun, it doesn't have to try to unfold. It doesn't need self-confidence or self-discipline or perseverance. It just unfolds. As a matter of fact, it can't help unfolding." — Barbara Sher[1]

Like plants, human beings need optimal growing conditions in order to thrive. Humans — and all forms of life — have basic needs. Sunshine, water, nourishing food, and fresh air are fundamental to health. So are regular exercise, rest, and sleep. If these needs are not met, it's hard to function at our best. Raising healthy children is our most important work: Creating and sustaining a positive ecosystem — a home in which they can survive and thrive — is essential to our task as parents.

Many kids today are exposed to toxins their bodies can't process. Many more miss out on crucial ingredients for growth and development. These conditions can lead to a negative outlook, either conditional — low blood sugar, dehydration, and nutritional deficiencies — or structural — disease, disorders, and neurodiversity.

Food, Mood, and Being Rude

My son had a preschool friend who was a sweetheart but sometimes would act out and hit other kids. His mother confronted his behavior with time-outs. "If you hit, you must sit," she'd say, putting him in a chair to cool down while she took care of his latest victim. He was embarrassed and ashamed at his impulsive behavior. After one conflict she noticed that his ears were red, and a lightbulb went off — she remembered that she'd first noticed his ears turning red when he was a baby crying for food. She asked, "Andrew, are you hungry?" He nodded. Her insight helped Andrew understand his body's unique signal, and he learned to listen to his body's needs and keep everyone safe.

Nutrition plays a larger part than we realize in regulating mood. Many serious disorders are connected to vitamin deficiencies. There have even been studies linking criminal behavior to nutritional deficits.

Theoretically, we should be able to get all our nutrition from our diet, but our cultural staples both starve and poison us. Long ago, a person ate 40 to 50 grams of fiber per day — now we're lucky to get 15 grams. Before industrialization, a person ate about 16 grams of sugar a year — now an adult eats 16 grams a day, and teenagers eat 34 grams a day.[2]

The US topsoil is severely depleted because of commercial farming practices. Nearly all of our country's wheat and corn has been genetically modified to grow in spite of poor soil, so many of us are malnourished, no matter how much we eat. Pesticides that help plants to appear healthy sneak into the food chain and poison beneficial microbes in our digestive tracts.

Our bodies face more stress than ever before. Pollution, light pollution (which dysregulates sleep), sugar, dietary toxins, sunburn, and emotional distress cause oxidative stress in our tissues, which causes dis-ease and disease that can last a lifetime. A recent study showed that if kids ate one more serving of fruit (loaded with antioxidants) each day, we would see a major reduction in all types of illness.

Our bodies need macronutrients (fats, fiber, and protein) and micronutrients (vitamins, minerals, and antioxidants) in every meal and snack. Kids with ADHD or other spectrum issues may have genetics that affect how they process nutrients. Protein wakes up their brains in the morning, and healthy plant carbs with fiber help them self-regulate. Everyone needs water when they wake up in the morning as well as throughout the day.

Bad mood foods spike blood sugar and trigger inflammation, causing everything from grumpiness to brain fog to self-disgust.

Read labels and avoid processed foods with
- added sugar and white (refined) flour,
- food additives and food coloring,
- high-fructose corn syrup, and
- hydrogenated fats and oils (trans fats).

Good mood foods put us at ease in our body and allow cells to do their work without interference. These include
- whole vegetables, grains, and legumes,
- probiotics (fermented or cultured foods) and prebiotics (vegetables, fruits, seeds, nuts, and whole grains), and
- healthy fats (avocado, olive, and coconut oils), which are also crucial for brain function.

If you or your kids are being negative, look out for these.
- Dehydration—headaches, irritability, reduced physical and cognitive functioning can all be symptoms. A dehydrated teen is as dangerous as a drunken teen behind the wheel.
- White spots on fingernails can indicate a zinc deficiency, which can make kids irritable. Most protein foods (nuts, seeds, meat, dairy, eggs, beans, shellfish) are high in zinc. So is dark chocolate! Copper kettles and pipes can cause zinc deficiency.
- B-vitamins are called "stress vitamins," partly because they wash out of our system when we're stressed and partly because our nerves and blood vessels suffer stress when we lack them. *Yellow pee? There goes B. Clear pee? You need B!*
- Feeling tired; getting sick often; and having tummyaches, back pain, muscle pain, and/or headaches are all symptoms of needing more vitamin D, which we get from the sun. Be sure kids spend more time outside than on devices.

> Kids with dark skin need even more sun to get enough vitamin D.

- Shallow breathing or overbreathing. Taking breaths into your whole body, breathing through your nose, and having out-breaths that last longer than in-breaths change the brain's chemistry from a reactive state into a calm one.

Just as seeds lie dormant for a long time until the environment improves — sun shines, rain falls, rocks are cleared away — a kid's brain, with attendant emotional and mental health, can make a big turnaround when its physical and nutritional needs are met.

Sickness vs. Self-Esteem

Every primary caregiver discovers the hard way that they aren't "allowed" to get sick. When little people rely on us, we feel guilty when we need time in bed. And when kids are sick, our lives stop or slow down until they're better. Things that aren't our fault can feel like our fault, and being unable to keep up with life causes great anxiety and negativity.

Kids who deal with chronic sickness also have to cope with emotional pain. My friend Maria's daughter, who was diagnosed with rheumatoid arthritis, has always had to struggle against her anger and sadness. Her first-grade student Shawna has diabetes, which also triggers big feelings of anger and frustration. She uses a blow-up clown as a punching bag instead of hitting people.

When the body loses function, people have to become reliant on others, which can be embarrassing and discouraging. Medication can change the body, which brings comments and reactions from others. Mastery builds self-esteem, and when we can't engage on the basis of what we do, we feel defined by our illness. It's hard to like yourself when you don't like what your body is doing. It's really hard to express these vulnerable feelings to family members.[3] Parents, friends, and teachers can support sick kids by helping them find activities they can handle, feel challenged by, and master so that illness is not all-encompassing.

Sometimes an illness is mental, not physical. In fact, this book was inspired by a graduate course Mom took in abnormal psychology. She realized that every single mental illness had low self-esteem as a symptom. Low self-esteem is commonly found in people with anxiety, depression, panic disorder, eating disorders, and substance use disorders. In fact, one of the driving forces behind development of these types of mental illnesses can be low self-esteem.[4] All of these can be treated with counseling.

Healthy self-esteem can prevent and heal many mental illnesses. People with severe mental illness (schizophrenia, bipolar disorder, or major depression) can still have healthy self-esteem. Those who feel connected to their families, have meaningful work, and have positive social relationships prove that people can experience well-being even as they manage their disease.[5]

All Kinds of Minds

Mom always resisted what she saw as pathologizing kids. Although all of her children could have been diagnosed with ADHD (which I finally was in my forty-eighth year), she chose to see us as individuals and taught us strategies for coping with weaknesses and using strengths. ADHD is less stigmatized now than it was in the 1970s (as a physician, my father could never reveal his struggles with it for fear of losing his status and his job) and is accepted as a normal human variation that includes powerful gifts as well as challenges.

Kids with ADHD, Aspergers, and autism were categorized as disordered because they responded, reacted, and behaved differently from other kids. It's true that tendencies like avoiding eye contact, hyperfocusing, and having difficulty finding words can be seen as disabilities, but kids who are different typically have unusual talents and intelligences that can greatly benefit society.

Kids with neurological or psychological differences like ADHD, dyslexia, PTSD, Aspergers, and autism can struggle with shame, loneliness, negative self-talk, and reactivity, with or without the label of *disability* or *disordered*. They are considered weird by neurotypical children and teased and bullied for their differences. When I was a girl, I was a daydreamer, and in spite of my intelligence and talent (or because of it), I often felt misunderstood and dismissed. Like most girls, I learned to control my behavior and frame my ADHD difficulties as my being ditzy and dingy: I'm blonde, so I coped with that stereotype, as well. Even though Mom always highlighted my greatness, I've struggled with low self-esteem driven by my differences. Temple Grandin, agriculture innovator, autism activist, and professor, describes how her mind "thinks in pictures" and solves problems mechanically. "The world needs all kinds of minds," she said in her TED talk. Her statement inspired a book title and then an organization.[6] Now AKOM (All Kinds of Minds) has become a driving philosophy in efforts to create dignity for kids with Learning Differences (LD). In the work world, talents associated with cognitive diversity are becoming more valued than they were in the past, when the world needed workers who fit "inside the box."

Other normal human variations that can affect self-esteem include Highly Sensitive Persons (HSPs), introverts, extroverts, and those who are gender nonconforming.

Hurt Brains

Trauma also affects bodies and brains. It occurs after we've been shocked unexpectedly by something that lies outside of our normal experience. If we don't immediately release shock by talking about it, shaking, or shouting, says Gabor Maté in the documentary *The Wisdom of Trauma*, it can settle into trauma and change our brains, even causing ADHD, anxiety, and depression. Trauma, says psychiatrist Bessel van der Kolk, is a fact of life, and the traces of stress it leaves in our muscles affect our minds. He writes, "At least one-third of couples, globally, engage in physical violence. The number of kids who get abused and abandoned is just staggering. Domestic violence, staggering. Rapes, staggering.

Psychiatry is completely out to lunch and just doesn't see this."[6] But parents can see it. Parents are sometimes confronted with what seems to be past-life trauma, and they can help release it from a child's body.

Trauma rearranges areas of the brain dedicated to pleasure, engagement, control, and trust.[8] When a parent, teacher, or therapist is completely present with a child, they build healing mindfulness and connection by comforting them, teaching them, and playing with them (see chapter 19, "Touch Is Vital").

Adoptive parents especially need to understand the effects of trauma and not take it personally. Those who adopt babies rarely know their genetic tendencies, and those who adopt older children don't know the experiences they have missed. This can be true of children to which we give birth. Craniosacral therapy (CST), emotional freedom technique (EFT), and neuro-linguistic programming (NLP) are noninvasive therapies that soothe and sort out troubled nervous systems, and Chinese medicine designates places for emotion in the physical body. Always give traumatized kids space for creativity; we are born with the ability to heal ourselves.

All children, whatever their type or state of mind, need support to understand and appreciate their bodies and brains, which provide a lifetime of unfolding mystery. Life is about finding balance and learning how to nourish our personal needs. When we take care of our brains, our whole being feels better, and we can better connect with our hearts.

Our Literal Heart

What is the connection between brain and heart? Believe it or not, the heart sends more signals to the brain than the other way around. The heart is a sensory organ, like our eyes and our ears. It is not a metaphor; our heart is the literal seat of our emotional reality. Teach your kid to pay attention to their heart, and send it feelings of love.

Try this meditation for building positivity, from the HeartMath

Institute.[9] Place your hands over your heart and take slow deep breaths. You can even imagine breathing in from the crown of your head and the soles of your feet, and then breathing out through your heart. Think about a time that you were happy or about things that make you feel happy: holding hands and singing, cuddling a puppy, chasing waves with bare feet in the sand, laughing with friends, inspiring speeches, sentimental movies, or music that make you want to dance. As you exhale, imagine those peaceful, strong images going out to people around you, the beings in your life.

This prayer-like meditation creates a measurable energy field around you. Try it and see if you find that it helps others shift out of pain and into a higher consciousness of love, ease, and well-being.

30.

The Fractured Family

"All happy families are alike, but every unhappy family is unhappy in its own way." – Leo Tolstoy, *Anna Karenina*

We added this chapter after readers advised us that self-esteem struggles arise most frequently in divided families. Sooner or later, every family becomes divided in some way. By divorce or separation; by ideology or politics; by disease or death; by personality or perception; by pain or trauma. A resilient family that can work through anything adapts to and overcomes most or all of these divides. But when a family fractures, traditional relationships are disrupted, uncomfortable rifts become chasms, and ruptures may split off branches of the family tree.

Before the twentieth century, divorce was extremely rare, ending only 3 percent of marriages, but it has been destigmatized. Now, 50 percent of marriages end in divorce. As families destabilize, kids face significant losses: time with parents, economic and emotional security, and physical health. They also typically experience greater emotional distress.[1] Within the last fifty years, there have been enormous splits in families — physically and emotionally — the two often go hand in hand. Important natural family connections have been seriously weakened or severed. It is perhaps no coincidence that we see a rise in the number of immune-system-related illnesses. A strong and flexible family network is a metaphor for the body's natural ability to maintain its resistance to disease.

I found a journal entry from my teenage years, from a time when tension in my main home had built up to the disaster point.

282

My father wasn't blind to his kids' pain, but he didn't know how to handle his own, much less ours. To him, we just needed to be nicer to our stepmother. Once, when she took me aside and explained, "Actions have consequences," a voice in my head said to me, "The consequence of your yelling (verbal abuse) could be my moving out and never speaking to you again. It could be my brother killing himself." But I kept my mouth closed, nodded, and promised to do better. Pouring my pain onto a page felt much safer than sharing it out loud.

My father, who had lived in an orphanage for several years, imagined that his wife and he could form a *Brady Bunch–* or *Cheaper by the Dozen*–type family, in which the parents considered all the kids "their children." But while my stepmother lavished attention on her own three kids, she was unable to relate to my brothers and me. Only when I became a mom could I fully appreciate how she managed to put delicious food on the table, create a clever laundry system, and provide endless taxi service, but when we were children, my brothers and I felt like intruders in our own home. Decades later, after she and I had forged a peaceful and cooperative relationship, I was shocked to hear her still calling my brothers losers in the background of a phone call with Dad.

Throughout my life, I've seen friends, relatives, and kids in the community devastated by divorce, but I've also been inspired by people who figured out how to separate and regroup in functional, even positive, ways that not only minimized trauma, but enhanced the lives of their kids.

Low-Drama Divorce

Some parents are able to keep their kids' self-esteem intact during divorce by resolving conflicts without exposing their kids to pain. This is more likely when separation is managed through mediation rather than through litigation, which elevates stress levels and lowers coping mechanisms.[2] Mediation is a process that finds win-win scenarios, and after divorce, regular visits with a mediator (even if it's a family member) or a support group can continue to help struggling exes and new partners navigate new relationships as co-parents.

Divorce changes the way children with growing brains form beliefs, truths, and realities. To avoid deep damage, it's crucial that adults stay connected with kids in positive, supportive ways. Parents caught up in drama can take things out on kids, and even use their kids as leverage or weapons. Giving kids space to listen and process their struggles can help reduce their stress. Talking about books and films is an easy way to do this.[3]

There are low-stress ways to structure a family after divorce. When I was in college, I visited a friend, Mira, whose divorced parents lived in opposite wings of one house. They'd designed a way to have separate lives and a family space at the same time. I was astonished by their functional friendship. Our family friends Joe and Tami sold their home and got separate apartments in the same building so that their kids could easily go back and forth between them. Mom's friend Judith and her husband didn't divorce, but chose to live on opposite sides of the world — "because it's our marriage, and we can do it any way we want to!" Their children had interesting international experiences. And finally, when my aunt and uncle divorced, they bought houses next door to each other and shared the value that "everyone is welcome at every table." Each of these situations allowed kids to feel like they had homes where they could always feel safe. I wish my parents had been able to see options like this.

Parents who decrease divorce stress on their children play fair, with guidelines such as the following.

- Refuse to talk badly about the other parent. Kids will be in relationship with them all their lives.
- Focus on win-win scenarios, or kids may become victims.
- Stay focused on the needs of the kids. That will guide you in your actions.

- When you find yourself in a power struggle, stop and connect.

Blended and Bonus Families

Divorce can free grown-ups to find the love they really want and need. But moving away from bad relationships takes courage and strength, and mixing broken families requires stamina, skill, flexibility, and love. Stepparenting is rarely smooth, but it can be. My friend Stephanie gave her stepsons love without trying to mother them, and they grew strong bonds. Mommy blogger JM Randolph had to become the custodial stepparent to five little ones, who are now growing up and moving on.[4] But there are no guarantees. Terri, an artist I know, gave her stepdaughter all the love she could and was heartbroken to still be considered "wicked."

My stepfamily had its good days, even singing a song with our names in it that sounded like the *Brady Bunch* theme. We traveled around the country by train and had a few very happy years creating a team identity before negative feelings overwhelmed us. As time passed, the term *stepfamily* was culturally replaced by the term *blended family*, but families don't always blend. When they do — either by luck of personality or by a conscious commitment to positivity practices — love and appreciation expand exponentially. One writer who experienced this phenomenon came up with the term *bonus family*, which became a new way of looking at added family members. With this idea, a family is a flexible space where everyone can be celebrated and differences can be honored.[5]

Remixed families can be exceptionally complicated, especially with different brains, beliefs, and values moving among different homes and different realities. It's difficult for kids to "code-switch" between different parental cultures, especially if there are widely different emotional tones and rules.

Parent Combat

In many divided families, there is one parent who is critical and judgmental—and another one who reads books like this! One parent might be able to keep commitments, and the other breaks agreements. One might have a prohibition against bad-mouthing, yet gets their reputation smeared by the other. One may be only concerned about the physical well-being of a child, and the other is conscious of a child's mental and emotional health. When one parent is incarcerated for a crime or has untreated or undiagnosed mental illness, or when there has been violence between parents, staying in relationship can be especially difficult.

In all cases where parents are unable to function as a team, a child struggles with their divided sense of self.

When I read my teenage journals, I see that I couldn't figure out how to twist myself into what my dad and stepmom needed me to be. I desperately wanted to advise them that they would get better results if they worked with who I was, who my brothers were, and who all kids were. "Don't make chores the most critical and important factor in the household. Don't judge kids on their ability to do or be concerned about chores. Coach and help us without exerting power and forcing us to buckle under your iron will. Try to understand each child's needs, other obligations, physical capabilities, and attention span, and allow reasonable leeway for these considerations. If anger should arise, restrain yourself, and under no circumstances call your children names." I felt proud to be writing such sage advice, even though I was just a teen. I shared these words with my mom, and she heard them. (Who knows, perhaps I inspired her to write a book!) The lesson here is that kids have hidden gifts.

Here are approaches that help parents cope with divided families.

Manage Expectations

In my Brady Bunch family, the first few Christmases were fun. Each child got a gift from Santa, and we got each other little presents. I learned that putting aside stress and creating happy moments during holidays built positivity that lasted long after they were over. I learned that divorced-family Christmas could be twice the fun and learned to use the season to tap into my own generosity. Then one Christmas, presents I gave to others were opened one after another, until there were no more packages under the tree. Christmas was over, and I hadn't received a present. Neither had my brothers. Disappointed and hurt, we tried to make sense of what had just happened.

Looking back, I realize I had been warned. That summer, I wanted to live with my mom before going off to college, which felt threatening to my stepmother. She said, "If you leave this house, you will never receive an ounce of support from your father again, financially or emotionally." I knew she was wrong because my father and I were deeply bonded. I had expected traditions to overcome divisions, but I didn't realize she was in charge of them. Our dad didn't have the bandwidth to shop for our gifts.

Expectations are dashed all the time. Sometimes Mr. Right becomes Mr. Has To Be Right. Or the apple of your eye has a worm. But joking aside, parenting is all about being flexible. I became a headstrong woman. My friend Genet's bright baby became an autistic toddler. My neighbor Josiah became a grandparent when his daughter was still a child herself. My friends Will and Janette let me know before their son joined us at a restaurant that he had become their daughter. What do we do when life does not happen the way it's "supposed to" and people don't act the way we expect them to? We may not like it, but do we accept it? The answer forecasts the future of our relationships.

Changed plans force us to choose between the images we have in our head and the reality in which we live. This shift allows us to let go of rigid expectations and look deep into another person, seeing his, her, their, or xer capabilities, looking beyond differences that separate us to commonalities that connect us.

Everyone has good and bad days. It's a relief to realize that we don't have to be perfect. When the people in your life accept who you are, you can be authentic. You don't always have to be on top of things; you don't always have to be strong. Instead of creating a false self to please them, discover and become who you really are. When adults accept humanness (even the yucky parts), kids more easily accept theirs—and will reveal their true brilliant colors.

Accepting differences

Simply being different surprises us and gets us into trouble. Good manners in one family can be bad manners in another. I found out the hard way that the people skills my mom taught me made some of my in-laws uncomfortable. It took a while to find ways to communicate that worked for all of us. The following five love languages are a starting place for understanding how to accept and honor differences.[6]

- **Words of Affirmation** feel crucial to some and intrusive to others.
- **Acts of Service** feel kind to some and obsequious to others. Doing helpful things feels wonderful to some and unhelpful to others.
- **Giving and Receiving Gifts** feels special to some and like *more stuff* to others.
- **Quality Time** feels meaningful to some but boring to others.
- **Physical Touch** feels nourishing to some and irritating to others.

Which language feels most natural to you?

Accept others' differences. This is true in both divided families and connected families.

Managing Change

We all have basic needs that must be met so that we will feel safe and well. But when we are feeling emotionally uncomfortable in the face of change, it's not always obvious what those needs are. Doctor of neuroscience David Rock teaches businesses how to manage employees' needs when companies undergo mergers and moves. Understanding and adapting the SCARF model of social needs helps us give our children and teens what they need when families are changing.

- **S** is for STATUS. Make sure your kids feel important and know what their place is in each family in relation to other family members.
- **C** is for CERTAINTY. The more you can predict the future, the better you can help your kids anticipate upcoming changes.
- **A** is for AUTONOMY. Kids need a sense of control over events and need to feel like they have choices.
- **R** is for RELATEDNESS. Create opportunities to build a sense of safety and belonging in new groups.
- **F** is for FAIRNESS. If things aren't fair, emotions will flare.[7]

In a new group or environment, if any of these areas are murky, people will naturally to pull away from the situation. When they are clear, people will naturally lean in. Observe how your kids relate to peers, adults, and YOU, according to this model. To check in, simply ask, "Are you feeling uncertain?" and then explain the SCARF model to open up much-needed conversation.

Build Good Communication

Parents are the adults, and they have to rise up to all challenges during and after divorce, even when they are exasperated or feel animosity. The frustrating truth about divorce is that you have less influence and leverage over a partner than you did when you were married. When there is no longer a natural desire to communicate, parents still must commit to doing so for the sake of the kids. Effective proactive tools include **checklists, conflict resolution, mediation, daily check-ins**, and **calendars**.

When my son was in middle school, I created a family **checklist** of all the things we needed to talk about each week. We talked about work, family obligations, school events, deadlines, sports, playdates, and creative pursuits. I developed a new appreciation for parliamentary procedure when I saw how sitting around a table and having each person speak in turn made sure every voice was heard. (Our formal Monday meetings may actually have kept us from becoming a divided family!)

Even when there's conflict, you can have good communication. Our son learned **conflict resolution** in middle school. One time when we were arguing, he asked us to sit down with him, and he astonished us by guiding us, step-by-step, through an effective **mediation** session, which looked something like this:

1. Each "side" takes turns stating, as simply as possible, their feelings and desires.
2. The other "side" listens, and repeats back what they understood.
3. When both sides are understood, there can be discussion.
4. Stay focused on each person's stated needs and desires.
5. Brainstorm solutions without jumping into any one of them.
6. Use nonthreatening, respectful language, for example, "I wonder if you might consider . . ." instead of "You have to . . ."; or, "Would you be okay with . . ." instead of "I need you to. . . ."
7. Choose the solution that feels right to all.
8. Check for agreement.
9. Write down the agreement.

(See *feedback*, aka *no-fault communication*, in chapter 12, "How Parenting Responses Affect Self-Esteem.")

Just as important as weekly meetings are **daily check-ins** with partners and kids. These don't have to be lengthy, just long enough to let each other know you care about how they're feeling and how they're doing with items on the checklist. Even a text a day about nothing can keep you connected with teens and co-parents; knowing little things builds trust, and a baseline of daily connection makes it easier when things get challenging.

Finally, when used faithfully, shared **calendars** (like those online at Coparently, Cozi, and Google) make it easy to know who is where and what is needed. The calendar becomes "the boss" instead of one of the parents. 2Houses is a well-reviewed app that helps reduce tensions.

My brother Joe, who has a high-functioning co-parenting relationship with his son's mom, says they text every day about their son's school, health, and social life. "I have to bite my tongue sometimes," he says, to focus on the business of raising a healthy kid together. "I remind myself to stop and THINK."[8] THINK is an acronym for

- True – Is it true?
- Helpful – Is it helpful?
- Inspiring – Is it inspiring?
- Necessary – Is it necessary?
- Kind – Is it kind?

Some circumstances make communication particularly difficult to have a good relationship with a co-parent. If, for example, the partner has a narcissistic personality disorder, it can feel impossible. Jenny Penland, a blogger at Scary Mommy, says, "You cannot co-parent with a narcissist. No matter how hard you try, every attempt to 'be the bigger person' or 'kill 'em with kindness' will ultimately fail."[9] Narcissism is the opposite of empathy, and some people simply cannot stop controlling, intimidating, name-calling, blaming, denying the feelings of others, or denying reality. Some parents will consciously or unconsciously poison the other, encouraging the child to alienate the other parent. Nonetheless, you are still in relationship to them because you share kids, and you have to keep trying and work hard to take care of yourself. If you notice a pattern of DARVO (Deny, Attack, Reverse Victim and Offender), seek professional advice.

Find a New Unity

What I longed for most of all during the first few years after my parents were divorced was to be in the same room with both of them again and for things to *just feel normal*. Some children want this so much that they get hurt, or hurt themselves, to bring their focus back together. My friend Laurie was proactive. She lobbied both of her parents to stay married for a few years so that she could have a stable life. Amazingly, they listened, and she succeeded. The warring parents found a way to arrange their differences for those few years. When Laurie graduated from high school, the family went their own ways, with good will and admiration for their strong daughter.[10]

Divided families that are agreeable (if not comfortable) with each other for the sake of the family during holidays, graduations, weddings, and other life events are a huge gift to children. This isn't applicable for families divided because of abuse, of course. But parents who can safely get along for one night a month, or even one night a year, can give their developing children a sense of ancestral wholeness. A birthday, holiday, or visit to a relative or a favorite place can calm kids and create positive emotions that sustain relationships in hard times.

Joe (above), who has never been married to his son's mother, says, "You don't have to be a couple to be a family." It's easier to get along when you're clear on the fact that you don't want to be together anymore. But leaving a past relationship behind doesn't mean you can't keep the good parts. Don't throw the baby out with the proverbial bathwater—keep what is valuable. See the good in each other. You can keep extended family relationships that are nourishing, even when a family is officially divided. For example, even though my dad and his new family isolated her, Mom kept good relationships with her former in-laws. One night, a friend asked her where she was going. "My son's ex-girlfriend and I are going to dinner with my ex-husband's brother and his third wife and . . ." She couldn't finish the sentence—they were laughing too hard! Consciously, and lovingly, my mom helped us create good connections with our cousins and estranged grandparents, which helped us all feel like we belonged.

The Family Forest

Some family trees are more like big bushes or ivy vines or whole forests with birds that hop from branch to branch and roots that share nutrients. Families with separation and divorce, death and regrouping, arguments and differences are families just the same. The question is, can a divided family still be a winning family? Of course it can. Even if it's in parts and pieces.

When parents from a divorced couple can heal their wounds over time and become friends with each other, a child's extended family can grow in positive ways, with less pain and harm to all. Mom has a friend who was on such good terms with her ex-husband and his second wife that she became godmother to their two children! If there's love, things work out. Winning families are made of people who constantly work to see themselves and others as dynamic, worthwhile persons, and not as objects or the roles they play.

Joe says he is proud of the "scar tissue on his tongue" from biting back the things he doesn't say. There are conversations you don't need to have if you don't have a marriage. He decided to become choosier about the words he spoke and get clear on their common purpose: to be excellent partners as co-parents. They both take this job seriously, and my nephew has all his needs met and double the joy of many of his peers. This divided, but not fractured, family is still whole, expanding the idea of winning far beyond the nuclear explosion in which we grew up.

"God's dream is that you and I and all of us will realize that we are family, that we are made for togetherness, for goodness, and for compassion." — Desmond Tutu

31.

Extending Your Family

*"The bond that links your true family is not one of blood,
but of respect and joy in each other's life."*
– Richard Bach[1]

Familia, ohana, aiga lautele, mishpocha — every culture and
language values the concept of extended family. A family is
technically defined by genetic connections, but everyone who has
created one knows that a family, related or not, is actually defined
by love. There are many ways to extend your family and many
reasons to do so. "Joy shared is joy doubled; sorrow shared is half
sorrow." People who have ongoing significant contact with
children — childcare providers, babysitters, and neighbors — can
become part of an extended family network. They all play
important roles in children's lives and development, broadening
external resources and building internal resources. People who are
with us throughout our lives, or at crucial moments, have special
bonds.

In the previous chapter we mentioned bonus families. Let's
look more closely at intergenerational families, intentional
families, and school families.

Intergenerational Families

My mom grew up in an extended family in Detroit. Her
German immigrant parents met and married shortly before the
Great Depression. Her father's brother, Franz, lived with the
family for twenty years. Uncle Franz was a barber. As a child,
Mom sat on his lap and combed his hair. They walked hand-in-
hand to visit his friends. She learned much from him and
developed a loving bond. His caring presence in her family was a

key to her self-acceptance, self-esteem, and sense of self.

My father also grew up feeling vitally supported by his extended family. He lost his mother at a young age, so he conveyed to us kids the old-fashioned notion that families open their arms and doors to each other.

Representing only 22 percent of families, the nuclear family model, in which a mother, father, and children live under one roof, is not the norm, though it may appear to be. Families come in many models: single-parent families, blended families, families with more than two parents, extended families, and three-generational families. According to the *New World Encyclopedia*, "The three-generational family, including grandparents in addition to parents and children, provides the greatest support for the raising of children."[2]

Grandparents can be natural self-esteem developers. They give us long-range perspective on life and a connection to family history. They know about raising kids, often have time and energy to spend, and want to love and share. Helen, a seventy-six-year-old grandmother who attended Mom's workshop, worked in a nursery school. After her own six children were grown, she got involved working with other people's kids. She loved doing it, and knew she was needed. Her loving presence, depth of experience, and wisdom enriched the children's lives. Before I had kids, my mom practiced being "Grandma Lulu" with a friend of mine who had baby triplets and whose own mother lived far away. And when I had my son, Mom moved to California to be there for us all.

This was healing for me, because when I was a child, my paternal grandparents moved west to Colorado so that they could be near us. We had a happy caring connection until my stepmother banished them from our house and forbade us from seeing them, judging them a bad influence. After seven years, it was my mother who finally reunited us.

In the case of divorce, the vital grandparent-grandchild bond is often interrupted or damaged at a time when kids most desperately need support and stability. Throughout history, aunts, uncles, and grandparents have filled in during times of crisis until families recover, giving kids a familiar place to rest and center throughout turmoil. Sadly, some parents play keep-away during and after divorce proceedings. Divorce stems from problems between husband and wife; it need not create a major rift between families. Kids are not divorcing a parent, grandparents, aunts, uncles, and cousins. These are life bonds, and it's enriching and protective for kids to develop strong, caring bonds with all nonabusive adults. Extended family gives kids caught in the middle time (high-quality visits) and attention (letters and phone calls), good listening, and compassion during and after divorce.

Every year in the United States, around forty million people move from one place to another.[3] They uproot themselves for a variety of reasons. Many move great distances, leaving grandparents, friends, and neighbors behind. Some move to withdraw from painful dysfunctional families. Some move to pursue job or educational opportunities. After they transplant their families to new settings, they must start over from the beginning — re-creating important connections with others.

Intentional Families

Both of my parents were open-hearted and welcomed friendships. When I was three, we lived in Guatemala, and Mom and Dad brought back a teenager, Shenny, to help me and my brother after a new baby came. When I was six, Paul, a sixteen-year-old boy from the South, came to live with our nuclear family for a summer. Paul did yard work and played with us. We all enjoyed our extended family so much that we invited him back the following year. Today, despite miles that separate us, a loving bond connects us; Paul is part of our family. Another guest, Joe Wions, came to stay with us, adding yet another enriching friendship full of laughter that would last beyond his lifetime. Joe's kids and I later published his book, *More Time to Love*, about how he and his loving family turned his nightmare of ALS into miracles.

Mom and Dad's extended family modeling has been an inspiration. When I went to college, I was "adopted" by a family for whom I babysat and remained close to Anne and Reese until the end of their lives.[4] Even in high school, when things in my blended family were too hard to bear, I felt good about myself because my friends were like family to me. I married one, and others became godparents to my son. The human connection is more important than any particular family role.

A strong social support network is crucial to well-being and high self-esteem for children and parents alike. New varieties of extended families are becoming more widespread. Consciously or unconsciously, people are seeking out others to fill the void created by the absence of family members. Coworkers may become siblings or cousins. Neighbors may fill in as aunts, uncles, or grandparents. Families like ours are sharing their kids, spreading around responsibility, creating the support they need, and enriching their lives.

After creating a "surrogate family," workshop participant Kathy reflected, "Our biological families contain structured roles that can lock us into a track of behavior, much like a rollercoaster. As we grow and change, it becomes difficult to break away from these predefined roles. The surrogate family, by contrast, begins at the point at which we leave the biological one. There are few preconceived notions about each other, and we're allowed to be ourselves. We can interact without the fear of criticism or comparison. We can choose our extended family members."

And, of course, parents can be each other's biggest supports. Another participant, Nancy, told me, "I have a friend whose husband works nights, as does mine. We each have two children. One night a week I have her kids over for dinner and to spend the night, and the next week she takes mine. This gives the kids some quality playtime and gives us each a night off to spend some quality time alone." This time together also builds connections between all four children that enhances their lives, as well.

Many couples, with or without children, choose to have another person share their homes with them, creating the potential for deep bonds. Well-matched roommates can live together through thick and thin and become part of each other's lives long after they have gone their own ways. Women and men have long forged tight-knit bonds in social clubs and work teams, and today many also bond around sports, hobbies, and healing communities. Friends become family after deep experiences, long times, and spoken commitments.

We form connections outside the family similarly to how we form them inside: by building trust and connection. We form connections outside the family when there is a need that's not being met within it. Aristotle described friendships for mutual utility and friendships for mutual goodwill. He claimed that the hallmark of true friendship was a reciprocal interest in each other's highest good.

We all need many caring people in our lives. We need to reweave the web that connects us so that we have a safety net when we slip. We need to come together in ways that sustain and enrich us. When we extend our families, we expand our lives.

Educational Communities

When my son was three, we enrolled him in a cooperative preschool that was as educational for the parents as it was for the children. Having a community of other trusted parents who shared the same win-win philosophy of being compassionate and not controlling with our children set us on a good path. Even though he's an only child, my son had the experience of having three brothers from another family. (And I sometimes had the experience of having four children!) I never had to pay for babysitters.

After that experience, we knew what we were looking for in a grade school. We found one that had the same community feeling, where all the teachers felt like all the kids in the school were "their kids." Parents at the school liked working together and making a difference. The love shared as our kids grew, went their ways, and found each other again unfolded discovery, enrichment, and belonging. These are also experiences people have in religious communities that cherish children. There is a continuum between an extended family and having the support of a community.

As a parent volunteer, I had a close-up look at how different schools operated and how different teachers within schools created connection (or not) in their classes.[5] When school is a place where everyone feels safe and where everyone knows that their rights will be honored, emotional bonds flourish and learning soars. When parents work together to create enriching experiences for children, from simple potlucks to elaborate fundraisers that support classroom instruction, a feeling of family grows. There is often a gap between parents who have free time and those who don't, and between those who want to do service and those who need services. It takes some intentional effort to bring out the family feeling among parents at a school, but it's worth it. Be Strong Families provides simple conversation cards and safe-space guidelines for "Parent Cafés" that open authentic, meaningful conversations between parents of similar or different cultures. Building emotional safety helps parents from different worlds let down their guards and find things in common. If you can hire a translator, cross-cultural connections get even more profound.[6]

A So-Mo Toolbox

The ability to keep and maintain friendships is the number one marker of a deeply satisfying life. Children build this capacity in their school days through lots of practice and guidance.

My husband is a public schoolteacher whose elementary school serves a diverse culture of immigrants and low-income students. In his twenty-five-year career, he's been through some fourteen principals, so I've been able to see, objectively, what works well in terms of student and teacher well-being and what doesn't. The community has been at its best with a principal who sees the school body as an extended family of scholars.

In schools, social-emotional (so-mo) learning is just as important as — if not more important than — book learning. Thousands of tools and methods are available. One particularly creative concept comes from the Toolbox Project, which provides a set of cards printed with pictures of actual tools. Each physical tool represents a conceptual tool that helps kids build resilience, self-mastery, and empathy, "creating a world of kind, connected human beings." These brightly colored oval laminated cards are prominently displayed in classrooms, and sometimes teachers even wear them around their necks. When kids have trouble, they can reach for a card or a teacher can offer them the deck to help choose the one they need.[7]

The following simple so-mo tools (and their representative images) can build an extended family where no one has to lose.

- **Breathing Tool** (a tape measure)
  I calm myself and check-in.
- **Quiet/Safe Place Tool** (head phones)
  I remember my quiet/safe place.
- **Listening Tool** (air quotes)
- *I listen with my ears, eyes, and heart.*
- **Empathy Tool** (a level)
- *I care for others. I care for myself.*
- **Personal Space Tool** (yarn)
- *I have a right to my space and so do you.*
- **Using Our Words Tool** (a pencil)
- *I ask for what I want and need.*
- **Garbage Can Tool** (a garbage can)
- *I let the little things go.*
- **Taking Time Tool** (a watch)
- *I use time wisely.*
- **Please and Thank You Tool** (a key)
- *I treat others with kindness and appreciation.*
- **Apology and Forgiveness Tool** (glue)
- *I admit my mistakes and work to forgive yours.*

- **Patience Tool** (a plane)
- *I am strong enough to wait.*
- **Courage Tool** (a task light)
- *I have the courage to do the "right" thing.*

The Toolbox is a great gap-bridger for traditional dads who spend more time with tools than with kids. There are even hand motions for an upset kid to signal what tool they are using.

When you use all the positive parenting principles and skills in this book, there are no limits to the opportunities to create love and friendship between grandparents and grandchildren, stepparents and stepchildren, stepsiblings and half siblings, stepaunts and stepuncles, and chosen family.

Extending family sends care out into the world, for the sake of our children. The idea of *kinship*, sharing characteristics or origins, acknowledges our bonds with each other beyond even our extended family. *Mitakuye Oyasin*, a two-word Lakota prayer, expands love even further. It acknowledges oneness and harmony among all forms of life: people, animals, birds, insects, trees and other plants, and even rocks, rivers, mountains, and valleys. They are "all our relations." A kindred community can heal the wounds of modern life.

32.

When Everybody Wins

"When we try to pick out anything by itself, we find it hitched to everything else in the universe." —John Muir[1]

When my mom began her parenting journey, her intended family included two or three kids, a dad who worked, a mom who kept the house clean, a two-car garage, a dog, and a washing machine. "Before I had my first child," she wrote, "I never really looked forward in anticipation to the future. As I watched my son grow and learn, though, I began to imagine the world my children would live in. I thought of the children they would have, and their children. I felt connected to life before my time and beyond it. Children are our link to future generations that we will never know."

Your Family of Origin

What was your family environment as a child?

- Did you trust your parents, knowing that they would take care of your needs (food, shelter, acceptance, and love) and protect you from harm?
- Were you respected and loved just for being you?
- Did your parents realize that you were unique and special and make you feel that way?
- Did they believe in you and encourage you to be your best?
- Did you feel that your ideas and opinions were taken seriously?
- Were you encouraged to discover and explore your special talents and interests?

- Did your parents encourage you to do things for yourself, including solving your own problems?
- Did they set limits and allow freedom?
- Were you told that you could be and do anything you wanted? Were you given support and encouragement to do so?
- Did you know that when you got in over your head you could turn to them for help — without reproach?

If you answered yes to many of these questions, you were lucky. When children feel like winners in their own families, they are on the road to a successful life.

If you answered no, you have had to work on your self-esteem. If you are struggling with forgiveness, consider the idea that your parents, like you, have probably given more than they have received. Like you, they probably did the best they could at parenting, which is, as you know, the most difficult and challenging job of our lives.

In their childhood environment, perhaps no one saw their beauty or made them feel beautiful. Perhaps no one saw their hidden greatness and the important gifts they had for the world. Perhaps no one believed in them, supported them, or encouraged them to become winners.

Your parents made mistakes, and you will too. Feeling grateful for the good things they gave you can put you on the path to the forgiveness that can set you free. Ask those questions from your children's point of view, and give yourself a pat on the back for turning any of these old patterns around.

In our recovery and personal transformation book *Wings of Self-Esteem*, Mom and I explore how we are all born to win, but life teaches us to think of ourselves as losers. We are born as butterflies, but life teaches us to think we are caterpillars. We describe how to renourish ourselves with important emotional nutrients we may have lacked as children. When we fill our areas of deficiency and learn new skills, we all become late bloomers.

We can always grow, blossom, and bear fruit. It is never too late to become the beautiful, healthy, and happy person you were meant to be.

Our parents' generation made a lot of mistakes. As I write this, the world is scrambling to put the brakes on environmental destruction. Scientists all agree that we have passed a tipping point and that without a collective turnaround in the next eight years, there is little hope our great-grandchildren will survive. Yet we can feel the pull toward a more spiritual approach right now. Like never before, we need to become aware of our strengths.[2] A commitment to positivity and possibility can heal our broken pieces. We need to imagine our descendants living rich and meaningful lives. We need to prepare the way for them.

All Our Relations

"We did not inherit this land from our fathers. We are borrowing it from our children." – Amish saying

I remember the first Earth Day back in April 1970. My school-aged brother and I proudly filled several bags of litter from our picnic area. When we were a little older, we marched to end the Vietnam War, wearing sandwich boards that proclaimed, "War is a No-No." These experiences, and many like them, instilled in us a sense of power, of taking responsibility for creating safety, beauty, and peace in our world. Having a child myself opened my eyes wider, like it did my mom's, to the world my children would live in. In my lifetime, the environment has gone from stable to chaotic.

When I was a child, the idea of glaciers melting was terrifying science fiction. When I had a child, it all became real. From disposable diapers to Halloween costumes to school commutes, I was constantly aware of the choices I had as a parent to use resources responsibly and teach my son to do so as well.

We cannot fully respect ourselves or our children without fully respecting our Home. We cannot continue to make choices that are destructive to the environment any more that we can continue abusing our kids. We need to make the connection and find a new paradigm. We need to help our kids shape their beliefs about life on Earth as well as their beliefs about themselves. If we say, "The problems we face are so immense, whatever we do doesn't matter," we overwhelm them and talk ourselves into being helpless and hopeless. If, instead, we turn our focus to new models that bring greater harmony, we can channel our passion for life and build energy.

Naomi Klein, author of *The Shock Doctrine* and *This Changes Everything*, faces the hard truth that "our [extraction-centered] economy is at war with many forms of life on Earth, including human life."[3] Countries such as Bhutan and Costa Rica have shifted their priorities to putting well-being, including the well-being of children and grandchildren, ahead of corporate profits. New Zealand has done this by making Māori an official and constitutionally protected language, honoring tribal culture in every aspect of public life. Infant classes called *kōhanga reo* or "language nests," welcome children into the greater concept of *whānau*, "family," an example of the Evolved Nest idea of parenting in community.[4]

This decision to protect a native language supports Klein's revelation that the key to slowing and stopping systems of environmental destruction lies in centering indigenous people and their human rights. Hawaii public schools are another inspiring example of an inclusive approach. The state centers the concept of *Nā Hopena A'o (HĀ)*. *HĀ* means "breath," the sharing of life and love. This framework focuses on the strengths of belonging, responsibility, excellence, aloha (which means hello, goodbye, and I love you), total well-being, and Hawaiian culture. language and history. Author of *Teaching with Aloha*, Damian Nash, states, "Hawaiian values provide educators around the world with a beautiful model of social and emotional learning, centered on *aloha*, which encompasses all the facets of love that are appropriate in the classroom, and necessary for thriving learning communities."[5]

Solutions to environmental, economic, political, and social problems become clear when we link them to the well-being of children. Imagine a world where children have all their needs met and are not set up to fail.

Dinner-Table Democracy

The first known use of the term *self-esteem* was in 1619, the year the first New World legislature assembled in Jamestown, Virginia — also the time and place the first enslaved Africans arrived in what was to become the United States. Although slavery was common in democratic ancient Greece, ultimately, it would not hold up to the modern revival of democratic government. The foundational idea of democracy is that everyone is equal, and self-esteem lies at the core of human rights. Everyone deserves to see themselves as sovereign, worthy, and part of a greater good, and for others to see them as such.

If empathy is the ability to share someone else's feelings or experiences by imagining what it would be like to be in that person's situation, then its opposite is isolated self-centeredness. Living in a family or society where the idea of self-esteem is used to justify selfishness or self-centeredness rather than empathy creates imbalance and inequality. Apathy, misunderstanding, disdain, hatred, indifference, insensitivity, hostility, and unkindness create suffering and pain. In our book *The Bullying Antidote,* we play with the Esperanto word *zorgos* ("I will take care") as the opposite of bullying. We need to fill our kids with zorgos![6]

The work you do as a parent to guard and build everyone's self-esteem and equality goes beyond your family — it teaches skills of democracy. The path of empathy shows us that respecting ourselves means respecting the Self in others. It is a spiritual path that expands our sense of self to include what's best for all.

As you create a healthier emotional environment for your children, you create one for yourself. As you create one for yourself, you create it for your children. And as you co-create a family where everyone wins, you upshift all of humanity.

Can Home be a Utopia?

Utopia seems like a mythical paradise that, like heaven, is out of reach in the real world. But the Greek root of the word *eu-topos* means 'a good place.' *Eu* means good, or well, and in a home where a family is healthy, a family is well. We hope this book has give you a new perspective and vision on well-being in the family.

Although it seems that the world is full of those who care only about themselves, in the bigger picture we are learning to leave behind old patterns of blaming, shaming, judgment, and control. People are seeking ways to feel safer opening up to each other with curiosity, care, positive connection, and all the dimensions of love. When we have the skills to create calm, peace, and joy in our families, anything is possible, and everyone wins.

Appendix A

"WONDER WORDS"
Simple ways to brighten a kid's day

These words work best when spoken with sincerity + a pat on the back, a thumbs up, and/or a warm hug.

Wow! • Way to go • Super • You're special • Outstanding • Excellent • Great • Good for you • Pretty neat • Well done • Remarkable • I knew you could do it • I'm proud of you • Fantastic • Super star • Nice work • Looking good • You're on top of it • Beautiful • Now you're flying • You're catching on • Now you've got it • You're incredible • Bravo • You're fantastic • Hurray for you • You're on target • You're on your way • How nice • You're smart • Good job • That's incredible • Hot dog • Dynamite • You're beautiful • You're unique • Nothing can stop you now • Much better • Good for you • I like you • I like what you do • I'm impressed • You are clever • You're a winner • Remarkable job • Beautiful work • Spectacular • You're precious • You're darling • You're terrific • Atta boy • Atta girl • Congratulations • You've discovered the secret • You figured it out • Hip, hip, hurray! • I appreciate your help • You're getting better • Yeah! • Magnificent • Marvelous • Terrific • You're important • Phenomenal • You're sensational • Super work • You're very creative • You're a real trooper • You are fun • You did good • What an imagination • I like the way you listen • I like how you're growing • I enjoy you • You tried hard • You care • You are so thoughtful • Beautiful sharing • Outstanding performance • You're a good friend • I trust you • You're important • You mean a lot to me • That's correct • You're a joy • You're a treasure • You're wonderful • Awesome • A+ job • You did your best • You're a-ok • My buddy • You made my day • I'm glad you're my kid • Thanks for being you • I adore you • I cherish you • I love you!

Appendix B

CRITICISM VS. FEEDBACK

	CRITICISM	FEEDBACK
Based on	External pressure or force.	Internal motivation.
	I have the correct opinion, and you must do things my way.	I accept and value you and encourage you to find a better way.
Based on	You statements that are often global. "This is how you are."	I statements that are descriptive, specific, and limited to the issue at hand.
Underlying message	Focuses on the person: the whole person is blamed, labeled, put down, rejected. Orders and manipulates. Interactions charged with emotion.	Focuses on behavior. Gives specific information based on personal experience, delivered in a matter-of-fact, neutral manner.
Language	It feels like an attack. Arouses fear, self-protection, compliance, and/or defiance. Defensive response.	Well delivered, it feels like a gift. Arouses curiosity, self-reflection, and/or introspection and/or inspires an "aha," or lightbulb, moment. Creates closeness.
Strategies	Focuses on past events that cannot be changed, even drawing in situations from years ago. Feels hopeless.	Deals with the present and focuses on the future and what can be done to improve things. Builds hope.
Responses	Disempowerment, damaged relationship, low self-esteem.	Empowerment, enhanced relationship, high self-esteem.
Timeframe	Little, if any, concern for receiver's self-esteem or well-being. Respect may be lacking.	Based on respect for others. Concern about relationship and receiver's well-being and self-esteem.

Appendix C

LEADERSHIP STYLES

"You get to decide how to lead your family!"
— Hand in Hand Parenting

	Autocratic (Authoritarian)	Democratic (Authoritative)	Permissive
Characteristics of Parents:	• Reactive • Only one right way • Control thru fear and punishment. • Make all decisions/rules; demand compliance • Little flexibility • Demands strict obedience • "Respect" means fear • Children have no rights • Emotional needs not met • Children should be seen & not heard	• Proactive; warm & kind • Physical & emotional needs are met (both self and kids) • Has rules; some are negotiable • Not punitive; notice, comment on good behavior • See kids as worthwhile • Encourage kids to think, to be who they are • Responsibility & respect • Good communication	• Reactive • No rules, structure lacking • Too much freedom; chaos • "Whatever"… • Believe they have no rights • Absent (physically or emotionally) • Are overwhelmed, or simply not interested • Neglect
Feelings of Parents:	• Superior (one-up) • Burdened with responsibility • Afraid of environment • Lonely	• Loving & accepting • Considerate of others' feelings • Respect, trust & warmth • In charge, yet flexible • Positive emotions	• Confused and angry • Disrespected • Fear of losing children's love

Feelings of Children:	• Powerless, out of control • Frightened • Guilty • Hostile and angry • Dependent and submissive • Fear of losing parent's love • Bottled up feelings • Low self-esteem	• Loved, safe, • respected • Worthwhile, accepted • Self-confident, self-respecting • Trusting & trusted • Eager to cooperate • Feel connected • Gratitude • Joy	• Afraid, angry • Unsafe • Confused, discouraged • Dependent, rejected • Low self-esteem
Characteristics of Children:	• Compliant or defiant • Self-rejecting • Second-guessing common • Always feel one-down, even when grown • *Emotional needs not met • Lack a sense of personal responsibility	• Responsible • Self-discipline • Self-determining • Creative • Understand cause-effect relationships • Can be friends with parents later in life • Develop a moral compass	• Don't respect feelings of others • Think they have a right to do exactly as they wish • Little awareness of social responsibility • Have trouble with limits, yet hunger for them
OUTCOMES	• Lack of love; fear • Disconnection/loneliness • Don't trust; don't feel • Unsafe • Power struggles • Use of force, punishment • Bullying	• Trust. Respect. Love. • Warm connectedness • Positive emotions • Safety, security • Communication • Kindness; firmness • Cooperation • Character strengths appreciated • Well-being & high self-esteem	• Lack of love; fear • Disconnection/ loneliness • Don't trust • Unsafe • Neglect, chaos, confusion • Powerlessness • Bullying

Appendix D

100 SOURCES OF JOY

This list was written by my mother-mentor, Anne Fullerton, who welcomed me into the family as a nanny and showed her, up close, how a two-parent winning family model worked. Anne found joy in so many little things. Let her list inspire you!

raspberry picking • moonrise • sunrise • ocean • money in your pocket • root beer float • a good book • a verse that transports • snuggling with my pet • a hot bath • a playful time • playing tennis • doing yoga • smelling the woods after a rain • walking with my family • learning new words • seeing new icicles hanging from trees • favorite songs • tasting new things • being outside • splashing in mud puddles • a mountain lake • a work of art • raindrops on the roof • raindrop races on the window • a cozy bed • hot bread • a special memento • singing a smile • a thoughtful note • anticipation of a happy event • an unexpected package • my friends • a soft scarf • the wind in your hair • camping • a driving trip • different cultures • wandering through a new place • autumn colors • a row of ducklings • a swan • a fuzzy blanket • spotting a toadstool • wildflowers • violets • slapstick comedy • a fire in the fireplace • animal tracks in fresh snow • fresh seafood • veggies from the garden • an herb garden • shelling peas • picnics • tea time • finding a birds nest • sound of the surf • fresh squeezed • a homemade valentine • a ginger bread house • crosswords • rainbows • a shooting star • an eclipse • tidal pools • coffee ice cream • snow w/ hot maple syrup • a pumpkin patch • a hike in the mountains • riding a bike on a trail • jumping rope • playing catch • playing a windy day • decorating the Christmas Tree • first flowers of spring • snow on the trees • hot homemade cookies • a frozen waterfall • family member • a shared memory • dressing up • dancing • a kiss and a hug • knitting • bubbles • bookstores • fabric & yarn stores • an organized desk • a chalk drawing on the sidewalk • hopscotch • feeling the wind in your hair • tree lined streets • a beautifully set table • leftovers • wandering leaves • a dandelion puff • finding shade on a hot day • candles • crisp clean bed sheets • a squishy pillow • walking in the dark • popcorn • seeing a wild animal • a fresh peach • scent of freshly mowed grass fresh • a purring cat • old photos • shelling peas • finding something you lost

—Adapted from "Life is Full of Treasures" by Anne Fullerton

Appendix E

THE ANTEATER

Yes, that's pasta on the door...this is how we test to see if it's done in our play-based, imperfectionist kitchen!

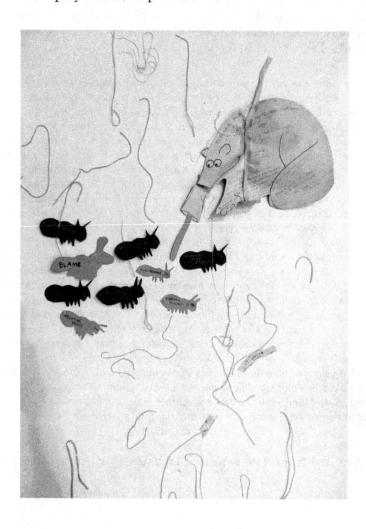

Notes

Preface – By Dr. Louise Hart

1. "Best Countries for Raising Kids," US News and World Report, https://www.usnews.com/news/best-countries/best-countries-to-raise-a-family.

2. US Surgeon General Vivek Murthy, NPR, Dec. 7, 2021 (Protecting Youth Mental Health: the US Surgeon General's Advisory, https://www.hhs.gov/sites/default/files/surgeon-general-youth-mental-health-advisory.pdf)

3. Cat Wise and Jaywon Choe, "Childhood Trauma Impacts Millions of Americans, and It's Having Devastating Consequences," PBS News Hour, December 14, 2020, https://www.pbs.org/newshour/show/childhood-trauma-impacts-millions-of-americans-and-its-having-devastating-consequences.

4. Centers for Disease Control and Prevention, "Creating Positive Childhood Experiences," CDC, https://www.cdc.gov/injury/features/prevent-child-abuse/index.html.

Chapter 1 - The Idea of Winning

1. Stated frequently on his 1984-85 Born in the USA Tour.

2. Kate Hefferon and Ilona Boniwell, *Positive Psychology: Theory, Research, and Applications* (Maidenhead: Open University Press, 2011).

3. Learn more and get your ACEs score here: "What ACEs/PCEs Do You Have?," at *ACES Too High News* (blog), https://acestoohigh.com/got-your-ace-score/.

Chapter 2 - You Are Creating a Masterpiece

1. From Louise Hart's workshop brochure *Building Self-Esteem in Children*.

Chapter 3 - The Greatest Gift: Self-Esteem

1. *Merriam-Webster Dictionary*, s.v. "self-esteem," www.merriam-

webster.com/dictionary/self-esteem.

2. This and other comments on children with special needs added with thanks to speech language pathologist Dawn Larson.

Chapter 4 - Building Self-Esteem

1. From a lecture by adult and child psychiatrist Foster Cline, Evergreen, CO, 1976.

2. Bruce D. Perry and Oprah Winfrey, *What Happened to You? · Conversations on Trauma, Resilience, and Healing* (New York: Flatiron Books, 2021).

3. Read more about attunement in Gabor Maté's *In the Realm of the Hungry Ghosts: Close Encounters with Addiction*, in which Maté states, "Attunement is a subtle process. It is deeply instinctive and is easily subverted when the parent is stressed, depressed, or distracted. A parent can be fully attached to the infant, and in love, but not attuned. The infants of distressed parents experience severe psychological stress not because they are not loved, but because their parents are not attuned with them. Attunement is likely to be lacking if parents missed out on it in their own childhoods" (Berkeley, CA: North Atlantic Books, 2010). *See also* Gabor Maté, *Scattered: How Attention Deficit Disorder Originates and What You Can Do About It* (New York: Plume, 2000).

4. Henry David Thoreau, *Walden* (1882).

5. Dorothy Corkille Briggs, *Building Self-Esteem in Children* (Garden City, NY: Doubleday, Dolphin Books, 1975).

6. Claudia Black, *It Will Never Happen to Me* (Denver: M.A.C. Publications, 1982).

7. Expanded from Briggs, *Building Self-Esteem in Children*.

Chapter 5 - Self-Esteem Protection Skills

1. Eleanor Roosevelt, *This Is My Story* (New York: Harper and Brothers, 1937).

2. Affirmation from Jack Canfield, *Self-Esteem: The Key to Success* (Self-Esteem Seminars, 17156 Palisades Circle, Pacific Palisades, CA 90272), six cassette tapes.

3. Rodolfo Mendoza-Denton, *The Unfair Self-Esteem Trap Faced by Minority Students*, at *Psychology Today* (blog), www.psychologytoday.com/us/blog/are-we-born-racist/201205/the-unfair-self-esteem-trap-faced-minority-students.

Chapter 6 - "I Know They Love Me, But I Don't Feel It."

1. Elizabeth Gilbert, Committed: A Skeptic Makes Peace with Marriage (New York: Viking, 2010).

2. Shere Hite, The Hite Report on Male Sexuality (New York: Alfred A. Knopf, 1981).

3. Gretchen Livingston and Kim Parker, "8 Facts about American Dads," at Pew Research Center, June 12, 2019, www.pewresearch.org/fact-tank/2019/06/12/fathers-day-facts/.

4. Mildred Newman, Bernard Berkowitz, and Jean Owen, How to Be Your Own Best Friend (New York: Random House, 1973).

5. Leo F. Buscaglia, Living, Loving, and Learning (Thorofare, NJ: Slack, 1982). Used by permission.

Chapter 7 - Listening Skills

1. Julie Rigg and Julie Copeland, Coming Out! Women's Voices, Women's Lives (Melbourne, Australia: Nelson, 1985).

2. No Bully restorative justice training in Oakland, California. Learn more about this excellent school program at www.nobully.org.

3. Parent Effectiveness Training (PET) teaches listening skills based on Rogerian counseling principles.

4. Leo F. Buscaglia, Loving Each Other (Thorofare, NJ: Slack, 1984).

5. Denise Olesky, "The Gift of Listening Develops Your Sense of Self," GoodTherapy (blog).

Chapter 8 - Asking and Refusal Skills

1. Pat Palmer, The Mouse, the Monster, and Me: Assertiveness for Young People (Oakland, CA: Uplift Press, 2011).

2. Adapted from Palmer, The Mouse, the Monster, and Me.

3. "Saying 'no' means . . ." and "the value of 'no' " exercises from

Claudia Black, It Will Never Happen to Me (Denver: M.A.C. Publications, 1982).

4. We recommended I Said No! A Kid-to-Kid Guide to Keeping Private Parts Private, by Kimberly King, Zack King, et al. (Weaverville, CA: Boulden Publishing, 2020).

Chapter 9 - Dealing with Feelings

1. Dr. Ani Liggett's book is for grown women leaving home. Endings... Beginnings. (Boulder" Be Me, 2009)

2. Dorothy Corkille Briggs, Building Self-Esteem in Children (Garden City, NY: Doubleday, Dolphin Books, 1975).

3. Claudia Black, It Will Never Happen to Me (Denver: M.A.C. Publications, 1982).

4. Laurel Hameon, teacher, Australia, 1992.

5. Louise Erdrich, "The Years of My Birth," New Yorker, January 2, 2011, www.newyorker.com/fiction/features/2011/01/10/110110fi_fiction_erdrich.

6. American Heritage Dictionary, s.v. "guilt" and "shame" (New York: Dell, 1976).

7. Per Dawn Larson. See also Enhancing Self-Esteem (Muncie, IN: Accelerated Development Inc., 1989).

8. Philip Oliver-Diaz and Patricia A. O'Gorman, 12 Steps to Self-Parenting: For Adult Children of Alcoholics (Deerfield Beach, FL: Health Communications, 1988).

9. John W. James and Frank Cherry, The Grief Recovery Handbook: A Step-by-Step Program for Moving Beyond (New York: Harper and Row, 1989).

10. "Helping Children Cope with Grief," Child Mind Institute, https://childmind.org/guide/helping-children-cope-grief/.

11. Leo F. Buscaglia, Loving Each Other (Thorofare, NJ: Slack, 1984).

12. Concept from Jack Canfield, Self-Esteem: The Key to Success (Self-Esteem Seminars, 17156 Palisades Circle, Pacific Palisades, CA 90272), six cassette tapes.

13. Based on the insights of Barbara DeAngelis and John Gray, the

"Love Letter Technique" recognizes that anger is "the tip of the iceberg" and maps out the emotions beneath it: sadness, hurt, fear, and responsibility/accountability, plus love, wants, needs, and desires.

14. Matthew Fox, Meditations with Meister Eckhart (Santa Fe: Bear, 1983).

15. Nancy Davis Kho, The Thank-You Project: Cultivating Happiness One Letter of Gratitude at a Time (Philadelphia: Running Press, 2019).

Chapter 10 - Coping Skills for Stress

1. Concept attributed to Hans Selye.

2. WholeHearted School Counseling (instagram), www.instagram.com/wholeheartedschoolcounseling.

3. Gabor Maté in The Wisdom of Trauma, producer-directors Zaya and Maurizio Benazzo (film), https://thewisdomoftrauma.com/about-the-film/.

4. Kellita Maloof (aka The Showgirl Shaman), I K(no)W (one-woman show), https://vimeo.com/316019772.

5. Jean Illsley Clarke, author of Self-Esteem: A Family Affair (Minneapolis: Winston Press, 1978).

Chapter 11 - The Power of Words

1. Matthew Fox, *Original Blessing* (Santa Fe: Bear, 1983).

2. Adapted from Jean Illsley Clarke, Self-Esteem: A Family Affair (Minneapolis: Winston Press, 1978).

3. Clarke, Self-Esteem.

4. Melissa L. Kamins and Carol S. Dweck, "Person versus Process Praise and Criticism: Implications for Contingent Self-Worth and Coping," *Developmental Psychology* 35, no. 3 (1999): 834–47. *See also* Carol S. Dweck, "The Perils and Promises of Praise," in *Best of Educational Leadership 2007–2008* 65 (Summer 2008): 34–39.

5. Thomas Gordon, Parent Effectiveness Training: The "No-Lose" Program for Raising Responsible Children (New York: P. H. Wyden, 1973).

6. *See* Daniel Amen and Brendan Kearney, *Captain Snout and the Super Power Questions: Don't Let the ANTs Steal Your Happiness* (Zonderkids, 2017).

Chapter 12 - Parenting Responses that Affect Self-Esteem

1. Adapted from Jean Illsley Clarke, *Self-Esteem: A Family Affair* (Minneapolis: Winston Press, 1978).

2. Robert Ricker, *Love Me When I'm Most Unlovable* (Reston, VA: National Association of Secondary School Principals).

Chapter 13 - Parents Are Leaders: Re-Visioning Your Family

1. Albert Schweitzer, in Edward F. Murphy, 2,715 One-Liner Quotations for Speakers, Writers, and Raconteurs (New York: Crown, 1981).

Chapter 14 - Parenting Leadership Styles

1. Marilyn French, *Beyond Power: On Women, Men, and Morals* (New York: Ballantine Books, 1985).

Chapter 15 - Parenting and Empowerment

1. Kaleel Jamison, *The Nibble Theory and the Kernel of Power* (New York: Paulist Press, 1984).

2. Riane Eisler, *The Chalice and the Blade: Our History, Our Future* (New York: HarperOne, 2011).

3. Naomi Klein, The Shock Doctrine: The Rise of Disaster Capitalism (London: Picador, 2008).

4. Mary Fran Gilleran, "Blowing the Whistle on Oppression," Kindred Spirits Newsletter (Detroit), 6, no. 3 (January/February 1988).

5. The Peace Alliance, Statistics of Violence and Peacebuilding in the US and Worldwide, https://peacealliance.org/tools-education/statistics-on-violence/.

6. National Bureau of Economic Research, "Does Child Abuse Cause Crime?," The Digest, no. 1 (January 2007), www.nber.org/digest/jan07/does-child-abuse-cause-crime.

7. "Most Violent Countries 2022," World Population Review, https://worldpopulationreview.com/country-rankings/most-violent-countries.

8. Anthony V. Bouza, "The Epidemic of Family Violence," Surgeon General's Workshop on Violence and Public Health (Washington, DC: US Department of Health and Human Services, May 1986).

9. Paula Gunn Allen, "Connecting with the Source," Creation 2, no. 6 (January/February 1987).

10. Child-Friendly Initiative was a group of San Francisco moms led by Michele Mason, a birth educator. Chapters around the country who provided guidelines for businesses to be more welcoming to moms with little ones. Their work inspired the United Nations in establishing the idea of Child-Friendly Cities, and is the reason restaurants have crayons on the tables and airports have nursing stations.

11. T. Berry Brazelton quoted in Chicago Tribune Tempo, October 21, 1988.

12. Jennifer Liu, "The U.S. Moved up in This Year's World Happiness Ranking—Here's Where It Ranks Now," CNBC Make It, March 19, 2022, www.cnbc.com/2022/03/19/world-happiness-ranking-2022-where-the-united-states-ranks-now.html.

Chapter 16 - Family Boundaries

1. Faith G. Harper, *Unfuck Your Boundaries: Build Better Relationships through Consent, Communication, and Expressing Your Needs* (Portland: Microcosm, 2020).

Chapter 17 - Discipline Without Damage

1. Attributed to seventeenth-century poet Samuel Butler, who paraphrased Proverbs 13:24: "Whoever spares the rod hates their children, but the one who loves their children is careful to discipline them."

2. Stacey Patton, *Spare the Kids: Why Whupping Children Won't Save Black America* (Boston: Beacon Press: 2017).

3. H. S. Glenn and B. J. Wagner, *Developing Capable People*, instructor's manual. Privately printed (n.d.).

4. Adapted from Donald Dinkmeyer and Gary D. McKay, *The Parent's Handbook: Systematic Training for Effective Parenting* (Circle Pines, MN: American Guidance Service, 1982).

5. Kenneth Blanchard and Spencer Johnson, *The One Minute Manager* (New York: Berkley Books, 1981).

Chapter 18 - Problem Solving

1. Jo Coudert, *Advice from a Failure* (New York: Stein and Day, 1965).

2. Gail Murphy, Director, Peter Pan Cooperative Nursery School.

3. Jesse Jackson, from a speech to Denver Public Schools Push/Excel Program, August 1979.

4. Richard Bach, Illusions: The Adventures of a Reluctant Messiah (New York: Delacorte Press, 1977).

Chapter 19 - Touch is Vital

1. Felix, Louise's son, at age thirteen.

2. James W. Prescott, "Body Pleasure and the Origins of Violence," The Futurist, April 1975, 63–74.

3. Natalie A. Cherrix, " 'Good Touch, Bad Touch' May Send Confusing Message to Children about Sexual Abuse," www.hollyshouse.org/uploads/3/2/0/9/32090669/notgoodbadtouch.pdf.

4. Linda Tschirhart Sanford, The Silent Children: A Parent's Guide to the Prevention of Child Sexual Abuse (Garden City, NY: Anchor Press, Doubleday, 1980).

5. Kimberly King, *I Said No! A Kid-to-Kid Guide to Keeping Private Parts Private* (Kimberly King Books), www.kimberlykingbooks.com/.

6. Cherrix, " 'Good Touch, Bad Touch.' "

7. Pam Leo, *Connection Parenting: Parenting Through Connection Instead of Coercion, Through Love Instead of Fear* (Deadwood, OR: Wyatt-Mackenzie Publishing, 2007).

8. Jules Older, "A Restoring Touch for Abusing Families," *The International Journal of Child Abuse and Neglect* 5, no. 4 (1981). Exercise devised by occupational therapist Franceska Banga.

9. Exercise adapted by Martha Belknap in *Stress Relief for Kids: Taming Your Dragons* (Duluth, MN: Whole Person Associates, 2006).

10. Learn more about using acupressure in the classroom or at home in Paul E. Dennison and Gail E. Dennison, *Brain Gym: Simple Activities for Whole Brain Learning* (Edu Kinesthetics, 1992).

Chapter 20 - Beliefs & Believing

1. Docuseries: *The Me You Can't See* – Prince Harry with Oprah Winfrey, https://www.themeyoucantsee.info/

Chapter 21 - Monkey Talk

1. Sy Safransky, *Sunbeams: A Book of Quotations* (Berkeley, CA: North Atlantic Books, 1990).

2. Daniel G. Amen, *Change Your Brain, Change Your Life: The Breakthrough Program for Conquering Anxiety, Depression, Obsessiveness, Anger, and Impulsiveness* (Crown, 1998).

3. Upward spiral is a cornerstone of positive psychology. To find out more, *see* Louise Hart and Kristen Caven, *The Bullying Antidote* (Center City, MN: Hazelden, 2013), or go straight to the source with Sonja Lyubomirsky, *The How of Happiness: A New Approach to Getting the Life You Want* (New York: Penguin, 2008).

4. Carol S. Dweck, *Mindset: The New Psychology of Success* (New York: Ballantine, 2007).

5. Adapted from Matthew McKay, Martha Davis, and Patrick Fanning, *Thoughts and Feelings: The Art of Cognitive Stress Intervention* (Oakland, CA: New Harbinger Publications, 1981).

6. *The Little Engine That Could* is an American folktale told in many forms by many authors. The book widely known in the United States is by Watty Piper, aka Arnold Munk, illustrated by Lois Lenski and first published by Platt and Munk in 1930.

7. Learn more about the science of self-talk in Martin E. P. Seligman, *Learned Optimism: How to Change Your Mind and Your Life* (New York: Vintage Books, 2006).

Chapter 22 - Who's Pulling Your Strings?

1. Charles Norman, *The Magic-Maker: E. E. Cummings* (New York:

Macmillan, 1958).

2. Attributed to Albert Ellis, an American psychologist and psychotherapist who founded rational emotive behavior therapy (REBT). Ellis also famously created the term "Musterbation."

3. Bernie Siegel, *Love, Medicine, and Miracles: Lessons Learned about Self-Healing from a Surgeon's Experience with Exceptional Patients* (New York: Harper and Row, 1986).

4. Joseph L. Wions, *More Time to Love: One Father's Extraordinary Journal of Living Longer with ALS* (Oakland, CA: Uplift Press, 2016).

5. Martin E. P. Seligman, *Learned Optimism: How to Change Your Mind and Your Life* (New York: Vintage Books, 2006). *See also* Seligman's books *Authentic Happiness* and *Flourish.*

6. Marilyn Ferguson, *The Aquarian Conspiracy: Personal and Social Transformation in the 1980s* (Los Angeles: J. P. Tarcher, 1980).

7. Joseph Campbell, *The Power of Myth* (New York: Doubleday, 1988).

Chapter 23 - Obsession With Perfection

1. Sy Safransky, *Sunbeams: A Book of Quotations* (Berkeley, CA: North Atlantic Books, 1990).

2. Ruthann Richter, "Among Teens, Sleep Deprivation an Epidemic," Stanford Medicine, October 8, 2015, https://med.stanford.edu/news/all-news/2015/10/among-teens-sleep-deprivation-an-epidemic.html.

3. The Center for Disease Control states that eighteen hours of being awake is the equivalent of having a blood alcohol content of two drinks in an hour (.05 percent). "Drowsy Driving," CDC, March 21, 2017, https://www.cdc.gov/sleep/about_sleep /drowsy_driving.html.

4. Diane Frey and C. Jesse Carlock, *Enhancing Self Esteem*, 2nd ed. (Muncie, IN: Accelerated Development, 1989), 365.

5. William Dodson, "How ADHD Ignites Rejection Sensitive Dysphoria," ADDitude, July 11, 2022, https://www.additudemag.com/rejection-sensitive-dysphoria-and-adhd/.

6. Sonja Lyubomirsky and Lee Ross, "Hedonic Consequences of Social

Comparison: A Contrast of Happy and Unhappy People," *Journal of Personality and Social Psychology* 73, no. 6 (1997), http://drsonja.net/wp-content/themes/drsonja/papers/LR1997.pdf.

Chapter 24 - Internal Barriers to Self-Esteem

1. Gloria Steinem, "A New Egalitarian Life Style," New York Times, August 26, 1971.

2. Jessica Cerretani, "The Contagion of Happiness," *Harvard Medicine*, Summer 2011, https://hms.harvard.edu/magazine/science-emotion/contagion-happiness.

3. US Department of State, *Trafficking in Persons Report 2012*, https://2009-2017.state.gov/j/tip/rls/tiprpt/2012/index.htm. *See also* "Slavery Still Exists?," The World Counts.

4. From a conversation with "David G," 2022.

5. Ruby S. Grewal and Tony P. George, "Cannibis-Induced Psychosis: A Review," *Psychiatric Times* 34, no. 7 (July 14, 2017), www.psychiatrictimes.com/view/cannabis-induced-psychosis-review. According to Juliann Garey, hallucinations while high are an indication kids may be prone to psychosis: "Marijuana and Psychosis," Child Mind Institute, https://childmind.org/article/marijuana-and-psychosis/.

6. Barry K. Weinhold and Janae B. Weinhold, Breaking Free of the Co-Dependency Trap (Walpole, NH: Stillpoint, 1989).

7. Co-Dependents Anonymous (CoDA; coda.org) is for anyone wishing to have healthy relationships.

8. For more support, read our recovery book, *Wings of Self-Esteem* (Uplift Press, 2023)

9. Bruce D. Perry and Oprah Winfrey, *What Happened to You? Conversations on Trauma, Resilience, and Healing* (New York: Flatiron Books, 2021).

Chapter 25 - External Barriers to Well-Being

1. Brené Brown, *The Gifts of Imperfection: Let Go of Who You Think You're Supposed to Be and Embrace Who You Are* (Center City, MN: Hazelden Publishing, 2010).

2. Jane Ellen Stevens, "The Adverse Childhood Experiences Study," ACES Too High, October 3, 2012, https://acestoohigh.com/2012/10/03/the-adverse-childhood-experiences-study-the-largest-most-important-public-health-study-you-never-heard-of-began-in-an-obesity-clinic/.

3. This has been measured by the Oxford Poverty and Human Development Initiative. D. Zavaleta, "The Ability to Go About without Shame: A Proposal for Internationally Comparable Indicators," *OPHI Working Paper* 3, University of Oxford, 2007, https://ophi.org.uk/wp-03/.

4. Ben Fell and Miles Hewstone, "Psychological Perspectives on Poverty," Joseph Rowntree Foundation, June 4, 2015, https://www.jrf.org.uk/report/psychological-perspectives-poverty.

5. Inspired by Monica Metzger, conversation about keeping children's spirits up when unhoused.

6. Daniel Kahneman and Angus Deaton, "High Income Improves Evaluation of Life but Not Emotional Well-Being," *PNAS*, September 7, 2010, www.princeton.edu/~deaton/downloads/deaton_kahneman_high_income_improves_evaluation_August2010.pdf.

7. From economists at the Federal Reserve, in Austin Clemens, "Eight Graphs That Tell the Story of U.S. Economic Inequality," Washington Center for Equitable Growth, December 9, 2019, https://equitablegrowth.org/eight-graphs-that-tell-the-story-of-u-s-economic-inequality/.

8. Children's Defense Fund, "The State of America's Children 2021: Child Poverty," www.childrensdefense.org/state-of-americas-children/soac-2021-child-poverty/.

9. Learn about the Pink Tax at Amy Fontinelle, "Pink Tax," Investopedia, February 12, 2022, www.investopedia.com/pink-tax-5095458.

10. See centerforpartnership.org, rianeeisler.com, and partnerism.org.

Chapter 26 - Cultural Barriers to Wholeness

1. Joshua Becker, "Why You Don't Need to Run with the Cool Kids," Becoming Minimalist,

https://www.becomingminimalist.com/much-cooler/. *See also* The Jay Austin Simply Be Kind Foundation, https://thejayaustinsimplybekindfoundation.com/.

2. Marilyn Ferguson, The Aquarian Conspiracy: Personal and Social Transformation in the 1980s (Los Angeles: J. P. Tarcher, 1976).

3. Malcolm Gladwell, "The Ethnic Theory of Plane Crashes," in *Outliers: The Story of Success* (New York: Little, Brown, 2008).

4. Ellie Lisitsa, "The Four Horsemen: Criticism, Contempt, Defensiveness, and Stonewalling," Gottman Institute, www.gottman.com/blog/the-four-horsemen-recognizing-criticism-contempt-defensiveness-and-stonewalling/.

5. Clarissa Pinkola Estés, "Newt Gingrich: And His List of Words," The Moderate Voice, January 5, 2012, https://themoderatevoice.com/newt-gingrich-and-his-list-of-words/.

6. Jane Fonda, *Jane Fonda's New Workout and Weight-Loss Program* (New York: Simon and Schuster, 1986).

7. A total of 1,679,943 combined surgical and nonsurgical procedures were performed in 1997, when social media emerged, and 10,663,607 in 2014. Cosmetic Surgery National Data Bank Statistics, *Aesthetic Surgery Journal* 35 (July 2015), 6.

8. Joshua Becker, "21 Surprising Statistics That Reveal How Much Stuff We Actually Own," Becoming Minimalist, www.becomingminimalist.com/clutter-stats/.

Chapter 27 – Guidance in the Digital Age

1. "Shaping Great Kids with Positive Parenting," presentation by Louise Hart.

2. Office of the Surgeon General, *Protecting Youth Mental Health: The U.S. Surgeon General's Advisory* (Washington, DC: US Department of Health and Human Services). (December 7, 2021.)

3. "Television and Health," Internet Resources to Accompany *The Sourcebook for Teaching Science*, www.csun.edu/science/health/docs/tv&health.html.

4. American Academy of Pediatrics, "Children, Adolescents, and

Advertising," *Pediatrics* 118, no. 6 (December 1, 2006), https://publications.aap.org/pediatrics/article/118/6/2563/69735/Children-Adolescents-and-Advertising.

5. Television's 'family hour' is turning into the violence hour... *USA Today*, September 11, 1986. https://www.upi.com/Archives/1986/09/10/Televisions-family-hour-is-turning-into-the-violence-hour/8971526708800/

6. Learn more at Fairplay: Childhood beyond Brands, https://fairplayforkids.org/beyond-brands/.

7. Jennifer Comiteau, "When Does Brand Loyalty Start?," *Adweek*, March 24, 2003, www.adweek.com/brand-marketing/when-does-brand-loyalty-start-62841/.

8. Antonia Quadara, Alissar El-Murr, and Joe Latham, "Effects of Pornography on Children and Young People," Australian Institute of Family Studies, December 2017, https://aifs.gov.au/publications/effects-pornography-children-and-young-people-snapshot.

9. "Time Flies: U.S. Adults Now Spend Nearly Half a Day Interacting with Media," Nielsen, July 31, 2018, www.nielsen.com/us/en/insights/article/2018/time-flies-us-adults-now-spend-nearly-half-a-day-interacting-with-media/.

10. Roxanne Nelson, "Children Face Higher Health Risk from Cell Phones," WebMD, 2014, www.webmd.com/children/news/20140819/children-cell-phones.

11. Watch Feminist Frequency videos to learn more about misogynistic tropes, https://feministfrequency.com/.

12. Pat Palmer, *Liking Myself* (Oakland, CA: Uplift Press, 2011).

13. Chapter 18, "Swept Away by Technology," in Louise Hart and Kristen Caven, *The Bullying Antidote* (Oakland, CA: Hazelden, 2013).

14. Adapted from Hilarie Cash, Cosette D. Rae, Ann H. Steel, and Alexander Winkler, "Internet Addiction: A Brief Summary of Research and Practice," *Current Psychiatry Reviews* 8, no. 4 (November 2012), www.ncbi.nlm.nih.gov/pmc/articles/PMC3480687/.

Chapter 28 - The Power (and Pleasures!) of Play

1. They claimed to have attended the Eastman Kazoovatory of Music . . . look them up on YouTube!

2. Visit the Strong National Museum of Play in Rochester, New York, www.museumofplay.org.

3. "Game Library," Playworks, www.playworks.org/game-library/

4. Roly-poly, also known as sow bug or pill bug: any of various small, terrestrial crustaceans of the genus Armadillidium or related genera, having convex, segmented bodies capable of being curled into a ball.

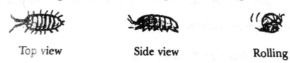

| Top view | Side view | Rolling |

5. Grab some ideas from the Hand in Hand Parenting Blog (https://www.handinhandparenting.org/2022/01/games-for-kids-all-ages/) or check out *Listen: Five Simple Tools to Meet Your Everyday Parenting Challenges* by Patty Wipfler

6. Penalty Flags for social behavior concept by David Bryce.

7. Cheryl Gorvie, *New York Times*, " 'Joys' of Parenting" virtual event, hosted by Jessica Grose, December 2021.

Chapter 29 - Bodies and Brains

1. Barbara Sher, *Wishcraft: How to Get What You Really Want* (New York: Ballantine, 2009).

2. Nutrition facts in this chapter provided by Dr. Mark Hyman and Neal Barnard M.D., from *Plate by Zumba* course and their YouTube interviews.

3. Informed by Megan Klenke, "How Chronic Illness Can Drastically Affect Your Self-Esteem," The Mighty, April 28, 2017, https://themighty.com/2017/04/how-chronic-illness-can-affect-your-self-esteem/.

4. Meghan Blackford, "How Self-Esteem Can Affect Mental Health," FHE Health, August 19, 2020, https://fherehab.com/learning/self-esteem-mental-health.

5. Carol J. Van Dongen, "Self-Esteem among Persons with Severe Mental Illness," *Issues in Mental Health Nursing* 19, no. 1 (January–

February 1998): 29–40, https://doi.org/10.1080/016128498249196.

6. QED Foundation, https://allkindsofminds.org/.

7. Zoe Williams, "Trauma, Trust, and Triumph: Psychiatrist Bessel van der Kolk on How to Recover from Our Deepest Pain," The Guardian, September 20, 2021, www.theguardian.com/society/2021/sep/20/trauma-trust-and-triumph-psychiatrist-bessel-van-der-kolk-on-how-to-recover-from-our-deepest-pain.

8. Learn more in Bessel van der Kolk, *The Body Keeps the Score: Brain, Mind, and Body in the Healing of Trauma* (London: Penguin, 2019).

9. HeartMath Institute, www.heartmath.org.

Chapter 30 - The Fractured Family

1. Jane Anderson, "The Impact of Family Structure on the Health of Children: Effects of Divorce," *Linacre Quarterly* 81, no. 4 (November 2014), www.ncbi.nlm.nih.gov/pmc/articles/PMC4240051/.

2. Melissa Heinig, "Divorce Mediation Basics," NOLO, www.nolo.com/legal-encyclopedia/divorce-mediation-basics-36180.html.

3. You will find useful resources at "Help for Kids of Divorce," Divorce and Children, https://divorceandchildren.com/resources/help-for-kids-of-divorce/.

4. Her blog is very funny: JM Randolph, accidentalstepmom, https://accidentalstepmom.com/.

5. Grab some great resources form Dr. Jann Blackstone at https://bonusfamilies.com/.

6. Gary Chapman, *The Five Love Languages: How to Express Heartfelt Commitment to Your Mate* (Northfield, 1992).

7. Adapted from the SCARF model. *See* Ed Batista, "Neuroscience, Leadership and David Rock's SCARF Model," March 25, 2010, https://www.edbatista.com/2010/03/scarf.html.

8. Conversations with Joe Baumgardner, 2022.

9. Jenny Penland, "You Can't Co-Parent with a Toxic Ex, but You Can Do This Instead," Scary Mommy, February 2, 2020,

www.scarymommy.com/cant-co-parenting-with-a-toxic-ex/.

10. Laurie Gordon, San Francisco, CA, interview with Kristen Caven.

Chapter 31 - Extending Your Family

1. Richard Bach, Illusions: The Adventures of a Reluctant Messiah (New York: Delacorte Press, 1977).

2. *New World Encyclopedia*, s.v. "nuclear family," December 13, 2018, www.newworldencyclopedia.org/entry/Nuclear_family.

3. American Community Survey (ACS) data in Riordan Frost, "Who Is Moving and Why? Seven Questions about Residential Mobility," JCHS (Joint Center for Housing Studies of Harvard University), May 4, 2020, www.jchs.harvard.edu/blog/who-is-moving-and-why-seven-questions-about-residential-mobility.

4. See appendix D, "100 Sources of Joy," by Anne Fullerton.

5. Find out how to evaluate a school's policies and culture in terms of whether bullying will occur or will be handled well in Louise Hart and Kristen Caven, "Towards a Bully-Free Culture," in *The Bullying Antidote* (Oakland, CA: Hazelden, 2013).

6. Conversation decks available at Be Strong Families, www.bestrongfamilies.org/cafe-supplies. Talk to your school about purchasing a deck or two.

7. Visit the Toolbox Project at https://toolboxproject.com. Tell your school about the program if they don't use it already. You can also get *The Toolbox Songs* on Amazon.

Chapter 32 - When Everybody Wins

1. Sy Safransky, Sunbeams: A Book of Quotations (Berkeley, CA: North Atlantic Books, 1990).

2. Take a fifteen-minute test to identify your strengths at the Via Institute on Character (www.viacharacter.org), where you will also find resources on strength-based parenting.

3. Naomi Klein, *This Changes Everything: Capitalism vs. the Climate* (New York: Simon and Schuster, 2015), 21.

4. Learn more about the concept at Darcia Narvaez's website, The Evolved Nest, https://evolvednest.org/.

5. Damian Nash, *Teaching with Aloha*, forthcoming.

6. Resources available on the Zorgos Reader, www.zorgos.wordpress.com

About the Authors

Kristen Caven and Dr. Louise Hart have been working on positive parenting education since the day Kristen was born, with Louise pioneering a new mothering style. Decades later, when they were in school at the same time, they both decided to be writers—Kristen was a freshman in college, and Louise was in grad school working on her doctorate in community psychology. Six years later, they worked together to revise *The Winning Family* for Celestial Arts, and the book was eventually published in six countries.

Their second book, *Wings of Self-Esteem*, was based on Hart's personal transformation from a "mousy doctor's wife" to an international speaker who soared beyond expectations. Its unique approach to self-esteem recovery was highly praised by many, including Jack Canfield, Jerry Jampolsky, Dr. Bernie Siegel, and Dr. Michele Borba.

As a professional speaker, Louise taught parents, teachers, and caregivers her earned wisdom, delivering over 400 presentations to communities and military families across the United States and in Germany and Japan, plus a conference in Russia, with visuals created by Kristen, who become an award-winning artist and writer known for her comics, literary works, and performances. Louise retired from speaking to live near her children and grandchildren.

The two continued writing together while Kristen was advising and leading organizations, such as Child Friendly Initiative, Oakland Parents Together, and PTA groups. They published newsletters and articles and brought Pat Palmer's children's books back into print. Their third book, *The Bullying Antidote: Superpower Your Kids for Life*, requested by Hazelden Publishing, was the first book to frame bullying as related to ACEs (Adverse Childhood Experiences). Kristen directed The Zorgos Project, which distributed 3,000 copies to parents in Oakland, California, where anti-bullying work was centered on social justice and building healthy community relationships. Kristen also earned a certificate in positive psychology, coming full circle through her mother's contributions to a greater understanding of the dignity of children.

The two share a passion for writing, children, and healthy families and societies. Kristen inherited Louise's love for travel, and Louise absorbed Kristen's love of dancing, starting Zumba lessons at age 75.

Acknowledgments

A book with this much history has been shaped by so much sharing, so much caring. This book is about all families and owes everything to our own core, bonus, and extended family members, who contributed support, wisdom, and experience over the years. You know who you are!

Among our beloveds we owe special gratitude to David and Donald Caven, Joe Baumgardner, Victoria Luibrand, and Alice Wertz, as well as flourishing maven Emiliya Zhivotovskaya, for inspiring and shaping the new chapters. This publication relied confidently on its strong foundation, with gratitude in remembrance of past publisher David Hinds, of Celestial Arts; friend and author Dr. Pat Palmer; the Fullertons; and the man who made our family possible, Jan Baumgardner. It brought us great delight to work with Lynn Meinhardt, whose sensibilities shaped both old and new editions, providing extra continuity through time.

We are grateful to all of the teachers who influenced this book, including all of the learners who shared their stories. Most of all, we'd like to acknowledge our readers and their children — you are the reason we wrote this book! When you see another parent who has a great connection with their kid, acknowledge they inspire you, ask them for their secrets, and share yours with them.

More from Uplift Press

By Dr. Louise Hart and Kristen Caven

On the Wings of Self-Esteem
A Practical Guide for Personal Transformation

The Bullying Antidote
Superpower Your Kids for Life

By Dr. Patricia Palmer

Liking Myself
Understanding and Managing Feelings

The Mouse, the Monster and Me
Assertiveness for Young People

Other Authors

More Time to Love
One father's extraordinary journal of living longer with ALS
By Joseph L. Wions

The Souls of Her Feet
A Novel Cinderella Story
By Kristen Caven

www.upliftpress.com

CPSIA information can be obtained
at www.ICGtesting.com
Printed in the USA
LVHW080758260822
726792LV00012B/336